FROM DICKINSON TO DYLAN

FROM DICKINSON TO DYLAN

Visions of Transcendence in Modernist Literature

Glenn Hughes

UNIVERSITY OF MISSOURI PRESS
Columbia

University of Missouri Press, Columbia, Missouri 65211
Printed and bound in the United States of America
 First printing, 2020.

Library of Congress Cataloging-in-Publication Data

Names: Hughes, Glenn, 1951- author.
Title: From Dickinson to Dylan : visions of transcendence in modernist literature / Glenn Hughes.
Description: Columbia, Missouri : University of Missouri Press, [2020] | Includes bibliographical references and index.
Identifiers: LCCN 2020025724 (print) | LCCN 2020025725 (ebook) | ISBN 9780826222206 (hardcover ; alk. paper) | ISBN 9780826274526 (ebook)
Subjects: LCSH: American literature--20th century--History and criticism. | Transcendence (Philosophy) in literature. | Modernism (Literature)--United States.
Classification: LCC PS228.T725 H84 2020 (print) | LCC PS228.T725 (ebook) | DDC 810.9/005--dc23
LC record available at https://lccn.loc.gov/2020025724
LC ebook record available at https://lccn.loc.gov/2020025725

∞™ This paper meets the requirements of the American National Standard for Permanence of Paper for Printed Library Materials, Z39.48, 1984.

Acknowledgment of permissions for this volume appears on pages 231–32

Typefaces: Caslon and Museo Sans

This book is dedicated to

CARL ADLER

BILL GRAY

PAUL KIDDER

and

DAVID SCHULDBERG

for love, welcome, and conversation

Mysticism keeps men sane. As long as you have mystery you have health; when you destroy mystery you create morbidity. The ordinary man has always been sane because the ordinary man has always been a mystic. . . . The mystic allows one thing to be mysterious, and everything else becomes lucid.

—G. K. Chesterton

CONTENTS

FROM DICKINSON TO DYLAN

INTRODUCTION

FOR READERS AND writers of literature in the twenty-first century, the most culturally imposing and influential literary "classics" are the masterworks of literary Modernism. This is true in part because they serve as a set of ideal types establishing the parameters of what is formally possible. But it is not merely because of the remarkable ways they break from traditional literary forms that they enjoy their status. They have become classics because, like the Homeric poems, like Virgil and Dante, like *Don Quixote* and the works of Shakespeare and the novels of Austen, Dostoevsky, and Tolstoy, they are inexhaustibly intelligent about the human condition and human experiences, with their inventions of style brilliantly serving their tellings, giving them like all classics an "eternal and irrepressible freshness."[1] These are the qualities that reward repeated returnings to Joyce's *Ulysses*, to T. S. Eliot's *The Waste Land* and *Four Quartets*, to Proust's monumental tale of remembrance, and to masterworks by Virginia Woolf, Rilke, Pirandello, Kafka, William Carlos Williams, Knut Hamsun, Hermann Broch, E. E. Cummings, Wallace Stevens, Marianne Moore, William Faulkner, Samuel Beckett.

The masterworks of these writers are peculiarly *our* classics, first because of their formal structures, which reflect a distinctly modern (and postmodern) sensibility, and second because of the subjects they treat.

As to form: in fiction the experimental structures created to represent the differentiated and disrupted consciousness of modern times include interior monologue, verbal collages of perceptions and symbols, and narration expressing incomplete understanding and unconscious motives. Poetry's innovations—especially *vers libre*, use of modern idioms, and startling patterns of image-association—yielded verse that had a vital sense of immediacy and mirrored the psychology of modern experience.

Drama increasingly found ways to express in the architecture of staged "stories" dreamlike inward states, social unmoorings, inconclusive narratives, and absurdities of felt existence. And experimentation was thorough: once traditional rules were overthrown, the newly possible was indulged in with gusto. It is difficult to imagine novels going further, formally speaking, than Joyce's *Ulysses* (not to mention *Finnegans Wake*), Woolf's *To the Lighthouse*, Alfred Döblin's *Berlin Alexanderplatz*, Proust's *In Search of Lost Time*, Andrei Bely's *St. Petersburg*, Flann O'Brien's *The Third Policeman*, E. E. Cummings's *Eimi*, and Beckett's *The Unnamable* and *How It Is*. In poetry one might say the same of the inventions of Pound, Eliot, William Carlos Williams, Marianne Moore, and Cummings. And Beckett's works for theater, taken together, push the possibilities of staged drama to extreme limits, within a larger Modernist movement embracing the formal innovations of Ibsen and Strindberg, Pirandello, Ionesco, Albee, and Pinter.

As to subject matter: the dominant concerns of Modernist literature remain to a striking degree (if not exclusively) our contemporary concerns. Modernist classics describe a world where moral and religious belief systems have been undermined by the impact of scientific, psychological, anthropological, and philosophical discoveries, leaving us to search for metaphysical satisfaction among "heaps of broken images" (Eliot). They explore how ever-more-sophisticated technologies, impenetrable bureaucracies, omnipresent commercial advertising, speed, and dizzyingly diverse and anonymizing urban living shape perception and personality. Theirs is a culture in which myths and artifacts of early peoples have become objects of fascinated study, and where history is no longer regarded as a spectacle of inevitable progress but as a confusing tangle of multiple narratives. Above all, they examine the events of the world as they appear to, or inside of, consciousness, rather than as a verifiable sequence of "objective" facts. This is still obviously very much the world of our own lives and storytelling, however profoundly personal experiences and the cultural landscape have continued to be altered by technological, political, and social developments.

But the masterworks of literary Modernism remain relevant most of all because they explore the human psyche with the expansiveness and discernment belonging to all great literature, while doing so with a modern sensitivity to the intricacies of interiority. As Declan Kiberd has remarked with regard to *Ulysses*, the major works of Modernist literature are a kind of "wisdom literature": they can be returned to repeatedly with cumulative reward because they keep telling us as humans who we are.[2] And this is why books *about* these works (like this one)—along with books about Greek and Roman classics or any other species of "classic"—continue to be written.

The present book is concerned with an often-overlooked element in the wisdom literature of Modernism: its exploration of human beings as consciously related to a "beyond" of meaning, timeless and possibly divine, which reveals itself to consciousness in its struggle to comprehend existence. One could describe this as the theme of spirituality in the authors discussed—Emily Dickinson, Marcel Proust, T. S. Eliot, Ezra Pound, Samuel Beckett, and Bob Dylan—though the terms "spiritual" and "spirituality" have in modern parlance become increasingly vague. It would be more precise to identify the topic at hand as visions of human involvement with, or immersion in, a mystery of sacred, transcendent meaning.

A common assumption about Western literature is that from the nineteenth century onward it reflects an increasingly secularized view of world and existence. That many major literary authors of the last two centuries have discarded traditional religious language and symbols as inadequate for representing their most profound experiences is obviously true. Nonetheless concern with the sacred, the transcendent, or the divinely mysterious remains central to the focus and inspiration of major figures of Western literature in both the nineteenth and the twentieth centuries. The most obvious nineteenth-century examples are groundbreaking authors of literary Romanticism, writing roughly during the period 1790 to 1830. Blake, Wordsworth, and Coleridge in England, for example, and Schiller, Novalis, and Hölderlin in Germany, are clearly attempting to defend and articulate authentic experiences of engagements with a sacred transcendence amid the growing popularity of Enlightenment-inspired visions of a mechanistic world created by an inaccessible "watchmaker" God or, more radically, the thoroughly disenchanted cosmos of philosophical materialism. In the twentieth century, those literary Modernists who affirm a mystery of transcendent reality find themselves in a cultural situation in many respects continuous with that of the literary Romantics: they too are reacting against mechanistic and instrumentalizing views of nature and human existence, responding to the weakening authority of Christian orthodoxies, and continuing the development, in a literary modality, of the modern "turn to the subject" in which the authority and inner freedom of the person is emphasized.

But the voices of literary Modernists addressing sacred transcendence also register a new, and tremendous, epochal shift with regard to basic existential assumptions and perspectives. The literary Romantics, for example, are confident in the harmony and oneness of the sacred with both nature's depths and the depths of the self, which leads to a tendency in the Romantic imagination to *merge* the supernatural with the natural, and for the superior artist—a Blake, a Wordsworth, a Hölderlin, or a Novalis—to regard himself, and to be regarded by others, as a seer-prophet in whom this merging is creatively conscious. A sort of self-divinizing, as Nicholas Riasanovsky puts it, is the "igniting romantic spark."[3] The Romantics are also confident about the interpretive stability and "transparency" of the symbols used for expressing enduring truths about self, nature, and the sacred; about the unity and internal coherence of the artistic consciousness that creates these symbols; and about human progress toward an ever-greater integration and reconciliation of natural and sacred realms of meaning. The disintegration of these confidences is central to the visions and voices of literary Modernism.

Modernist authors devoted to exploring the mystery of sacred being are writing in a cultural world where interiority, in advancing self-differentiation, has discovered its inwardly fractured nature and unconscious layers, and feels sharply its discontinuity with nature and the sacred; where the "linguistic turn" has made the artist acutely aware of the fragility and historicity of language, and of the unclosable gap between linguistic representation and reality (sign and signified); and where the complexities of science and technology, urban speed, and impersonal bureaucratic interactions have become far more intrusive and alienating; all of this leading to personhood being experienced both as decentered and as discrete. Such a self is no longer assimilable into, or capable of assimilating into itself, nature, on the one hand, or a sacred realm of meaning, on the other. The stable and unified personal identity of the literary Romantics has been replaced, in the literary Modernists, by a "stream of consciousness" belonging to a self that is simultaneously single and many as it develops over time (Proust, Joyce), fragmented and fluid (Joyce, Woolf), and an "I" that is always also "an other" (Rimbaud). The epiphanies of transcendence communicated by their works are thus not those of self-apotheosizing subjects. Writers such as Eliot, Woolf, Pound, and Joyce are properly termed *counter-Romantics*, as they are no longer capable of sincere belief in the overcoming either of alienation between self and world or of alienation within consciousness; and they reject as naïve the Romantics' exaltation of the literary maker as a holy seer.[4]

The Modernist literary author engaged in exploring transcendent mystery, then, is always aware of (1) the internal disunity of the self; (2) the instability and relative inadequacy of linguistic symbols; and (3) the radical alterity of any sacred "beyond" it might try to evoke. These assumptions have a direct impact, of course, on ideas about human development and human history. History is never conceived by literary Modernists in terms of a steadily redemptive course of civilizational or universal progress; such a notion has fallen apart in Modernist visions (Yeats: "Things fall apart; the centre cannot hold"). As we shall see, the idea of secular historical progress which is so basic and consolidating for the literary Romantics is ignored by Dickinson and Proust; critiqued by Eliot and Pound; contemptuously dismissed by Beckett; and replaced with (traditional) religious apocalypticism by Dylan.

Thus one finds in those literary Modernists who remain faithful to a mystic sense of reality an insistence that the sacred realm of meaning must be accorded its proper transcendence. As we shall see, in Dickinson, Proust, Eliot, Beckett, and even in Dylan (Pound represents something of a special case, in his insistence on the *imaginability* of divine Otherness), there is a kind of perilous re-recognition of the transcendence of transcendence, with the result that their literature ceases to be "spilt religion," in the famous phrase T. E. Hulme used to define Romanticism.[5] Literature becomes (again) merely art—though still, *as* art, a crucially important locus of epiphanies of transcendence suited to its epoch. In other words, insofar as literary Modernism exhibits mysticism—the exploration by consciousness of the mystery of the transcendent "ground" of nature and consciousness—it has had to become more *deliberate* in its mysticism.

A clarification at this point about the term *mystery* will be useful. A mystery in the existential or ontological sense is not a blank of unknowability. It is a depth of meaning in which humans know themselves to be involved but which is understood to transcend full human comprehension. True mysteries are *realities* in which we are involved, discerned at the border where they disappear beyond human capacities for insight. For example, we know that we are not the creators of our own existences; we are, as Kierkegaard writes, "derived" beings.[6] But derived from what? Or (to speak analogically) from whom? This is the mystery of ultimate human origins. About this "ground" of existence people can develop (or there are revealed) apprehensions, surmises, deductions, arising from both affect and insight, but whatever its essence or nature is, this is understood to lie beyond any possible human understanding. Again: history is the unfolding of significant human action in time, in which persons find themselves participating. But what is history's ultimate meaning or goal? And what purpose does each of us serve as an actor in its drama? This is the mystery of history—and though we may attain insights into many of the meanings that structure historical process, we understand that we cannot grasp the meaning *of* history, for history is both unfinished and also it, too, has emerged from and participates in the unknowably transcendent origin of the cosmos.

Anyone who attends with courage and consistency to the mysteries of transcendent meaning that inform existence, and who illuminates for self or others the truths of that participation, is by definition a certain kind of "mystic." To assert that Dickinson, Proust, Eliot, and the other writers discussed herein are mystics, as I do here, and that they are *deliberate* in their mysticism, does not of course mean that they are to be understood as mystics in the narrow sense that pertains to figures such as St. John of the Cross or Teresa of Avila or Julian of Norwich. It affirms instead three things. First, it underscores their acknowledgment that they are existentially involved in dimensions of meaning that they will never fully understand. Second, as discussed earlier, it recognizes their acute awareness that any language descriptions or symbols they use to convey the meaning of their experiences of mystery are (a) contingent carriers of meaning, (b) easily misunderstood, and (c) inadequate to what is mysterious in these mysteries. And third, it honors their appreciation of the fact that, in the disturbingly novel circumstances of modern life, radically new forms of literary expression are needed to communicate the self's involvement in transcendent meaning—just as modern painters, sculptors, and musicians had to break with earlier forms in order to communicate experiences of a sacred transcendent to a modern sensibility for whom traditional symbols serving that purpose had become stale and ineffective.

In describing mysticism as sensitivity toward and existential witness to transcendent meanings, one must take care that the term *transcendence* itself is not misunderstood, as it so easily is. The most typical misapprehension is that it is meant to refer to some kind of entity (as in so-called "onto-theological" notions of God), or to some kind of place, a heaven (or hell) spatially beyond the spatiotemporal universe. Such imaginings are simply blunders. The term *transcendence* is not a description of anything, but rather signifies a *dimension of meaning* that consciousness becomes aware of when it is open and faithful to "the elementary matter of raising further questions."[7] We question, for example, why we exist, or why a universe exists, or what purpose there may be to striving and failing and hoping. This is a "further questioning" that is propelled in part by emotions: we are anxious to be happy, to live well, to live meaningful lives; we are frightened of missing the true direction in existence; we long for a perfect and infinite goodness because we are dissatisfied with all the goods the finite world might offer. It is driven also by intelligence: if the universe gave rise to us, then what gave rise to the universe? And an elementary fact about this affective-intelligent human questioning is that it is formally unrestricted: that is, it is not satisfied with answers that do not completely explain why we ourselves or a universe exist, or that fail to settle our most intense yearnings for moral coherence and justice. But the universe in which we live, the universe proportionate to what we know and might know under the conditions of existence, cannot provide us with such answers or assurances. The contingent universe cannot provide an account for its own being; and morally, whatever apparent advances history might show us, the arc of the known universe promises no resolution. So our "further questioning" proceeds, quite reasonably, to out-question the universe—it brings us through its own natural dynamism to the notion of a meaning "beyond" everything intrinsically conditioned by space(s) and time(s), to the notion of a mysterious reality, in which we participate, that can account for *everything* because it is itself unconditioned and unrestricted, and that in fact must be real if existential and cosmic meaning are to be complete and make sense.

Neither the mind nor the heart is truly at rest until such a notion, however mysterious, suggests itself as a reality—although both the notion of an unrestricted reality, and the trustworthiness of the unrestricted human question that heads toward the conceiving and naming of such a notion, may be existentially suppressed, ignored, or dismissed for ideological reasons, especially in an intellectual culture permeated by the influence of the "cultured despisers of religion" (Schleiermacher). *Transcendence*, the term, is simply a name for this notion—but a name that has the advantage, for philosophical purposes, of being purely heuristic. It says no more than that this reality that is the ground of the universe and ourselves lies beyond what we can understand with human understanding, and it is a dimension of meaning distinct from finite, spatiotemporally conditioned realities.

Despite the fact that a consciousness with unrestricted questioning is inherently mystical in orientation, however, minds find ways to avoid an apprehension of a "beyond" of knowable meaning. This avoidance is principally due to the awareness of existential uncertainties that invariably attends recognition of transcendence. As the Czech philosopher Jan Patočka explains, awareness of transcendent mystery uncovers a meaning "which cannot be mastered, delimited, grasped positively, and dominated," and therefore it causes a "constant shaking" of all certainties about metaphysical and existential matters.[8] To sustain this awareness requires accepting, or rather requires *being*, a tension of openness toward certain unsettling facts—for example, that the ground of the universe and ourselves is a mystery that can never be known or named with certainty; that the significance of one's own moral and spiritual efforts is always uncertain; and that the process of history is contingent on future uses of human freedom and thus unpredictable. This constant uncertainty is "too heavy a burden," as Eric Voegelin writes, for the many "who lust for massively possessive experience" with regard to ultimate matters, and who consequently replace their innate orientation toward transcendent mystery with one of two forms of certitude: religious certitude, or anti-spiritual certitude.[9]

Religious presumption of certitude about ultimate matters has been an omnipresent feature in the history of social life, most obviously manifested in modernity in the statements and attitudes of religious literalists and fundamentalists who claim to be in possession of definitive answers concerning God, the afterlife, how to secure personal attunement with the ground of being, and the historical future. The core attraction of such presumption is that it grants the soul its awareness of the reality of transcendence; what it betrays is only the ultimate *mysteriousness* of transcendent being. But this "only" alters everything. The spiritual consciousness that closes itself to the mysteriousness of the "beyond" of the meaning of the Whole in which it participates has corrupted its own nature, since its essence is an unrestricted questioning that out-questions the entirety of the knowable. It has substituted a comforting fantasy for an authentic vision of the human situation. Such souls, though, have a secular counterpart: those who presume to possess certitude that there is no transcendent meaning at all and that the human ability to out-question finitude has no significance. *This* certitude can bring with it an energetic confidence built on the epistemologically unsound supposition that spatiotemporally conditioned reality is the whole of reality, and that therefore eventual comprehension of all important truths, and perhaps even eventual human mastery of history, is possible.[10] This is the dream of scientistic and technocratic partisans who wave off intimations and symbols of transcendent mystery as irrelevancies or delusions, and of radical progressivists who consider the political perfecting of society to be possible. The point is that consciousness in each of these cases, religious and anti-religious, remains closed to the dynamism of its own questioning—and therefore to some degree deformed. Only mysticism is realism.

It is important to recognize, of course, that there are vast numbers of religious believers—Christian, Jewish, Muslim, Buddhist, Hindu, and those of other traditional or syncretistic or non-specific "spiritual" faiths—who practice or pray or meditate or seek attunement with a spiritual ground of being with a vibrant awareness of the mysteriousness of that ground. A Catholic who understands the dogmas expressing the "mysteries of the faith" *as* mysteries, or a Buddhist who habitually directs attention to the incomprehensibility and paradoxical-to-human-thinking quality of the ultimacy described in Buddhist literature as "nothing" or nirvana, consciously dwells with and within primordial mystery. Very large numbers of people, too, are self-proclaimedly agnostic ("not-knowing") with regard to a spiritual ground of being, recognizing with a greater or lesser degree of concern that they live in existential tension toward an ultimate reality whose character or truth lies beyond their ken. Even plenty of what might be called "easygoing atheists," who are deeply skeptical about any religious formulations or symbols like "God," wouldn't claim to be *absolutely* certain about the soundness of their inclinations regarding ultimate truths.

Yet, openness to mystery is difficult. More people, especially within the communities of religion, embrace false certitudes than those who consistently attend to the horizon of unknowabilities that encompasses human understanding. One might say that *forgetfulness* about genuine mystery, whether in a religious or an anti-spiritual mode, functions as a default mode of existence for many. And this forgetfulness is certainly encouraged in our day by a culture bombarding us at all times with inducements and distractions, along with the up-to-date directive to dismiss, with suspicion or amused irony, any sincere suggestion that a mysteriously transcendent reality not only grounds and embraces us but *requires* something of us. Still, transcendent reality never goes away; it only becomes, in certain cultures and at certain times, more difficult to attend to.

The antidote to forgetfulness is remembrance. And for remembrance of elemental mysteries, we rely above all on evocative images that shake us from absentmindedness, that recall us to an explicit apprehension of a fact always "known" by consciousness, however buried or occluded: that the drama of being in which we are all actors is grounded in a reality whose ultimate meaning is beyond our knowing. What kinds of images do this? Sometimes images of nature, when its sublimity and beauty quicken imagination. Images arising from memories of childhood also have the capacity, often, to stir up in us a sense of the numinous and a boundless depth of possibility. Religious or philosophical myths and symbols, of course, can keep sensitivity and conscience from slipping into forgetfulness of the mystery of being, when doctrinalism and literalism don't interfere. And also, of course, effective imagery may address us from the world of art: when music, for example, or painting—or literature—awakens in us a sense of wonder about mysteries, about the surplus of unknowable meaning "deep down things" (Hopkins).

It has often been declared that the highest or noblest function of art is to do just this: to create images that remind us of our spiritual nature and aspirations, renewing in us the wonder within which intimations of transcendence reside. That the greatest artists of every era are those who provide what consciousness needs to explore the utmost of meaning discernable is a view expressed over the centuries by philosophers from Plato to Levinas and by artists from Dante and Bach to Kandinsky and Rothko. If music, of all the art forms, has the most immediate psychological power to perform this function, it is also the most abstract or nonspecific; music creates worlds of feeling, often of uncanny intensity, but it lacks the differentiated specificity of meaning that words can convey. Likewise, painting and drawing, sculpture, dance, architecture, photography, and other non-verbal art forms offer us images that may have extraordinary power to suggest the inexplicable, the surplus of meaning in things and experience, but they do so without the nuanced, detailed articulation that only words can provide. Literature, however, in modes of poetry, drama, dialogue, and fictional tales long and short, is able to wed the existentially restorative power of artistic symbols to discursive precision about the human relationship to ultimate mysteries.

The Modernist authors discussed here are notable for the importance and influence of their writings generally, but also for the fact that each of them offers a vision of existence that places the struggle to pay attention to transcendent reality, and to interpret the human situation accordingly, at its heart. Each author's work is marked by mystical remembrance, and as a consequence by existential humility—for to remember transcendence is to remember the limits of human knowing and human power. Emily Dickinson's work reveals a continual examination of her involvement with divine transcendence, and tracks both her existential uncertainties and her oscillations between spiritual faith and despair. The cornerstone of Marcel Proust's novel *In Search of Lost Time* is the mysterious epiphanies of eternal being within the narrator's consciousness.

T. S. Eliot's *Four Quartets* is a poem cycle Christian in orientation and substance but rooted in mysticisms East and West. Ezra Pound's *Cantos* consistently express the need for consciousness to open itself to the enlightening influence of the mysteries of divine presence. Samuel Beckett's mature work is an extended meditation on human ignorance and impotence, which are lamented precisely in their relation to an idea of a perfect, transcendent reality. And Bob Dylan's lyrics consistently embed the listener in intrigues of spiritual mystery and acknowledgment of transcendent power.

This book pursues explanatory accounts of these authors' visions—only partially, of course, and in some cases more selectively than in others. As explanatory accounts, they serve as (very lowly) handmaidens to the art expressing those visions, which like all art speaks first of all to our *feelings*, however verbally dexterous and expansive it may be. One doesn't read literature for the dry logic of analysis, but to be moved, inspired, transported by a work's dynamic images, symbols, narrative arcs, detailed observations, exposures of consciousness, verbal music and rhythms. But the richest, most profound literature leads us also to consider: What are the crucial experiences and insights integral to this vision of existence? What affirmations and denials about the human condition, what appreciations and condemnations, give this illumination of human life its cohesion? Explanations arising from such questions emerge naturally from a long and loving encounter with such artworks. Thus, the following chapters serve their part as continuations, not abandonments, of encounters with the artworks themselves. These particular ruminations were inspired by each author's extraordinary articulation of the sorts of experiences of transcendent meaning that our contemporary world often shrugs aside as irrelevant to a properly sophisticated post-Modernist self-understanding, and as belonging to a less mature epoch of great literature. But there is nothing immature or passé about these authors. On the contrary, each has taken up, in his or her own way, one of the most difficult and important challenges of modern literature: how to be a mystic in contemporary times.

CHAPTER ONE

Emily Dickinson

Transcendence, Love, and Terror

EMILY DICKINSON'S STAR continues to rise. Her poetry is more popular, and her significance as a cultural figure more acclaimed, than at any time in the past. Why is this so? First, appraisal of her poetic achievement has repeatedly been revised upward: her originality, scope, linguistic inventiveness, intellectual brilliance, emotional richness, and psychological sophistication are respected as never before. Today, it is common to find her placed with authors such as Walt Whitman, T. S. Eliot, and Robert Frost as one of the four or five greatest American poets; the critic Harold Bloom has gone so far as to name her one of the thirty greatest writers of the Western world. Second, though her poetry was written in the middle of the nineteenth century, it often appears and sounds Modernist in style. In its original wording and eccentric punctuation, she appears as an innovative poet experimenting effectively with a variety of techniques: slant rhyme, irregular forms and rhythms, startling metaphors, and a mode of expression at times so lapidary and oblique that one must work hard to puzzle out the meaning. Such a description brings to mind Modernist poets such as Eliot, Hart Crane, Wallace Stevens, Ezra Pound, and E. E. Cummings—and most of her poems indeed seem quite at home in the world of post-traditional verse. And third, and perhaps most important, her sensibility feels contemporary; her poetry seems to be the testimony of an artist whose horizon of thought and feeling overlaps with our own—and this feels especially true with respect to her lifelong spiritual journey, which was radically idiosyncratic and probing.

Any reader of Dickinson's complete poetic ouevre will recognize that it is not sufficient to describe "religion" as just one of her perennial themes, along with nature, love, death, despair, and consciousness, because Dickinson's poetry on these other subjects regularly explores their meanings in relation to her *spiritual* experiences, doubts, and hopes. Surveying all of her nearly 1,800 poems and poetic fragments, one may reasonably agree with Charles R. Anderson's conclusion that "the reader today sees the ultimate purpose of all her explorations as religious in the profoundest sense of that term," centered as they are in Dickinson's continual engagement with the mystery of transcendent reality and the terrible adventure of illuminations, calamities, forsakenness, assuagement, and furious curiosity that it entails.[1]

As is well known, Dickinson's engagement with transcendence as detailed in her poetry reveals an ongoing struggle with, and aversion to many core tenets of, the Christian religion to which her family and the great majority of her friends and acquaintances subscribed. In her poems and letters she clearly rejects, often in tones of mocking contempt, teachings central to the Calvinist-based theology of her Congregationalist community, including the doctrines of original sin, hell and damnation, election, and redemption. Her poems make clear that to her the Bible is not truth in any traditional Christian sense, but essentially a repository of evocative symbols. On the promise of a personal afterlife she is inconsistent; while she often hopes it could be true, she remains convinced that human beings can't know anything about it, and she returns in her poems obsessively to the possibility that death means annihilation. Most importantly, as she strives to understand the spiritual significance of her experiences of self and world, she finds it all but impossible to believe in the Creator-God of justice, mercy, and love as taught in biblical and Christian tradition. All of this is fully apparent in her poems, and Helen Vendler is correct to state that Dickinson's "defiant critique of Christianity and her uninhibited scrutiny of its concepts . . . is unequaled among the poets of her day."[2]

Still, one must not be too quick to distance Dickinson's religious life and personality, as expressed in her poetry, from the comprehensive Christian vision of reality. It is obviously the Christian vision that provides the metaphysical framework for Dickinson's understanding of human being, nature, and cosmos. More specifically: her spiritual questions, doubts, discernments, and affirmations all unfold against background notions of (1) an omnipotent, singular, personal, and transcendent God, who created both nature and her individual soul; (2) a unique and once-only personal life on earth, which may or may not be succeeded by a permanent afterlife; and (3) a Jesus whose exemplary love and suffering offers her crucial orientation for interpreting and communicating her most extreme spiritual experiences. It is fair to say, then, that Dickinson battles Christianity from within. Even as she scoffs at many Christian doctrines and at most of the presumed certitudes of the *soi-disant* faithful, she nevertheless begins and ends her spiritual quest within the orbit of its metaphysical delineation of the universe and the human situation.

This same point must be applied to understanding her poetic use of Christian symbols and images. Her constant reliance on biblical and Christian language—on terms such as *heaven*, *immortality*, *paradise*, *Jesus*, *Gethsemane*, *Eden*, *crucifixion*, *grace*, *glory*, *God*, *spirit*, *covenant*—to communicate her experiences and thoughts is not simply a matter of her lacking any other religious vocabulary. While she regularly bends the meanings of such terms to suit her own expressive purposes, and not infrequently employs them ironically or even subversively, they are nevertheless indispensable to her, and she often uses them sincerely and without ironic detachment, because they genuinely *resonate* with her spiritual experiences. In other words, she is not simply forced by cultural circumstances to stay in the home of the Christian linguistic universe; she also chooses to live there, because many of the essential truths of her spiritual life find adequate expression through its language.

But given her rejection of many core doctrines of Christianity, what in fact *did* she hold to be the essential truths of an honest, and appropriately critical, spiritual life? Above all this: that there is a reality of divine transcendence in which her consciousness, along with all of creation, participates. Though from one poem to the next she may vacillate on whether God is good, or whether death is the end of personality, or whether suffering is ultimately meaningful, she never disavows that conscious existence and natural creation are suffused and circumscribed by a dimension of divinely grounded meaning that transcends the plane of the physical and transitory. In poem after poem we find the truth of transcendence affirmed. Examples are easy to find:

> This World is not conclusion.
> A Species stands beyond –

Invisible, as Music –
But positive, as Sound –
[. . .] (373)[3]

And:

The only news I know
Is Bulletins all Day
From Immortality.
[. . .] (820)

And:

The Infinite a sudden Guest
Has been assumed to be –
But how can that stupendous come
Which never went away? (1344)

Quotations from her poetry affirming or alluding to a divinely transcendent reality could extend into the hundreds.

Are these affirmations logically consistent, though, with Dickinson's many poems that describe experiences of spiritual despair and terrifying existential isolation? The answer is yes, they are consistent, because of the *reality* of transcendent meaning she is never in doubt. Indeed, the poignancy of her psychological traumas entailing loss of hope and extremes of pain, depression, terror, and fear of madness derive precisely from her loss of felt *connection* to, and inability to understand the meaning of her life or suffering *given the fact of*, a mystery of divine reality. To put it another way: Dickinson is never, either in her most extreme periods of anguish or in her most contemptuous flights of anger at the presumptions of Christian faith, tempted by philosophical materialism, or "immanentism." In joy, anguish, anger, and reflective calm alike, she acknowledges and accepts a reality of transcendence.

In fact it is precisely Dickinson's appreciation of transcendence *as transcendence*—that is, as a reality that is a mystery to human intellect, as a "beyond" of meanings and truths that we cannot ever know—that above all structures and guides her lifelong spiritual quest. It is this that grounds her outlook on the distinctive peculiarities and challenges of the human condition; her understanding of the self or soul; her relationship with the natural world; her grapplings with the idea of "God"; and her attitude toward many Christian doctrines, preachings, and presumptions. The main purpose of the present chapter will be to support and elucidate this view.

An appropriate first step is to explain how Dickinson's commitment to a truth of divine transcendence crucially shaped her relationship to two streams of "anti-Christian" critique that strongly influenced the intellectual culture of her time and place. The first of these was the local, and relatively short-lived, movement known as New England (or American) Transcendentalism; the second was the broad, accelerating impact of nineteenth-century scientific thought. A few comments on Dickinson's relationship to each of these phenomena will help clarify the unique manner in which, on the one hand, she breaks in a liberalizing and modern way from core Christian teachings while, on the other hand, she continues to adhere to the essence—and to central symbols—of a Christian metaphysical vision.

Dickinson's youth coincided with the rise, centered precisely in her western Massachusetts locale, of New England Transcendentalism, a literary and philosophical phenomenon associated most famously, now, with the writings and views of Ralph Waldo Emerson and Henry David Thoreau. The Transcendentalists emerged from within the Unitarian religious world as a more radical development of that community's rejection of Calvinist-based Christian orthodoxy and its theological metaphysics. Calvinist doctrines had been the bedrock of New England Puritan religion, but Calvinist teachings on predestination, eternal damnation, the depravity of human nature, biblical infallibility, and Trinitarian divinity had during the eighteenth century been increasingly challenged in New England churches by liberalizing theological preachers and writers. Liberal theological movements, including that which began to identify itself as Unitarian within the Puritan Congregationalist churches, with eastern Massachusetts as a center of activity, emphasized the benevolence of God, the fundamental goodness of human nature, universal salvation, the concordance of revelation and reason, the importance of the sciences, scholarship, and philosophy to the understanding of the natural world and divinity, and, above all, the oneness—the unitary character—of God. Unitarianism replaced Trinitarianism with an emphatically monotheistic theology. American Unitarianism as a denominational institution formally invested churches and declared its official status in Massachusetts during the second and third decades of the nineteenth century; from there it spread to the rest of New England, and eventually to the mid-Atlantic states and beyond.[4]

Unitarianism had scarcely coalesced organizationally, however, before it produced from within its midst a further rebellion in the New England Transcendentalists, with Emerson as a principal spokesman.[5] The Transcendentalists taught that individuals have no need whatever of organized religion or intercession, textual or ministerial, in order to develop a proper relationship with the divine, since every human being already participates in the divine oneness whose meaning and goodness permeate the universe, and which is experientially available to persons as an immediate (if evanescent) presence. Indeed, according to Transcendentalist teaching, each person can advance, through individual intuitive "Reason" and advancing self-interpretation alone, to sublime heights of human-divine insight and harmony. Regarding such "self-reliance" as the key human power, Emerson went so far as to describe religious creeds as "a disease of the intellect."[6] Together with other Transcendentalists, Emerson did emphasize the ultimate mysteriousness to human consciousness of the divine reality (which he famously referred to as the "Over-soul"); and a hint of Calvinism remains in his late declaration that "for every seeing soul there are two absorbing facts,—*I and the Abyss*," where we catch a residual glimpse of Puritan theologian Jonathan Edwards's pit of hell.[7] But together with the other Transcendentalists Emerson finally stressed, in a Romanticist vein, that we should recognize the whole universe inclusive of the human mind as a sacred *harmony* grounded in divine intelligence and goodness, and the natural world in which we live as an Eden—if only we could recognize it.

Dickinson read Emerson's prose and poetry from an early age, and throughout her life expressed deep admiration for him; Thoreau's writings influenced her as well.[8] She was clearly engaged by, and found solidarity with, elements of Transcendentalist teaching. She strongly sympathized with its rejection of both Christian doctrinalism and the need for institutional mediation of a personal relationship with the divine; its condemnation of ideas of innate human sinfulness and depravity; its assertion that spiritual development is the result of personal experiences of divine presence and the unfolding of original, individual insights; and its encouraging of mystical speculation.

This said, however, Dickinson's spiritual perspectives and conclusions remained in many respects at odds with those of Emerson and the other Transcendentalists. Transcendentalist optimism and Emersonian serenity conflicted with her recognition of the dreadful and terrifying aspects of spiritual life, and of the unjustified sufferings and inexplicable evils that riddle human existence. Instead of her spiritual insights revealing ever more clearly a grand harmony between the soul's experiences, the natural world, and divinity, they revealed instead profound and unresolvable paradoxes and disjunctions manifested most vividly, for her, in personal experiences of divine presence that alternated between loving communion and intense alienation, thus inspiring both elation and despair. And while at times she saw divinity in nature, and could find in her experiences of the natural world occasions for ecstatic "transport," more typically she experienced Nature as an alien realm, as a threatening and indifferent universe. In sum: Dickinson's poetry often testifies to a painful awareness of a radical ontological divide between her self and the ultimate divine ground of being, and to a similar divide between nature and the divine ground. That is, it witnesses—often in modes of anxiety and despair—to the radical *otherness* of divine reality, to its genuinely *transcendent* quality; and it continually articulates the many problems this radical otherness poses for our spiritual comprehension of self and universe and for the achievement of any kind of existential serenity. Thus, in a manner quite true to traditional Christian metaphysics, she rejects the pull toward the pantheist and "Eden here" tendencies of the liberalizing spiritualism of the Transcendentalists.

Dickinson's commitment to a truth of divine transcendence also informed her assimilation of, and the nature of her response to, advances by the natural sciences in the nineteenth century. Dickinson paid close attention to scientific discoveries and developments—including Darwin's theories and their impact—and her poems display a remarkably sophisticated knowledge of geological, chemical, botanical, and astronomical processes and technical terminology.[9] Consistent with this assimilation and her customary intellectual probity, her poetry reflects a clear grasp of how advances across the sciences constituted, in her day, a composite and cumulative challenge to traditional Christian beliefs—to belief in the existence of a Creator-God who omnipotently governs natural processes and is lovingly concerned with every human being's welfare, as well as in teachings concerning the divinity of Christ, miracles attributed to him, the Resurrection, and the promise of eternal life. Dickinson was at one with a growing cultural skepticism, abetted by science, regarding claims about "miraculous" events, which she rejected as consistently as she did Calvinist doctrines concerning original sin, salvation, election, and damnation; and, as we shall see, some of her poems express abandonment of belief in the Christian God of ultimate benevolence, a dispossession of hope in a personal afterlife, and even despair over whether the human struggle on earth is finally meaningful.

At the same time, even when Dickinson seems most in attunement with the growing nineteenth-century skepticism about traditional Christian beliefs in the face of attacks on them from adherents of either a purely scientific or a naturalistic worldview, she retains an undiminished religious sensibility and supra-natural orientation—shown often enough in poems (as well as in comments in letters) that scorn the notion that scientific discoveries could ever contradict or delegitimize the fact of a sacred, or divine, realm of being. This was due, it should again be emphasized, to her continual recognition, grounded in experience, of a *mystery of transcendence*—a genuine "beyond" of the material universe—which she experienced alternately as compellingly wondrous or frighteningly unfathomable.

While it is true that interpreting the mystery of transcendence as the God of Christian teachings repeatedly challenges her credulity, still transcendence for Dickinson has an inescapably divine character; that is, it has the character of *personhood*, however metaphorically or analogically this notion is to be understood. Transcendent reality, for Dickinson, could never be conceived as having only a "naturalistic," or impersonal, character, as it does in, say, Brahmanic Hinduism or philosophical Taoism, principally because, as her poems make clear, it is incomprehensible to her that her own personhood, or self, could have as both its originating source and its deepest ontological identity a creative principle lacking personhood. More concretely, as her poetry attests, her most intense experiences of transcendence are those involving loving desire and its (temporary) fulfillment, on the positive side, and those of anguished abandonment and emotional terrorization, on the negative side—and these are experiences of a divine "Other" who loves, abandons, and tortures. Thus her most meaningful experiences, resulting from her passionate desire for communion with what she perceives as both the origin of her self and the ultimate object of her longing, could in her view never have been caused by an impersonal transcendent principle. Such a notion is foreign to Dickinson's *experiential* horizon, which constantly rediscovers, and crystallizes in the symbols of her poetry, a *divine* transcendence—however difficult it is for her to entertain the belief that this is, indeed, the God espoused by the Christian traditions.[10]

Transcendence and Mystery

A sound interpretation of the spiritual quest expressed in Dickinson's poetry, one of the most extraordinary and challenging in all of modern literature, requires paying detailed attention to what she tells us in her poems (and occasionally in her letters) about what she sees as an honest understanding of the human relationship to divine transcendence. We may begin by noting three crucial aspects of that understanding.

First, one of Dickinson's recurrent poetic themes is that it is misleading and foolish to imagine the realm of divine transcendence, what she calls *Eternity* or *Paradise* or *Heaven*, to be some kind of place, or thing: some kind of "somewhere" or "elsewhere." This is because the very nature of transcendent reality is—to use two terms from her poetry—"Illocality," or "Boundlessness" (824). And how is such a reality discovered? She tells us: only by way of its *presence* in consciousness. It is in the invisible, intangible interiority of consciousness—and only there—that the discernment of a timeless and imperishable realm of meaning reveals itself. This discernment, importantly, is not a matter for her of the mind's *deducing* that the conceptions it entertains of divine eternity and imperishability refer to something real. It is rather the mind's recognition of the *presence* in consciousness of the divine basis of its own existence, the presence of a transcendent reality that reaches into consciousness from a "beyond" of consciousness, giving the human soul the ontological constitution of human-divine *co-presence.* A number of Dickinson's poems strive to make clear that what she variously calls *Eternity*, or *God*, or *Immortality*, or *Infinity* is only revealed to us as just such a truth of constitutive divine presence in consciousness. For example, she writes:

> The Blunder is in estimate
> Eternity is there
> We say as of a Station
> Meanwhile he is so near
>
> He joins me in my Ramble
> Divides abode with me
> No Friend have I that so persists
> As this Eternity (1690)

The ontological intimacy of personal consciousness and divine presence is so profound that Dickinson presents them in some poems as an identity.

> Heaven is so far of the Mind
> That were the Mind dissolved –
> The Site – of it – by Architect
> Could not again be proved –
> [. . .] (413)

And more famously:

> [. . .]
> The Brain is just the weight of God –
> For – Heft them – Pound for Pound –
> And they will differ – if they do –
> As Syllable from Sound – (598)[11]

This ontological identification, however, does not make Dickinson a kind of gnostic who equates human knowledge with divine knowledge; and she is certainly not a Feuerbachian type of reductionist who equates the divine with human imaginative projections. For while divine transcendence is revealed only interiorly—as it must be, being spaceless and timeless—and as ontologically interpenetrative with consciousness, it also remains *transcendence*. That is, while divine reality is distinctively constitutive of human consciousness, it is not contained by consciousness. So it is that in many of her poems Dickinson is at pains to convey how divine reality immeasurably transcends, with overwhelming mysteriousness, the limitations of human consciousness and comprehension. In fact, Dickinson's acute sensitivity and reactions to the unknowability of the "beyond" of meaning that co-constitutes consciousness is in the end the single most important factor in the spiritual journey depicted in her poetry.

This becomes obvious when we consider her interpretation of the nature of the self, or soul. Her scrutiny of her own consciousness informs much of her poetry, and one of the most prominent features of her view of self is that, because consciousness is, experientially, a limited participation in a boundlessness of transcendent meaning it can know itself only very incompletely. This is most directly stated in an undated poem in which Dickinson affirms both the divine creation of, and presence in, her mind, and her awareness that this divine depth of reality extends unassessably beyond any awareness or knowledge of it she might attain:

His mind of man, a secret makes
I meet him with a start
He carries a circumference
In which I have no part

Or even if I deem I do
He otherwise may know
Impregnable to inquest
However neighborly – (1730)

These lines bring to mind the fragment of the pre-Socratic philosopher Heraclitus, "You could not find the limits of the soul, even if you travelled every path; so deep is its logos."[12] The difference in Dickinson, of course, is the biblical divine personalization of the transcendent depth onto which each soul opens, a personalization emphasized in another poem whose first quatrain again emphasizes that divine presence is both co-constitutive of human consciousness and radically transcends all that humans can know and experience. Here she employs one of her favorite synonyms for God, the word "awe," which connotes both the divine reality itself and her feelings of fear and fascination in the face of divine power:

> No man saw awe, nor to his house
> Admitted he a man
> Though by his awful residence
> Has human nature been.
> [. . .] (1342)

Dickinson, then, knows where to search for the divine: in apperceptions and encounters within the interior of her own consciousness. But she also knows this search leads directly into the insoluble mysteries of transcendent meaning. This is the human situation she describes with her usual metaphorical nimbleness and wit in a prose fragment of 1872:

> Paradise is no Journey because it (he) is within – but for that very cause though – it is the most Arduous of Journeys – because as the Servant Conscientiously says at the Door We are (always – invariably –) out –.[13]

Paradise, *Eternity*, *God* is not an elsewhere; it is a placelessness revealed in the "within" of the soul's longing and reflection. And yet the seeking soul can scarcely know it beyond the mere fact of its reality, because transcendence must remain, in its substantial meaning, a beyond and an absence.

Second, the unknowability of transcendence dominates Dickinson's experiences and interpretations not only of the interior but also of the external world. It has often been noted that, for all her sympathetic delight in nature—in its bees and birds, flowers and trees, sun and moon, sunset and dawn—reminiscent of certain veins in Romantic poetry, Dickinson's relationship with the natural world, as revealed across the spectrum of her poems, shows itself to be deeply ambivalent. Her poems frequently express an alienation from nature, an experience of being "Homeless at home" in the world (1603), and an acute awareness of nature's indifference to human striving and suffering. But both her joyful responses to natural beauty and her alienated reactions to it derive from the same root cause: her recognition that every natural object is an ephemeral creation of and participation in a fuller and imperishable dimension of meaning, a divinely transcendent reality revealed to the self through the within of consciousness, whose purposes with and for nature seem sometimes glorious and sometimes dreadful but are always ultimately unknowable.

At times, Dickinson emphasizes the pleasures and comforts in apprehending nature as numinous, as in a poem about a tree near her house, which begins:

> By my Window I have for Scenery
> Just a Sea – with a Stem –
> If the Bird and the Farmer – deem it a "Pine" –
> The Opinion will do – for them –
> [. . .]

and ends with her assimilation of the tree into all of nature as the manifestation of a divine reality worthy of her worship:

> [. . .]
> Was the Pine at my Window a "Fellow
> Of the Royal" Infinity?
> Apprehensions – are God's introductions –
> To be hallowed – accordingly – (849)

More often, however, it is the uncanniness, even ominousness, of the sacred "otherness" suffusing the world of nature that Dickinson stresses. The penultimate quatrain from a much-anthologized poem expresses this vividly:

> [. . .]
> But nature is a stranger yet;
> The ones that cite her most
> Have never passed her haunted house,
> Nor simplified her ghost.
> [. . .] (1433)[14]

"Simplified" here means "clarified." Dickinson is saying that, for those with eyes to see, nature is haunted with a numinous presence that is unnerving and alienating because it is radically unknowable—and she concludes the poem with the terse assertion "That those who know her, know her less / The nearer her they get." For Dickinson, one sign of an undiscerning, or self-deluding, mind—whether of poetic, practical, or scientific bent—is that it presumes to be able to fully define and understand what the creatures and objects of the natural world are and mean. Dickinson's view is the opposite. In the words of James McIntosh, for her, if the soul is to be both honest and open to growth, "[t]he intellect needs not to know definitively and permanently the things it observes because they exist in time and space *and* disappear into an unknowable realm."[15] Existential openness to supervening mysteriousness, in nature as in the depths of the self, is a basic criterion of both intellectual and spiritual honesty for Dickinson.

Third, and most important, it is Dickinson's unwavering commitment to the truth of the unknowability of transcendent meaning that guides her critical, sometimes angry and often scornfully dismissive, reactions to Christian writing and preaching that present the nature and purposes of God as adequately revealed and clarified. In her poems she challenges, one after another, religious doctrines and presumptions that in her view claim to know the humanly unknowable. While she is not unsympathetic to the *urge* to believe in religious answers that, if they were indeed instances of knowledge, would give us great comfort, her honesty and self-respect compel her to be a witness to her own generically human ignorance about transcendent meanings.

For example, she bases her rejection of the doctrines of original sin and redemption on a straightforward confession of unavoidable human ignorance:

Of God we ask one favor, that we may be forgiven –
For what, he is presumed to know –
The Crime, from us, is hidden –
[. . .] (1675)

[. . .]
Is heaven an Exchequer?
They speak of what we owe –
But that negotiation
I'm not a Party to – (1260)[16]

Again, her contempt for the idea that divine reality is a God who listens to and answers human prayer, and who answers by way of comfort or insight whenever the human seeker knocks, is based on long experience of the frustration of her desire for spiritual comprehension:

There comes an hour when begging stops,
When the long interceding lips
Perceive their prayer is vain.
"Thou shalt not" is a kinder sword
Than from a disappointing God
"Disciple, call again." (1768)[17]

And the presumptions of prayer are, of course, part of a larger presumption in many Christian theological and church traditions that divine ultimacy is a God who is not merely all-knowing but also unfailingly merciful and just. This evokes incredulity on Dickinson's part, not only because of the unwarranted human pretension to comprehend what is transcendent but because it is belied by overwhelming evidence of unjust suffering, inexplicable calamity, and the indifference and cruelty built into the natural order of things. In a poem from her late twenties, she refers to children who have died young as "Sparrows, unnoticed by the Father –" (91), a simple but stern rebuke to Jesus' affirmation of God's omniscient care as related in the Gospel of Matthew; and in a poem written four years before she died, she delineates a divinity unmoved both by the destruction that attends the processes of the natural world and by human dismay at the seeming arbitrariness and amorality of divine action:

Apparently with no surprise
To any happy Flower
The Frost beheads it at it's play –
In accidental power –
The blonde Assassin passes on –
The Sun proceeds unmoved
To measure off another Day
For an Approving God – (1668)[18]

But if God cannot be known to be just or merciful, or attentive to human desire and distress, can God be known to be "God"?—that is, can the "Thou" of divine transcendence be more than a blank to a human ignorance honest with itself? In one of her most provocative poems on the theme of religious seeking, one that brings to mind advancing secularization in the nineteenth century and has a Nietzschean echo, Dickinson compares the faith of earlier times with her own incapacity to apprehend the divine nature:

Those – dying then,
Knew where they went –
They went to God's Right Hand –
That Hand is amputated now
And God cannot be found –
[. . .] (1581)[19]

The undiscoverability of divine character, so startlingly asserted here, is repeated in a famous sentence from her second letter to Thomas

Wentworth Higginson, the Unitarian minister, abolitionist, and writer to whom she wrote seeking advice on the publishability of her poetry, and who became to her a kind of mentor or "preceptor," where she states of her family, "They are religious – except me – and address an Eclipse, every morning – whom they call their 'Father'."[20] Now, this comment and the just-quoted poetic stanza can easily be misread as declarations that there is no God, that is, as confessions of atheism. But an "Eclipse" is not a metaphysical nothingness; rather, it is the hiddenness of something real. Likewise, just because God cannot be "found" by the human intellect doesn't mean the divine personhood within the hiddenness of transcendence is an illusion. Dickinson's spiritual position, rather, is characterized by the often-agonizing tension between her tenacious adherence to the truth that human existence participates in a reality whose ultimate ground is a divine Creator and her conviction that finite human understanding can know nothing, finally, of what this participation means or portends, or of the divine essence that is the ground of being.

This precise tension, it should be noted, has a long history of experience and symbolization within mystical strains of Christianity, in apophatic theologies that stress that God is ultimately a "Hidden" or "Unknown" God, a conceit with roots in the Hebrew scriptures and even further back in Egyptian antiquity.[21] The term *apophasis* literally means "denial" or "non-saying" or "non-sayable," and indicates in theological contexts the inability of human speaking or knowing to grasp divine transcendence. Dickinson's poetry, as William Franke notes, "continually approaches and even coincides with characteristic themes of negative" or apophatic theology in Christian (as well as Jewish and Islamic) textual traditions.[22] This being the case, a quick comment on Christian apophasis will not be amiss.

An apophatic mystical strain emerged early in the Christian theological tradition. Its first systematic developer and expositor was Pseudo-Dionysius the Areopagite (ca. 500), whose works, which were to become immensely influential, drew on centuries of Neoplatonic apophatic philosophy as well as on the writings of earlier church fathers such as Gregory of Nyssa. Dionysius's procedures and formulations for guiding attention to the mysteriousness and unapproachability of God by way of exacting indications of the unknowability of His essence became normative for many later Christian negative theologies.[23] The edifice of Christian apophatic theology is monumental; well-known Christian apophatic mystics include the medieval thinkers John Scotus Eriugena, Meister Eckhart, and Nicholas of Cusa; the Spanish mystics St. John of the Cross and Teresa of Avila; the anonymous English author of *The Cloud of Unknowing*; Jacob Boehme; and, closer to our own time, Simone Weil and Jean-Luc Marion. Comparison reveals that Dickinson's recurrent and inventive uses of all the devices of poetry to express the inability of human thought and words to apprehend the transcendent mystery of the divine Creator is close in spirit, if not at times identical, to a long-standing stream within Christianity—a stream that often flowed underground in the landscape of mainstream Christian churches and doctrinal orthodoxies such as those that dominated the social world of Dickinson's Congregationalist upbringing. Dickinson's understanding of her conscious existence as a tension toward a divine Beyond that she is convinced is real but whose essence and final designs she knows she cannot know remains, then, within the boundaries of long-standing Christian mystical tradition. But in her this tension toward an Unknown God leads to a relentless existential questioning and experiential testing of every Christian truth she encounters.[24]

Nowhere is this tension more apparent in her work than in poems in which she questions what happens to human beings in death. Again and again she brings into conjunction the possibility that death means personal annihilation with her awareness that the participation of human consciousness in divine transcendence suggests the possibility of some kind of personal afterlife. This tension is especially vivid in a poem from 1862:

> I know that He exists.
> Somewhere – in silence –
> He has hid his rare life
> From our gross eyes.
>
> 'Tis an instant's play –
> 'Tis a fond Ambush –

Just to make Bliss
Earn her own surprise!

But – should the play
Prove piercing earnest –
Should the glee – glaze –
In Death's – stiff – stare –

Would not the fun
Look too expensive!
Would not the jest –
Have crawled too far! (365)

This is not a poem, as some would maintain, in which Dickinson changes her position, as she reflects and writes, from an assertion of religious faith—"I know that He exists" (a first line ending with a rare full stop)—to a loss of that faith, in which the poem's mordant ending contradicts its confident beginning. The thinking in the poem, although anguished, is self-consistent. Dickinson begins with an affirmation of the fact of transcendent divinity; but in the context of that affirmation, she ponders the *possibility* that personal existence ends only in "death's stiff stare," which if true would reveal the drama of the self to be a grim "jest" perpetrated, presumably, by a cruel or indifferent God. This idea is posed as a question—one that Dickinson, as an honest spiritual questioner, cannot evade. But it remains a question; and what the poem shows is her awareness that not knowing what our participation in divine transcendence *means* can be the basis not only for hope in a personal afterlife, but also for a Macbeth-like despair in light of the possibility that, in the end, human existence on earth "signifies nothing."

Dickinson's principal spiritual fidelity, then, is always to the *mystery* of transcendent reality: to the unknowability of what it finally is, and of what our participation in it signifies. When she critiques Christian doctrines and corresponding pieties and presumptions of Christian believers, she is following in every point the evasion, or the obscuring, or the denial, of that mysteriousness. Because she experiences her own consciousness as—and from this experience, understands all of creation to be—the "intersection of the timeless with time," to use T. S. Eliot's phrase from *Four Quartets*, she has no doubt that creation is shot through with the divinely grounded transcendent meaning that she variously calls *Heaven*, *Eternity*, *Paradise*.[25] Every implication or consequence of what this ultimately means, however, in her view must remain uncertain. So she writes:

> Of Paradise' existence
> All we know
> Is the uncertain certainty –
> But it's vicinity, infer,
> By it's Bisecting Messenger – (1421)

Thus authentic spirituality, for Dickinson, means abjuring the so-called faith that oversteps the tight circumference of essential human ignorance. Genuine faith is, rather, the embrace of divine transcendence together with every uncertainty and doubt that recognition of the impenetrable mysteriousness of transcendence brings. As she wrote in a letter-poem late in her life to her closest friend and confidante, her sister-in-law Susan Gilbert Dickinson: "Faith is *Doubt*."[26]

Love and Terror

Given the foregoing, we should not be surprised to find the poems in which Dickinson describes both the most gratifying and the most dreadful extremes of her experience—poems of desire most richly fulfilled, and of pain most terribly suffered—to be lyrics in which her recognition of divine transcendence plays a central part. That this is the case can readily be shown by considering, first, poems whose topic is love (and as her writings make clear, love is for Dickinson the ultimate existential value) and, second, a few of the many poems describing Dickinson's experiences of terror, psychological trauma, emotional numbness, and despair, poems in which the acknowledgment of divine transcendence typically plays a sinister or distressing, but still crucial, role.

When Dickinson wants to describe what she has found to be of supreme worth in the drama of existence, she employs the term *love*. It is in "the revelation of love," as Helen Vendler describes it,[27] that Dickinson finds a reality to which she is willing to grant the status of an absolute value:

> Love – is anterior to Life –
> Posterior – to Death –
> Initial of Creation, and
> The Exponent of Earth – (980)

At their most sublime, experiences of love give her a fleeting sense of communion with what she cannot help but imagine as a divine and transcendent love that entices her with the allure of promise, even while she remains haunted with uncertainty about her ultimate destiny in relation to it, and even though experiences of agony may serve at times to eclipse or destroy that image. All of these elements are suggested in what may be Dickinson's most eloquent poem on the subject:

> The Love a Life can show Below
> Is but a filament, I know,
> Of that diviner thing
> That faints opon the face of Noon –
> And smites the Tinder in the Sun –
> And hinders Gabriel's Wing –
>
> 'Tis this – in Music – hints and sways –
> And far abroad on Summer days –
> Distills uncertain pain –
> 'Tis this enamors in the East –
> And tints the Transit in the West
> With harrowing Iodine –
>
> 'Tis this – invites – appalls – endows –
> Flits – glimmers – proves – dissolves –

Returns – suggests – convicts – enchants
Then – flings in Paradise – (285)

Love's overwhelming significance for the self is carefully delineated here, especially in the last stanza's cascading verbs, which confirm moments of paradisal joy while indicating how unstable the living soul's love-based relation with transcendence always remains, and how uncertain its ultimate destiny in relation to it.

Still, in poem after poem she identifies love as the highest realization of our positive relation to transcendence. "Love is like Life – merely longer" (287), she writes, and "Love – is that later Thing than Death –" (840). Given her biblically informed imagination, such a view inspires Dickinson on numerous poetic occasions to use the figure of Jesus to symbolize love in its utmost human capacity, and also to symbolize how a personal afterlife, should it be possible, can only rightly be conceived as love's fulfillment. While Dickinson always rejects authoritarian images of Jesus and the doctrine of his substantial identity with "God the Father," she is nevertheless powerfully drawn to the image of a human Jesus whose courage, compassion, and love show human participation in divine transcendence at its most completely realized.

In one particularly telling poem, which envisions a Jesus whose loving openness to reality extends even to the embrace of death through stating that "Christ – stooped until He touched the Grave – ," Dickinson allows herself to imagine this as an act of ". . . love annealed of love / Until it bend as low as Death / Redignified, above" (273). That is, she shows how the idea of a love unremittingly tempered and strengthened by further love makes sense of the imagined possibility of Christ's transfiguration, and thus of love as the means of a mysterious spiritual transformation—a transformation very much longed for by Dickinson—into a life beyond this life of suffering. Another poem revisits the theme:

To know just how He suffered – would be dear –
[. . .]

[. . .]
Was he afraid – or tranquil –
Might He know
How Conscious Consciousness – could grow –
Till Love that was – and Love too best to be –
Meet – and the Junction be Eternity (688)

Dickinson, of course, knows that she cannot know how Jesus suffered, or whether he experienced such a communion. But his example attracts her like no other for illustrating that it is love that enables us best to remain in attunement with the divine transcendence that is always present in consciousness and suggested by nature. As she writes in a letter of 1878, "Love makes us 'heavenly' without our trying in the least. . . . [and] its low 'Come unto me' begins in every place."[28]

Given Dickinson's profound association of love with transcendent reality, one might expect that her many poems describing experiences of psychological pain, deprivation, and emotional numbness, where the quickenings and comforts of love are agonizingly absent and in which a principal theme is the terror of life's meaninglessness, would register also a falling-away of confidence in the truth of transcendence. But such is not the case. Dickinson always remains acutely aware that her consciousness is a participation in a mystery of spaceless and timeless meaning; but the deeps of this mystery become, in periods of intense suffering, a terrifying abyss rather than an alluring unknown, a source not of spiritual hope and comfort but of spiritually originated affliction. In her famous poem beginning "There's a certain Slant of light," she emphasizes that the "Despair" she feels to have been placed like a "Seal" on her soul is "An imperial affliction / Sent us of the Air –" (320)—that is, it has a divine or transcendent source, sent for reasons unknown. Likewise in two of her most powerful and unsettling poems of psychological anguish, "'Twas like a Maelstrom, with a notch" (425) and "The Soul has Bandaged moments –" (360), she uses a language suggestive of spiritual agency, referring to "Goblin" and "Fiend" to convey her sense that the ultimate origins of her pain are uncanny and spiritual, and that whatever purposes her suffering might have, their basis lies in her soul's participation in the mystery of transcendence. In sum, extreme pain—like extreme joy—always directs Dickinson's imagination toward the unknowable depths of spiritual reality in which her consciousness is aware of participating.

She states this with precision, in a diction of typically Dickinsonian metaphorical and syntactical concision, in a two-stanza poem from 1864:

> A nearness to Tremendousness –
> An Agony procures –
> Affliction ranges Boundlessness –
> Vicinity to Laws
>
> Contentment's quiet Suburb –
> Affliction cannot stay
> In Acres – It's Location
> Is Illocality – (824)

The "Illocality" and "Boundlessness" toward which intense pain directs our consciousness transcend the "Laws" that govern "Contentment" in two senses. First, the *social* laws, or mores, to which everyday living is properly subordinated lose their relevance to a soul in "Agony." More profoundly, to the complacent and untroubled soul, the *laws of space and time* that structure the natural world can appear to circumscribe the whole of reality; but these laws are revealed to govern only a "Suburb" of the cosmos once extreme "Affliction" forces us to address the mystery of transcendence.

Inevitably, the spiritual questioning provoked in Dickinson by intense suffering guides her poetic imagination to Jesus' passion and crucifixion. Her frequent references to Calvary, in which she associates her own suffering with that of Jesus' crucifixion—she describes herself as "Queen of Calvary" (347) and "Empress of Calvary" (194)—are meant to suggest not only the intensity of her anguish but also her identification with the unrestricted openness of Jesus' human consciousness to transcendence, both in his extremity of doubt and in his hope for consolation. Calvary and Gethsemane are symbols that stand for how acutest anguish opens up—inwardly and invisibly—the abyss of transcendent mystery in the core of every spiritually self-aware soul. As she writes:

> [. . .]
> Gethsemane –
>
> Is but a province – in the Being's Centre –
> Judea –
> For Journey – or Crusade's Achieving –
> Too near –
>
> Our Lord – indeed – made Compound Witness –
> And yet –
> There's newer – nearer Crucifixion
> Than That – (670)[29]

Still, such experiences do not lead Dickinson to embrace the idea at the heart of Christology, and so central to much Christian self-understanding, that undeserved suffering is redemptive: that—as made manifest through and enacted by Jesus—it serves to reconcile sinful human nature with the just, merciful God of all Creation. That doctrine makes no more sense to her than it does to Ivan Karamazov. The only spiritual comfort her honest assessment of her experiences of anguish will allow her is recognition of the fact that, because the purpose of conscious participation in divine transcendence is impenetrable to human understanding, our experiences of both love and suffering in this life *may* hold an ultimate meaning in the economy of human-divine participation that, for now, we cannot surmise. Her credo of ignorance, and the utmost she can manage of cautious hope, are nowhere better distilled than in lines written in a letter to her cousins about the death of her mother, only four years before Dickinson's own death:

> She slipped from our fingers like a flake gathered by the wind, and is now part of the drift called "the infinite."

> We don't know where she is, though so many tell us.
>
> I believe we shall in some manner be cherished by our Maker – that the One who gave us this remarkable earth has the power still farther to surprise that which He has caused. Beyond that all is silence . . .[30]

As these words make clear, Dickinson's principal spiritual allegiance—and this holds true from her teenage years to the end of her life—was neither to any identifiable set of spiritual claims nor to a self-assured discrediting of the Christian vision in its entirety, but to the mysteriousness, the unknowability, of what the reality of divine transcendence and human participation in it finally mean. Nowhere does she express this point more succinctly than in a letter written, again to her cousins, about a year before her death: "That we are permanent temporarily, it is warm to know, though we know no more."[31] To claim to know more, in this as in other matters pertaining to transcendent meaning, would be to retreat from the truth of mystery and lose "the resilience not to be overcome by" its uncertainties, which is something her sense of spiritual authenticity will not allow her to do.[32]

It is due to this resilience, too, that she is no more approving of materialists or atheists than she is of her Christian neighbors who are convinced that they know ultimate truths. Of those who devote themselves exclusively to what is earthly and its rewards, and who ignore or deny what is—to her—the obvious fact of our participation in a divine infinite, she writes mockingly:

> How much the present moment means
> To those who've nothing more –
> The Fop – the Carp – the Atheist –
> Stake an entire store
> Opon a moment's shallow Rim
> While their commuted Feet
> The Torrents of Eternity
> Do all but inundate – (1420)

Dickinson laughs wryly at the blindness and silliness of those who are awash in evidence of transcendent reality—evidence glaring in the "awful residence" of the presence of timelessness within consciousness as well as in the natural world's perpetual testimony to a beyond of its own origins—but who insist that the material world is all. The "present moment" is all that they have, the hedonists and aesthetes, the sarcastic belittlers of religious vision, the adherents of scientism and other immanentist perspectives. Their desires and imaginations have, Dickinson holds, betrayed them into investing the here and now with the boundless value and meaning of the eternal—a ridiculous confusion, in her regard, if sadly understandable given the emotional and intellectual challenges of authentic spiritual openness, in addition to the impact on imagination of nineteenth-century cultural currents of "secularization."

Dickinson's spiritual position, then—while it can be confusing to readers of her poems who find her now worshipful of her Creator, now describing a negligent, indifferent, or cruel God; now hopeful of and curious about a personal afterlife, now resigned to despair or even dread of it; now confident that her experiences of love and joyful transport are revelatory of essential divine nature, now horrified by the thought that her experiences of anguish have their origin in divine malignancy—does have a coherent center, and is not self-contradictory. That center is her simultaneous affirmation of (1) the fact of divinely transcendent reality and (2) the mystery of what human participation in it means. Authentic spiritual faith, for Dickinson, is a steadfast acknowledgment of both of these facts—and such a faith is a first requirement, in her view, for any person's responsible embracing of their spiritual situation within reality:

> Faith – is the Pierless Bridge
> Supporting what We see
> Unto the Scene that We do not –
> Too slender for the eye
>
> It bears the Soul as bold
> As it were rocked in Steel

With Arms of steel at either side –
It joins – behind the Vail

To what, could We presume
The Bridge would cease to be
To Our far, vascillating Feet
A first Necessity. (978)

Faith is the confidence, born of love, that allows our "far, vascillating feet" to proceed not aimlessly but along the invisible bridge that links the world to the mystery of a divinely transcendent beyond. If we could "presume"—if we could take for granted—the "what" of that mystery, faith would be unnecessary. As it is, the invisible bond of faith that connects us to "things hoped for" and "things unseen" (Heb. 11:1) is a "first necessity" for a person's spiritual beginning and orientation, but wondrously enough a bond that feels as solid as "steel" as long as the seeking soul doesn't lose heart or vision.

These affirmations, and Dickinson's highly original grappling with transcendence within the context of a Christian culture and Christian imagination, place her literarily in a curious historical position. She appeals to us as a literary Modernist, or proto-Modernist; while as we know, the direction of much Modernist literature, both in poetry and prose, entails a turning aside or turning away from Judeo-Christian imagination and symbolism (obvious exceptions include Eliot and Auden). How attractive or persuasive that attempt at redirection is among Modernist giants such as Joyce, Pound, Woolf, Proust, William Carlos Williams, Beckett, Musil, and Stevens depends to a significant degree on the existential scope of the author's account of the human situation—that is, on how open to the full range of human experiences his or her works are. The greatness of each of these authors obviously relies on an appreciation, and some appropriation, of the enormous legacy of spiritual testimony and its literary expression in Western culture, which informs their attempts to exercise a spiritual imagination that is both non-Judeo-Christian and existentially convincing. Whatever the specific vision, though, it is a convincing literary expression of spiritual imagination only because it evokes, in some manner, mysteries too deep for human penetration.

If a recognition of truly transcendent reality and its mystery *do* inform a major Modernist author's vision, and he or she has recourse to an imaginal horizon other than the Judeo-Christian (which extends to the horizon of Islamic literature and mysticism), what options are available? For one, there is the world of philosophical symbolization in the classical Greek manner. For another, there is the imaginal world of cosmological polytheism. The first of these options we will see explored by Marcel Proust, the second by Ezra Pound. It is also possible to rely on Judeo-Christian symbols for expressing what is acknowledged to be an inescapable *idea* of transcendence, but to reject these as suspicious allurements and comforts on the agnostic assumption that the *reality* of transcendence remains cognitively and existentially inaccessible. That is the path of Samuel Beckett's mature work. We will take a look at each of these choices—although the road along Modernist literature's struggle with interpreting experiences of transcendence will lead us also to a consideration of T. S. Eliot's reclamation of the Christian vision, and to Bob Dylan's intermittently Christian evocations of the mysteries of "ulterior significance" that encompass human existence.

CHAPTER TWO

Marcel Proust

In Between World and Eternal Being

TO TURN FROM Emily Dickinson to Marcel Proust in an analysis of modern literature might seem strange at first glance. Proust's great work, the seven-volume novel *In Search of Lost Time* (originally titled in English *Remembrance of Things Past*), although largely set in the late nineteenth century, feels as if it belongs to a much later world than Dickinson's, although she wrote up until her death in 1886. Dickinson's poetry may be proto-Modernist, but Proust's novel is one of the founding works of Modernism itself; despite its outdated period settings, costumes, and customs, its voice and psychological perspectives have no whiff of literary quaintness about them—as Dickinson's poems, for all their striking originality and experimentalism, often do. But in fact it is quite appropriate to turn to Proust after a study of Dickinson, largely because of two qualities their works have in common. First, Dickinson and Proust are two of the most astute analysts of human consciousness in the history of literature; further, these are analyses of distinctively *modern* consciousness. Each explores with a rare combination of discernment and courage the interiority of the self in all its modern strangeness as polymorphic and fragmented, alone in its uniqueness, often alienated from nature, society, and itself, filled with self-doubt, and acutely aware of the status of personality as a project, a *becoming*. Second, as articulate explorers of the depths of consciousness, they are each enthralled by the self's encounter with the transcendent reality—the mystery of the beyond—that is discovered interiorly, when the self pays due attention to its most illuminating experiences; and thus Proust continues, albeit in a quite different mode and manner, Dickinson's hyper-attentive examination of the self's involvement with timeless meaning.

This continuity between the two authors, however, is easily obscured by two factors, one formal and one substantive.

The formal element that leads one to relegate them to separate literary spheres is not simply a matter of Dickinson being a poet and Proust a novelist. Rather it concerns Dickinson's working toward utmost concision of expression, her lapidary concentrating of meaning into linguistic units of greater and greater specific gravity, producing a nearly telegraphic mode of communication. Proust, by contrast, is the most discursive writer imaginable, in whose sentences and paragraphs nuances of insight and tangents of explanation unspool at hypnotic length. The character of mental attention one must bring to bear on Dickinson—focusing on metaphors and phrases as starbursts, concentration absorbed by brief explosions of compressed meaning—is very different from that demanded by Proust: a patient, undulant, ever-forward-oriented attention, like that of a long-distance swimmer, in a slow-moving accumulation of continually self-expanding and self-correcting thought.

And then there is a substantive difference, of a metaphysical nature, which can obscure the continuities in their analyses of the self. This pertains to their respective accounts of transcendent reality. In brief, Dickinson's transcendence is personal; it may or may not be the Christian God, but the encounter is with a transcendent *who*, not a *what*. By contrast, Proust's discoveries of transcendence reveal an impersonal reality—a dimension of meaning that is eternal, but not a Creator, a Friend, a Lover, or a Tormentor. Dickinson finds at the core of the universe and of her own existence a divine "Thou." Proust finds a truth of Eternal Being.

Considering all that separates the two writers' respective historical and cultural worlds, one might be tempted to view this latter difference as a reflection of the falling away, in Western modernity, of a certain provincialism of Christian imagination and metaphysical presumptions. But as we shall see in the case of T. S. Eliot, such a simplified explanatory trajectory is not convincing. Later we will have occasion to consider this difference between Dickinson and Proust as rooted principally not in their respective relationships to a cultural parochialism, but in mysteries of psychology, temperament, and accidents of biography. And at any rate, much more important for an understanding of spirituality in major modern literature is the common denominator that *unites* Dickinson and

Proust: their experiences of human consciousness as an interpenetration of temporal and timeless reality, of conscious existence as a reality "in between" world and transcendence. Both agree that human existence is, in the words of Eric Voegelin, "a temporal flow of experience in which eternity is nevertheless present" and in which at every moment "there persists the tension toward eternal being transcending time."[1]

Proust's Description of Existence as an In-Between

The elements of Proust's portrayal of the human condition in *In Search of Lost Time* that most often receive philosophical attention are his presentations of different types of memory; the complexity and multiformity of the self; the subjectivity of impressions; and the vagaries of desire and possessive longing, sexuality, and jealousy. Although such themes will be touched upon below, my principal focus will be Proust's vision and explanations of human conscious existence as an In-Between of immanence and transcendence. Of course, *In Search of Lost Time* is a novel, not a philosophical treatise, and as a literary artist Proust's principal obligation is to show—not to explicate in a systematic, explanatory way—the truths he wishes to convey about human existence and the self's relation to society, nature, language, art, time, and eternity. At the same time, this showing in Proust's work often takes the form of the "I" of the novel reflecting on such truths and explaining them at length—sometimes at great length. Since Proust's work is a novel, however, one may ask how far one is justified in taking the thoughts of the novel's "I," specifically as pertaining to the vision of human life as an existence in between world and transcendence, to be an accurate representation of Proust's own view.

Addressing this question requires, I think, recognizing three distinct authorial "voices" in the novel. The first voice is that of the Narrator. Structurally, the entire novel is the narration, in the first person singular, of one character recounting his childhood, growth to adulthood, and—most importantly—his formative experiences. A second voice belongs to the Narrator's younger and developing self, and reflects feelings, thoughts, and perceptions from within the viewpoint of that self at some stage in his development—a self referred to by the name "Marcel" at two points in the novel. Only at the very end of the novel's seven volumes do Marcel's voice and the Narrator's converge and become one, when the Narrator-now-Marcel, having discovered his vocation, prepares to begin writing the novel we have just read. And finally, to confuse matters, there is a third voice in the novel: the voice of Proust himself, which can to some degree be isolated from both that of Marcel and the Narrator, because a good deal of what Marcel says and does and what the Narrator writes about his own life does *not* correspond with important facts and details in Proust's biography, while at the same time it is possible to find in Proust's letters and essays sincere, often impassioned, expressions of judgments and viewpoints that are *exactly* reproduced in comments made by Marcel or by the Narrator in the novel.[2] In the novel, one finds certain assertions and assessments about consciousness, the self, society, and the metaphysics of the human situation carefully repeated and elaborated upon; and when these same assertions and assessments can be found in writings where Proust speaks for himself, we may conclude that they represent Proust's own considered judgments. Importantly for us, this is the case for all important passages explaining the structure of human participation in a reality beyond time and space—that is, to the elaborated account of human existence as an In-Between.

But why emphasize this distinction between the Narrator's or Marcel's voice, and Proust the writer's voice? Because there is some significance, it seems to me, in removing the *novel's* vision of human existence in the In-Between from the "what if" status of the point of view of a fictional Narrator. It is useful, that is, to understand the novel's philosophical anthropology as Proust's own, and to be able to rely on the novel's presentation of the In-Between of existence as Proust's own testimony, based on his own mystical experiences.

If the affirmation of human consciousness as an In-Between of immanence and transcendence is central to Proust's personal vision of existence, it is also of utmost importance, artistically, to the unity and integrity of his novel. The novel is the story of a life, which, like every existence, is lived and suffered in time; and in the reading it soon becomes clear that time as lived is the theme of the novel. But time lived, Proust reveals, can be seen to have an integral ontological form, to constitute a genuine *story* rather than being just an aggregate of disconnected chronological episodes that are perishable, contingent, and finally meaningless, because existence is at all times lived in the intersection of worldly time and a unifying transcendent meaning. Therefore just as in Proust-the-author's view human participation in eternal being grounds and integrates human existence, so the written story of Marcel's life, as created and presented by Proust, gains its distinctive *novelistic* unity and integrity from the author's slowly unfolding presentation of Marcel's existence as the In-Between of (1) a temporal, always-changing, worldly self and (2) some dimension of that self which continually participates in eternal reality—a novelistic motif which, one finally comes to understand, integrates all of the novel's episodes.

This is why it is to the point to emphasize that Proust's novel, in its vastly digressive way, and amid many other objectives, most fundamentally tells the story of Marcel's ongoing intimations, and eventual explicit discovery, that human existence participates in eternal being "outside of time." However, because this discovery does not take place (and thus the unified meaningfulness of both the narrated existence and the formal integrity of the novel are not revealed) until the final volume, *Time Regained*, the reader is left in the dark for a very long time about how the novel and the life whose story it tells "make sense" as a whole. Given that the novel's seven volumes were published over the course of fourteen years (1913–1927), up until the time the final volume appeared (five years after Proust's death) the whole work appeared to many readers and critics to be formless and disconnected—not to mention endless. As Roger Shattuck points out, "It looked at first like a conspiracy against readers."[3] But the concluding volume's clear and extensively elaborated account of the in-between structure of Marcel's existence effectively radiates backward over the whole work; elucidates many earlier passages that can then be recognized as hints of what is to come; and shows that Proust carefully planned the novel's integrated form and—for all of his expansions, as he added and added to its original length during the years between appearances of various volumes—successfully kept the unity of this form under strict control through its grounding in his vision of human life as participation in eternal meaning.[4]

Proust's portrayal of human life as an "in-between" existence may be illuminated by addressing in turn his affirmation in the novel of four points: first, that there is a transcendent reality that humans participate in and can know of; second, that humans experience transcendence only from within the perspective of the interpenetration, the mixture, of spatiotemporal and timeless reality; third, that Proust's (or Marcel's) own existence in time is revealed to be a meaningful story only because it participates in eternal meaning; and fourth, that there is no logical proof, or *need* of any proof, that the transcendence in which humans participate "exists." After investigating these topics it will be possible to explain why Proust is properly described as a mystic, and to identify some of the existential paradoxes belonging to the structure of human self-understanding that Proust's mystical account of the human situation shows to be unavoidable and irresolvable.[5]

To begin with, then: Proust is unequivocal, in the novel's final volume *Time Regained*, in his assertion that there is an eternal ground of reality, unconditioned by space and time, and that humans can know of their participation in it. Marcel states that there is a "being within [him]" that is able to undergo certain experiences only because, in the course of having them, this being consciously exists "outside time." In such moments, "freed from the order of time," "liberated from the contingencies of time," Marcel is able to taste, he says, the "contemplation . . . of eternity," and thereby is revealed both "a portion of our mind more durable" than the temporal self and a reality "whose value [is] eternal."[6] The literary critic Harold March aptly devotes a section of his book *The Two Worlds of Marcel Proust* to an analysis of Proust's account of "Transcendent Reality"[7]—a reality that Marcel describes wistfully, despite his joyful moments of participation in it, as "remote from our daily preoccupations," a reality "which it is very easy . . . to die without ever having known" and yet which is "all the time immanent in [men] . . ."[8]

Second, Proust also makes it clear that transcendent reality is only experienced in the medium of the In-Between—that is, the human being who experiences it is not only immersed in time, but also apprehends eternal reality only *through the medium of sensations and perceptions* that belong to the human body embedded in the world of space and time.

This fact directs our attention to the novel's famous "epiphanies": the ecstatic moments of existing simultaneously both in and outside of time, which Proust calls at one point in *Time Regained*, in an inclusive reference, *impressions bienheureuses*—"happy impressions," or "blissful moments," or "privileged moments."[9] The most famous of these *impressions bienheureuses* is described early in the novel when Marcel, as an adult, tasting crumbs of a madeleine in a spoonful of tea, is suddenly immersed in intense and, to his mind, *present* realities of certain childhood experiences—experiences he relives with a completeness and fullness of perception and feeling (experiences in their "first, full effulgence") that no effort of voluntary memory, or effort at intellectual recollection, could ever have come close to evoking.[10] The novel describes, depending on how one chooses to define them, somewhere between eleven and fifteen such *impressions bienheureuses*—not accounting for episodes where Marcel appears to turn away from, or somehow abort, such an experience.[11] Most critics agree that there are seven or eight such *impressions* that are crucial for understanding what Proust intends to convey, which is this: that *through the medium of certain sensory experiences*, often trivial enough, we can attain to glimpses of eternal reality and our participation in it; and, further, that the joy such moments almost always evokes in us, together with the certitude that we participate in an eternal reality, assures us that our lives have meaning and value. As a result of such *impressions bienheureuses*, we no longer need fear that our lives are nothing but pointless affairs of living, suffering, aging, and perishing within an exclusively spatiotemporal reality.

As described in the novel, there are three sources of *impressions bienheureuses*. One is the contemplation of nature and world (including human-made structures); a second is experiences of art (literature, painting, and music are particularly important in Marcel's story, but architecture, theater, sculpture, and other arts play their parts); and the third—and by far the most important source—is experiences of "involuntary memory," such as the experience provoked by Marcel's tasting of madeleine crumbs in spoonfuls of tea.

To treat the most important source first: in the episodes of involuntary memory, a sensory experience in the lived present brings flooding into Marcel's mind a similar sensory experience from his past life, but in a manner that is uncanny and deeply meaningful because the past sensation is not experienced as located in the past but as *present*. That is, the self suddenly becomes "the self that originally lived" the past sensation while still remaining the self living and experiencing the similar or analogous present sensation.[12] In this "magnetism of an identical moment," the self is not merely aware of but *is*—this is Proust's central point—the self of both "times."[13] His explanation of how such a phenomenon can occur centers on two affirmations.

The first affirmation is this. A present sensation—for example, the first *impression* of the five linked epiphanies in *Time Regained*, which entails Marcel's experience of standing on "uneven paving-stones" in the courtyard of the Guermantes mansion in Paris—can, involuntarily and with an overwhelming vividness and thoroughness of remembrance, evoke a past sensation—in this case a *precisely similar* feeling of standing on "two uneven stones" in the baptistery of St. Mark's Cathedral in Venice—because the two sensations share a common, timeless "essence," and Marcel has suddenly and involuntarily gained access to this essence.[14] The second affirmation follows: the self can in truth apprehend and "enjoy the essence of things," essences that constitute the true and timeless reality "behind" what we experience through our bodies, because there is a dimension of the self that is itself "extra-temporal." These two affirmations are the result of Proust's reflections on his most singularly profound *impressions*, as recounted in *Time Regained*. In that volume, the *impressions bienheureuses* of involuntary memory lead Marcel, through careful and prolonged reflection on their nature and meaning, to conclude that "real" personal life, which is our enduring, timeless self, and "real" truth, which consists of the timeless essences of meaning, may be discovered by us when, experiencing "a quality common to two sensations, we succeed in extracting their common essence and in reuniting them to each other, liberated from the contingencies of time . . ." When this occurs, consciousness rises to an apprehension of timeless and essential reality through the "miracle" of the self's "escape from the present," which is an escape from being bound to the merely temporal dimension of change, decay, and death.[15]

However—and contrary to what Samuel Beckett asserts in his 1931 essay on the novel—this escape described by Marcel does not constitute an "obliteration" of time. That is, it is not an experience whose result is that "Time is dead."[16] Time is very much alive in the *impressions bienheureuses* of involuntary memory, even as the self "escapes from time," because the events are based on *sensations experienced through the time-bound body*. The *impressions bienheureuses* are sensorily drenched, and therefore drenched in time. In other words, they are moments of being *simultaneously in time and outside time*, in which time is experienced in a strange "contradiction of survival and annihilation," as simultaneous attention to sensations of time present and the regaining of sensations of a time past produce a "synthesis of [the] survival and annihilation" of time.[17] Proust's account of human access to timelessness is a portrayal of human existence as an In-Between of immanent and transcendent reality: only *in* time and *through* time, Proust's descriptions and explanations show, can timeless, eternal reality be humanly experienced. In the *impressions bienheureuses* of involuntary memory, consciousness experiences—in the phrasing of T. S. Eliot—the intersection of the timeless with time.[18]

That the revelation of the eternal occurs only in the medium of this "intersecting" is underscored by Proust through his emphasizing that in moments of involuntary memory the self becomes intensely aware of the particularity—the individual and unique existence—of the sensorily experienced objects of "time present." This awareness differs from our everyday sensations and memories because, he explains, we habitually perceive and understand things only in terms of abstract and general concepts. But apprehension of the timeless essence of a thing produces in us a momentary lifting of this veil of habit and abstraction, bringing a sudden, illuminating recognition of the utter originality, the pure individual existence, of a thing, place, or person—what Duns Scotus and later Scholastics called the *haecceitas*, the unique being, of some worldly thing. In the course of the novel, Marcel repeatedly expresses his longing for, his desire to sense and feel and know, the pure individuality of what he encounters without "abstract ideas of things" constituting a barrier between himself and objects, places, and people.[19] One of the wonders of the *impressions bienheureuses* of involuntary memory is that, through revealing a sensed object to be a truly singular manifestation of a timeless essence, the object sensed is suddenly shot through with pure particularity, is glimpsed not through the lens of an abstract concept but encountered as concretely unique. As Marcel puts it in *Time Regained*, the *impressions bienheureuses* of involuntary memory induce "shocks to the senses" resulting in his perceiving, in the memory-triggering things, the "concept of 'existence' which they usually lack," thus making it possible for him "to secure, to isolate, to immobilize—for a moment brief as a flash of lightning—what normally it never apprehends: a fragment of time in the pure state."[20] What this last phrase means is that Marcel recognizes, in light of his reflections on the significance of the *impressions*, that a worldly object is only apprehended in its true reality, in its "pure state," when it is seen as an absolutely unique thing in space and time that manifests an invisible, eternal essence. This vision secures two crucial truths at once: the ineluctable reality of the thing or place or person in its uniqueness (since it is no longer known as merely a "conceptual abstraction"), and the reality of the timeless essence of which it is a manifestation. Thus Proust's vision of the in-between character of his existence occasioned by the *impressions bienheureuses* of involuntary memory makes simultaneously indisputable the real meaningfulness of the singular particularities that make up the world and the genuineness of timeless being.

As already noted, the sources of *impressions bienheureuses* include not only experiences of involuntary memory, but also experiences triggered by certain experiences of natural or worldly objects and those that arise from encounters with great works of art. Accounts of both of these latter types of experience are scattered throughout the novel, and some of them give rise to important *impressions bienheureuses*, such as the young Marcel's response to viewing the steeples of Martinville described in the first volume, *Swann's Way*, and the adolescent Marcel's reaction to the "musty smell" in the little water-closet pavilion in the Champs-Élysées described in volume two, *Within a Budding Grove*.[21] Usually, however, Marcel's accounts of significant experiences entailed in spontaneous mystical responses to the world or arising from his engagements with art are described as merely preludes to, or hints of the possibility of, more profound *impressions*, through his describing them as experiences in which timeless reality is vaguely sensed as a "mystery" beneath or behind the "outward appearance" of things.[22]

For example, with regard to contemplative responses to the world, in *Swann's Way* Marcel describes how, as a child, he would continually be drawn by a vague and passing apprehension of some "mystery that lay hidden in a shape or a perfume . . . a mass of disparate images—the play of sunlight on a stone, a roof, the sound of a bell, the smell of fallen leaves," which only much later in life he will discover to have been a jejune apprehension of essential, timeless reality.[23] Again, in the adult life described in later volumes of the novel, Marcel is attracted and invited by many such apprehensions of mystery: the "mystery of a place," the "mystery of personality," the mystery of names, attractions that usually end in disappointment, but which in *Time Regained* are revealed to have all along been "presentiments" of the mystery of eternity that is revealed in its climactic *impressions bienheureuses*, and fully understood only by the mature Marcel after a strenuous effort to elucidate for himself the meaning of all these epiphanies.[24]

With regard to art, it is unsurprising that Proust is particularly interested in, and describes repeatedly in the novel, the manners in which art in all its forms can evoke a sense of the mystery of eternity, since in *Time Regained* Marcel will find his vocation in producing a work of literary art—the novel we have been reading—in whose creation and worth he can now believe because he has clarified for himself, and is certain, that the artistic evocation of the mystery of eternal truth is the revelation of a genuine reality: that human beings, whether they understand it or not, live in the In-Between of immanence and transcendence. Proust's understanding of the role of art in spiritual life will be addressed later in this and the next chapter.

This brings us to our third topic. It is the revelation of eternal reality, and Marcel's participation in it, that alone for Proust can give his novel its integrative and narrative unity, because its essential subject matter is existence in time, and it is only participation in eternity that gives existence in time metaphysical unity or identity. The *impressions bienheureuses* not only reveal to Marcel that his existence has a greater significance than mere existence in space and time; they also enable him to perceive the disparate episodes and stages of his life as having an ontologically interrelated significance. Thus Marcel eventually realizes and is able to affirm (as related in *Time Regained*) that his entire life—his sensations, feelings, thoughts, encounters, his disappointments and pleasures, his sorrows and joys, his intellectual efforts, his vague apprehensions of mysterious depths of meaning, his aesthetic experiences, his social life, even his thwarted attempts at attaining satisfaction in romantic love and the ensuing tortures of jealousy—all add up to something meaningful as a whole, that his life constitutes a genuine *story*. And the central motif of this story, the existential motif that guides its unfolding pattern and grounds its coherence, is, unsurprisingly, Marcel's *search* for the eternal meaning that from childhood he continually glimpses and eventually in adulthood comes to explicitly identify. In the end he finds what he had always been searching for: "verities pertaining to a world more real than that in which I lived."[25] And so he describes the afternoon of the five climactic epiphanies in the final volume as "this most wonderful of all days which had suddenly illuminated for me not only the old groping movements of my thought, but even the whole purpose of my life."[26] And there can then ensue, for Marcel (now merging into the Narrator) the decision to fulfill his call to be a literary artist—a call he had long suspected of being an illusion both in terms of his talent and the value of literary art—by writing a novel about a person's (that is, his own) "search for lost time": his search for the meaningfulness of time passed, time forgotten, time wasted, but which in the end is revealed to be not lost at all, because all of its meaning has been preserved and has a narrative integrity through its participation in eternal truth and value.

Fourth and finally, however, Proust/the Narrator makes a point of stating in numerous passages that there is no proof—no logical, philosophical, or scientific proof—that eternal and "essential" reality exists, and that we participate in it and can know of it. Nor does it matter that there is no proof. It is a truth whose verification and "indisputable evidence" lie in three aspects, or characteristics, of the *impressions bienheureuses*.[27] These are (1) the *special joy* that typically floods his being in his experiences of "escape from time"; (2) the *feeling of certitude* about eternal reality and about the meaningfulness of world and existence that this joy brings with it; and (3) the accompanying complete *evaporation of all anxieties* about the future, "the vicissitudes of life," and death.[28]

Proust works hard to communicate the elevated kind of happiness, the distinctive joy, that almost always accompanies the *impressions bienheureuses* by using a variety of expressions to emphasize its special character. It is an "exquisite pleasure," an "all-powerful joy," "felicity," an "unreasoning pleasure," a "positive rapture," and again and again simply a "special pleasure."[29] At times his expressions elevate this pleasure to a supernatural status: he describes it is an "extra-temporal joy," a "supraterrestrial joy," and even at one point surmises that it might be the "boldest" human approximation to that "bliss of the Beyond" of which religious teachings tell.[30]

Marcel experiences many types of pleasure, but this is the only joy that satisfies and answers the search that has shaped his existence. And it is the intensity and purity of this joy that leaves him without question that he is genuinely experiencing timeless reality. In the joy, the rapture, of the *impressions bienheureuses* all "intellectual doubts" about eternal reality, and thus about the value of living, disappear; the joy itself is "like a certainty," and Marcel cannot imagine a man who would not "have confidence in [such a] joy."[31] Doubts about what the joy signifies are made impossible, above all, by the fact that every time he experiences it death immediately becomes "a matter of indifference," along with all anxieties about life's slings and arrows.[32] This is most fully and beautifully expressed in a passage from the account of the first, and most famous, epiphany, which tells of effects of tasting crumbs of a madeleine soaked in tea:

> An exquisite pleasure had invaded my senses, something isolated, detached . . . And at once the vicissitudes of life had become indifferent to me, its disasters innocuous, its brevity illusory . . . I had ceased now to feel mediocre, contingent, mortal. Whence could it have come to me, this all-powerful joy?[33]

This last, key question, located near the start of the novel, will be answered only in its final volume: the origin of this "exquisite pleasure" is the experience of timelessness, of the self "freed from the order of time," who can look upon suffering, failures, disasters, death, and the perishability of all temporal things with indifference because these no longer constitute a threat to his search for meaning.[34] The meaningfulness of existence is assured because life is existence in the In-Between: immanence participates in, and is comprehended by, transcendent truth and value; and the experienced revelation of that truth and value causes *necessarily* the instant evaporation of despair and uncertainty about life's meaning.

The four elements just analyzed clarify beyond doubt that for Proust human life is always lived, to borrow the language of Eric Voegelin, "in a temporal flow of experience in which eternity is nevertheless present" and in which "there persists the tension toward eternal being transcending time."[35] It also suffices to justify describing Proust as a mystic. Most critics have no hesitation in referring to the *impressions bienheureuses* as "mystic experiences" or "mystical experiences"; even Samuel Beckett, so temperamentally averse to the non-ironic use of such spiritual language, applies the phrase straightforwardly three times in his essay on Proust.[36] What is not at all clear is what type of mystic Proust is. He repeatedly affirms joyful personal experiences of a transcendent mystery that he asserts to be the "true" or "essential" reality; but as mentioned earlier, one fails to find in his reports of these experiences anything like an "encounter" with God or a divine "person." Although adjectives such as "celestial," "supernatural," and "divine" are dotted throughout his passages explicating the *impressions bienheureuses*, at no time does he ascribe "personhood," in the sense of the Western religions, to the transcendent reality he testifies to with such emphasis and at such length. For this reason Edmund White identifies Proust as a "mystical atheist" and Harold Bloom describes Proust's spiritual posture as "secular mysticism"—reasonable enough descriptions, but ones that raise a number of questions and issues that will be addressed briefly below.[37] First, though, it will be useful to note a number of existential paradoxes that Proust's mystical account of the human situation, "secular" though it may be, reveals to be necessary ingredients of an accurate self-understanding of existence in the In-Between.

A first paradox pertains to self-understanding. It is paradoxical that, when authentic self-recognition takes place through acknowledging the fact that one's very being as a human is existence in the In-Between of immanence and transcendence, this entails at the same time discovering that the most intimate ontological core of the self is permanently unknowable because it is the element of one's being that belongs to the mystery of what is beyond space and time. Proust highlights this fact in a number of passages (usually in the context of accounts of *impressions bienheureuses*) by referring to that part of himself that is "freed from the order of time" not as "I," but variously as "a being whom we carry within us," "the being which at that moment . . . was an extra-temporal being," a being that "was myself and something more than me," and, most tellingly, the being that is "the only part of ourselves that is real and incommunicable"—identified here as unqualifiedly "real" because it participates in imperishable reality beyond space and time, and as "incommunicable" because it is participatorily identical with the mystery of transcendence.[38] To know oneself truly, Proust indicates, is to know that the essence of oneself is unknowable.

A second existential paradox illuminated by Proust is that we can only come to feel the truth of death—that is, bear the full emotional cognizance of death, and accept with clarity the "destructive action of Time" that leads to death—once death has ceased to feel like a threat to the meaningfulness of life in time by our discovering that we participate in eternal reality.[39] This paradox is brought out most clearly in Marcel's account of that *impression* of involuntary memory when, returning in later adolescence to the seaside hotel in Balbec where previously he had stayed and been cared for by his now-dead grandmother, upon touching the top button of his boot to begin undressing he is flooded with remembrance of the first night of a prior arrival there with her. At that moment, through involuntary memory, she becomes for him utterly real, genuinely "alive" for the first time since she had had the stroke leading to her death, *present* to him in her actual and complete particularity—but only at the same time through his suddenly discovering, at the deepest emotional level, that she is *truly dead* and so learning that he has "lost her forever." While this "sudden revelation of death" breaks his heart, it is nevertheless an experience of participation in timelessness, a "crisis which annihilates time and space," although at this youthful stage in his development he has no explicit understanding of this truth.[40] Thus here we do not hear of an "exquisite joy" or "special pleasure" arising from this particular *impression bienheureux*, but rather of a "painful synthesis of survival and annihilation"—a simultaneous recognition that death means irrevocable passing ("annihilation") but also an awareness that both she and he participate in a dimension of meaning beyond world and perishing ("survival").[41] Only later, as a result of the joyful epiphanies described in *Time Regained*, will Marcel, through his efforts to understand the meaning of the *impressions bienheureuses*, explicitly make the connection between (1) the vision of a reality beyond death which removes death's threat to life's meaningfulness and (2) the ability to see clearly, and embrace emotionally, the always-particular and grim actuality of mortal aging and death and to recognize time—"ordinarily without qualities in our normal lives"—as the ravaging, "destructive demon" it truly is.[42]

A final existential paradox worth noting is that the *impressions bienheureuses* that reveal life to be existence in the In-Between are carefully described by Proust as "given"—as not achieved but rather granted, triggered spontaneously and suddenly, and typically when Marcel is in a downcast and resigned mood—while at the same time this "givenness" is in some sense the consequence of Marcel's ongoing search for the meaning of his life, which constitutes the dynamic core of conscious existence.[43] Are we meant to understand, then, that the *impressions bienheureuses* are "gifts" over which Marcel has no control but at the same time are a result of (one might say a reward for) his continually resurgent efforts to understand the meaning of his existence? The paradoxical answer to this is yes. Roger Shattuck has phrased the issue well: everything Marcel has gone through and struggled toward, he writes, "has imperceptibly shifted the odds in his favor [for experiencing the *impressions bienheureuses*] until *chance has the force of fate*."[44] Marcel's lifelong responsiveness to the allure of, and attempts to reflectively penetrate the meanings of, the "mysteries" he continually encounters in things and persons—the "signs and secrets"[45] beneath and behind and within things and people—eventually make it his "fate," his destiny, to attain to conscious experiences of transcendence; at the same time, the epiphanies are *gifted* to him when he has no inkling of their approach, given even "against [his] will"—an unbiddenness, he notes, that serves as another "mark of their authenticity." Thus one could say he "was not free to choose them," but still his persistent search for the true ground of meaning, for eternal being, has practically guaranteed their emergence.[46] One of the paradoxes of existence in the In-Between, then, is that the explicit discovery of the metaphysical truth of existence as the intersection of world and eternal meaning is at once the consequence of efforts of will and the gift of revelation.

Gifts Without a Giver

Yet the gift of the revelation of transcendent reality, notably for Proust, has no Giver. Proust never symbolizes transcendence as "God," even though he uses adjectives such as "divine" and "supernatural" to refer to eternal being. His affirmations of transcendence sidestep, one might say, all religious traditions that account for experiences of transcendence by acknowledging a *presence*, a "Thou," who has drawn the human seeker along the journey toward revelation. Dickinson, in her idiosyncratic way, stands firmly within this tradition: for her, the love of reality that has guided her to experience a "beyond" as its (and her) origin is incomprehensible except as a transcendent Lover and Creator (and Abandoner); her longing for experiences of ultimate communion require, in order to make sense, a divine partner (however mysterious), a transcendence who as Love can be a divine *answering* to unrestricted human love. *Cor ad cor loquitur.* But Proust's revelations of eternal being are not the unveiling of divine presence; transcendence for him is an impersonal and unanswering dimension of meaning.

Nowhere in Proust's novel is it explained *why* eternal, transcendent reality should not be symbolized in personalistic terms—why it is inappropriate to refer to a "Giver" of the gifts of the *impressions bienheureuses.* It is true that here and there in the novel Proust's language seems to hint at, or indulge in brief, hesitant glances toward, the notion that transcendent reality might be a "divine partner." For example, describing in *Swann's Way* Marcel's youthful fascination with things giving rise to sensory impressions whose power and beauty intrigue him—"a gleam of sunlight on a stone, the smell of a path"—he recalls that they "appeared to be concealing . . . something which they invited me to come and take."[47] This ascription of an invitation is intensified later in the novel, when he describes how, as a mature man, in certain artworks he was "able to apprehend the strange summons" they presented to him "as the promise and proof that there existed something other" than the perishable, merely temporal world.[48] "Summons" and "invitations": however metaphorical Proust's use of the words are, they cannot help but hint at a summoner and inviter. Finally, there are two isolated passages worth noting with regard to the issue. In one, Marcel/the Narrator rather surprisingly (given the portrayal of love in his novel) refers to a "universal love" of which his perennially disappointed efforts at loving another person he "knew" to be a "tiny fragment." In another, he mentions a "universal spirit" to which the "portion of [his] mind more durable" than the part of the self that can die should "give [the] love, [and] the understanding of this love" that he has instead been directing repeatedly and frustratingly toward individuals.[49] But there is no follow-up to or expansion on these references to a "universal love" and a "universal spirit" to which the undying part of his self should, or will, offer his love. In the end Proust's vision of transcendence remains impersonal.

This fact should not be taken to indicate that Proust was merely a peculiarly gifted and articulate representative of the growing European cultural elite who looked down on traditional religious belief as superstitious and passé, or that he had only slight acquaintance with those traditions, or that he felt antipathetic toward religious practitioners. Proust's father, Adriene, an eminent physician and specialist in epidemiology and hygiene, was raised Catholic and his mother belonged to a middle-class Parisian Jewish family; and although neither parent, nor much of their immediate families, was religiously devout, Proust (himself baptized Catholic) grew up in an extended family milieu that enabled him to absorb knowledge of both Jewish and Christian scriptures, doctrines, and rituals, and their respective treasure-houses of artistic, literary, architectural, and other modes of symbols.[50] In an article written at the age of twenty or twenty-one, "L'irreligion d'état" (1892), Proust proclaimed his belief in Christianity and rejection of all materialist worldviews,[51] and though this identification with Christianity as an absolute truth soon faded, throughout his adulthood Proust inhabited a "very wide circle of Catholic, Jewish, and Protestant friends and contacts" with whom he carried on discussions and correspondence on spiritual topics.[52] In his novel's portrayals of religious believers, whether casual or rigid in their devotion, Proust is often satirical but never mean-hearted; on the contrary, what is often conveyed is a deep sympathy for the impulses of faith and respect for the beauties of spiritual life. The best way to characterize Proust's overall attitude toward Christian faith in his mature writings, states Barbara Bucknall, is to describe it as a "mixture of exasperation and affection" not uncommon in those "who have been taught in their youth to love a religion which in their maturity they have left behind."[53]

With his loss of faith in the personal God of Christianity, Proust became a mystic of a different order. Precisely what type of mystic is not a simple question to answer. The mysticism of Marcel whose genesis and development is so carefully described during the course of *In Search of Lost Time*, and so elaborately explained in its concluding volume, has been characterized, on the basis of its presentation of transcendence and the relationship of the Narrator's self to Eternal Being, as essentially

Buddhist by the scholar of Eastern religions R. C. Zaehner; as more or less Hindu by Harold Bloom and Roger Shattuck; as compositely Hindu-Buddhist but with a residue of Christian longing for eternal life by Barbara Bucknall; and as Platonist by nearly everyone.[54] Each of these interpretations has its merits, and perhaps it is in viewing Proust's mysticism as a kind of idiosyncratic Modernist amalgamation of ideas that correspond in different facets to elements in Platonist, Hindu, and Buddhist teachings that one hews most closely to the evidence, especially considering the impact on Proust of Schopenhauer's Plato-inspired and Eastern-admiring philosophical mysticism.[55] Schopenhauer's aesthetic theory, also, which describes art as the one refuge and salvation from the struggles and sufferings of life, had a significant influence on Proust; and it was a central inspiration to the French Symbolist poets whose attitudes toward both art and the mysteries of existence were a major influence on Proust during his formative years and into the time of his early career. Indeed, in attempting to understand Proust's mysticism, a brief consideration of Proust's relation to the French Symbolists will be of use. It not only will help to explain one of the most important literary sources of his Modernist achievement, but also will illuminate the nature of Proust's carefully articulated mysticism—his reflectively lucid account of transcendent mystery and the temporal self's relationship to it—by contrasting it with the elaborately evocative but deliberately unclear mysticism of the earlier Modernists of the Symbolist school.

In poetry, Symbolism refers to a movement that gained an official designation and a program of literary ideals in the mid-1880s, but which retroactively embraces the four mid-century French poets who are recognized as the originators of the perspectives, styles, and aims of those who came afterward: Baudelaire, Mallarmé, Verlaine, and Rimbaud. In the poetry of literary Romanticism, the "symbol" had already been given an elevated significance, usually referring to a natural object or place or an occurrence that was presented, more or less straightforwardly, as "the embodiment of some greater truth."[56] The Symbolists advanced and complicated this elevation in a number of ways. For Baudelaire, as for later Symbolists, *all* natural objects may be "read" as symbols; also, any symbol stands for, and evokes, not only one but a multiplicity of meanings, and is intended in a poem to interact within a complex of related symbols to awaken an "almost infinite suggestion" of associations and memories.[57]

The Symbolist turn to interiority, as in the Modernists generally, sharpens and deepens as well. The poetic language continually refers to its own genesis in the artist's perceptions and creative imagination, as well as to the singularity of the artist's mind. Ambiguities of meaning and obscurities, expressed through such devices as new stylizations of syntax, dream-imagery, and evocations of synesthesia saturate the poetry and direct attention both to the naiveté of supposing that direct and accurate description of external objects is possible (which was the supposition and artistic goal of writers of the Naturalist school, exemplified most famously by Zola, against whom the Symbolists positioned themselves) and to skepticism concerning the ability of consciousness to obtain clarity or certainty about its own inward being. The reader is drawn intentionally into a web of shadowy mysteries of signification. The feelings and confused, imprecise perceptions that flood inner life find outward expression in the overdetermined symbols of the poems; and yet these are not offered as mere contortions of the imagination, representative of nothing but the auto-stimulative play of an isolated psyche, but as articulations of spiritual mysteries that engulf and transcend the world known by reason: the sacred obscurities that the artist's consciousness apprehends and, in an inevitably singular and doubting way, expresses in distilled symbols organized into poetic form.

Proust was deeply influenced both by the great Symbolist forerunners—above all, his "mind and sensibility" were "steeped" in Baudelaire's poetry—and by their heirs.[58] He read and admired (though quarreled in print with) Mallarmé.[59] The Symbolists contributed to his acquaintance with Schopenhauer, also, and he shared their enthusiasm for Wagner. Of course he was far from alone among early twentieth-century literary giants in drawing inspiration and guidance from the Symbolists; it is a company that includes Ibsen, Chekhov, Yeats, Joyce, Woolf, T. S. Eliot, and Ezra Pound. But Proust was the first writer of fiction to apply the Symbolist technique and ideas to a novel, a work in which the "shifting images of the Symbolist poet, with their 'multiplied associations,'" are transformed into the very "characters, situations, places, vivid moments, obsessive emotions, [and] recurrent patterns of behavior" of the narrative.[60] Proust's novel reflects the passions of the Symbolists for exploring the regions of interiority most difficult of reflective access; for following associative webs of impressions and memories along the most obscure pathways of detail and triviality; and for expressing in richly allusive symbols, grounded an idiosyncratic imagination, mysteries of spiritual meaning evoked by things and persons and events that resonate in, and even define, the center of the self.

And yet Proust's artistic vision and aims, and his style too, diverged from those of the Symbolists in crucial respects. Already in 1896, a dozen years before he began shaping the narrative of *In Search of Lost Time*, in his article "Contre l'obscurité," Proust criticized the Symbolist devotion to obscurity for its own sake, rejecting its presentation of mystery as "false." Accurate knowledge of the external world is indeed possible, Proust argued; although an artist has no choice but to perceive and interpret it from the relative perspective of his individual mind and sensibility, its truths do exist and can be ascertained, and the artist can successfully represent them.[61] "The shape of everything is individual and clear," he wrote, and Nature "enables every man, during his passage on earth, to explain the most profound mysteries of life and of death clearly."[62] This conviction underlies the construction and artistic intentions of *In Search of Lost Time* from first to last. The elaborate detail of the long-flowing sentences that register, sometimes in exuberantly branching ways, the Narrator's impressions of people, names, places, natural objects, human creations, and social activities as well as the emotions, memories, and reflections continually shaping and altering his own consciousness—all serve Proust's intention to show exactly the existence of things.[63] There is not the slightest tendency toward solipsism or obscurantism in Proust; on the contrary, he is a realist to the core. And those particular realities concerning what is truly inexplicable, truly mysterious, about the universe and ourselves should, he holds, be presented by the artist with as much clarity as any other elements of experience. So it is that in *Time Regained*, once the Narrator has undergone his climactic series of *impressions bienheureuses*, the experiences that reveal transcendent being to him are subjected to a reasoned analysis of profound scope and exactitude, representing a remarkable effort of sustained reflection that clarifies, with rare exegetical precision, the ontological situation of his own consciousness (and representatively that of every other human being) as participating simultaneously in Time and Eternity.

All this gives us a more informed understanding of Proust's mysticism. He is a very *careful and deliberate* mystic—one who, unlike the Romantics, does not incline toward the merging of transcendence with nature or the self, and who, unlike the Symbolists, neither injects into symbolizing language a distorting mysteriousness that blurs the relation between objects and transcendence, nor values artistic symbols over the realities symbolized.[64]

Despite these facts, some notable critics have argued that Proust practices and advocates an identifiable "religion," *aestheticism*, since throughout the course of his novel he continually presents works of art—works of painting, music, architecture, and other arts, but especially of literature—as the profoundest mediators of sacred reality, and crucial catalysts for experiences of redemption from the existential wastage of lost and misused time. In Barbara Bucknall's *The Religion of Art in Proust*, for example, many passages in the novel are presented as evidence that, for the Narrator, art and art alone provides the "spiritual nourishment" human beings require, and that therefore artistic creation and appreciation must for him be the occasions and ultimate goal of spiritual "faith."[65]

The problem with viewing Proust as a priest of art, however, serving a cult in which artworks of genius are venerated as sacred in themselves, and seeing his once-Christian passion for the absolute as displaced into a worship of aesthetic objects and their creation, lies, as Roger Shattuck points out, in the disregarding of Proust's repeated reminders in his novel—primarily through the mouthpiece of the Narrator but sometimes through the voice of another character (such as the painter Elstir)—that the true value of art lies not in the works themselves, in the symbols themselves, but in their capacity to assist in the discovery of that which is *genuinely real*, both in ourselves and beyond ourselves. Thus it is only a "partial truth," as Shattuck notes, to claim that Proust regards art as the ultimate value and the creating of it as the highest human activity; great artworks and their creating only have value insofar as they assist their authors and those who respond to them to *make real* the lives they have lived.[66] Proust's immense dedication to writing his own novel lies not in a snobbish absolutizing of art and artistic genius, but, as the Narrator explains in *Time Regained*, in his desire, first, to illuminate his life both in its labyrinthine complexity and unity so that he can consciously grasp the deeper, transcendent reality that grounds it, and second, by doing so to help all future readers discover what is both peculiarly true and transcendently real about *their own existences* and so to *unify their own lives* using the tool of the "finely ground lens" of his book.[67] The novel, in other words, like all art for Proust, is not an end in itself, not a matter of "art for art's sake." Proust wishes it to serve, as does all important art in his view, as a means by which his readers can remember and recover their own stories as individual narratives whose meaningfulness is grounded in their participation in Eternal Being. Though it is not wrong—as will be discussed in the next chapter—to describe Proust's principal concern as "aesthetic" rather than "religious," this is only true insofar as the latter term refers to commitment to religious devotional practice within an institutional religious community. Proust's devotion to art is due to his viewing it as the most profound means for developing a relationship to the reality beyond the world, and beyond art itself.

So there is no posture of religious worship or adoration toward anything or anyone in Proust. Only a God (or gods), or their manifestations in icons or hierophanies of object or place, can be religiously loved; Proust's mysticism does not lead him along a path of affective (much less ecstatic) devotion wherein a loving deity draws him, by redemptive grace, toward human-divine communion.

And here a question arises. Given that the spiritual experience of loving and being loved by the ground of being is so prevalent in the literature of mysticism, one might reasonably wonder if Proust's reluctance, in his maturity, to analogically personalize transcendent reality could have some roots in his formative experiences of love, and in his interpretations of the meaning and potentialities of love—experiences and interpretations presented and discussed at length in his novel. As is obvious to all readers and critics, the only authentic love, the only normative love, one might say, in the novel is the love between the personages of grandmother, mother, and Marcel; romantic love and friendship are, for the Narrator/Proust, enterprises that are doomed to disillusion and disappointment. As Edmund Wilson points out, there is a genuine "spiritual nobility" in the love displayed by Marcel's grandmother and mother, examples "from which Proust's narrator sets out"; but these examples bear no fruit in Marcel's capacities to properly love anyone other than these two.[68] One could say of Marcel's intersubjective relations to all other persons in the novel, including the most important for his emotional and intellectual life, that there is, to use Martin Buber's terminology, not a single normative "I-Thou" relationship, or reciprocity of loving encounter, among them.[69] And this perhaps sheds light on Proust's description of his relationship with transcendent being. Eternal reality is the "true" reality, and it reveals itself dramatically to Marcel in his major epiphanies; but an "eternal Thou" could be disclosed only through experiences of loving and being loved by a "divine partner" in being.[70]

If this is seen, as it is by some readers and critics, as a deficiency in Proust's portrayal of human existence with regard to both the normative possibilities of intersubjective relationships and the understanding of what in-between existence finally means, the psychological sources of that deficiency lie too deep for confident analysis. But it is a deficiency that can be usefully brought into association with another significant feature of Proust's portrayal of Marcel's existence in the world: Marcel's almost complete lack of interest in moral considerations, and his total lack of interest in problems of justice. At one point in the fifth volume of the novel Marcel himself comments on this characteristic: "What was more," he writes, "the notion of justice, *to the extent of a complete absence of moral sense*, was unknown to me. [The extent of my morality was that] I was in my heart of hearts entirely on the side of the weaker party, and of anyone who was in trouble."[71] And this is indeed the only "moral" trait that Marcel regularly (if not consistently) evidences: kindness, and a sympathy for the underdog. But *responsibility* for anyone, responsibility to enact or promote justice, is foreign to him. The only obligation he ever confesses to recognizing is the duty of an artist toward his work—including, of course, the obligation to write his own novel, which falls upon his conscience with urgent intensity in the latter part of the final volume.[72]

Building on this point, one might make a final diagnostic surmise. Should one consider Proust's novel through the lens of what is common to the philosophies and anthropologies of Martin Buber and Emmanuel Levinas, Marcel's lack of interest in justice, the absence of any sense of responsibility to come to the *aid* of anyone in trouble (however he might sympathize with him or her), his inability to experience reciprocally loving "I-Thou" relations with other persons besides his grandmother and mother, and his inability to find in his experiences of transcendence an affective dimension of addressing or being "addressed" by a God or an "eternal Thou," are all of a piece. For Buber and Levinas, the personhood of transcendent reality is grounded in and apprehended through responding, in *loving responsibility*, to the vulnerability and infinite value of other persons.[73] Every human other makes an ethical claim on us, in this view, because of that vulnerability and value; and it is through responding to that claim by embracing our obligations to other persons (however limited our abilities in fact are to help others) that we come to care about personal, social, and legal justice, and as well come to recognize the reality of a transcendent Other who is infinite and has become manifest through the infinite value of persons.[74] From this philosophical perspective it would not perhaps be inaccurate, then, to attribute Proust's general refusal to be drawn toward personalistic symbolizations of eternal being at least *in part* to an existential developmental lacuna entailing a turning-away—for reasons unknowable—from the burdens and opportunities of responding in loving responsibility to persons other than, as represented in his novel, his grandmother and mother.

Proust's vision of human life as existence in an In-Between of world and eternal reality remains, whether one finds refreshing or wanting his view of transcendent reality, a profoundly important phenomenon in the world of Modernist literature. With utmost rigor of psychological acumen, Proust's novel reminds us that the more general intellectual and literary trend in recent times to ignore transcendent reality is countered by the visions of not a few Modernist literary masterpieces. To deepen appreciation of the variety of such visions, the next chapter will juxtapose Proust's descriptions of experiences that reveal a truth of transcendent reality with those presented in T. S. Eliot's mature poetic work *Four Quartets* (1936–1942).

Eliot, younger than Proust by only seventeen years, was another founding genius of literary Modernism. His breakthroughs in verse form, content, and poetic "voice," introduced most famously in *The Waste Land* (1922) and culminating in *Four Quartets* a generation later, altered the literary landscape no less radically than did Proust's innovative novel. Significantly, both *Four Quartets* and *In Search of Lost Time* may be understood as projects of self-exploration: the principal subject matter of each work is the development of its author, although in each what might be called the adventure of self is transmuted, as in all good art, through the "impersonalizing" artistic alchemy by means of which private experiences, impressions, discoveries, and growth are rendered universally relevant and resonant. Also, in accordance with the increasingly differentiated interiority of Modernism, Eliot's *Four Quartets*, like Proust's novel, is concerned to represent the polymorphous character of personal consciousness; the inevitability of gaps and errors in self-interpretation; the unavoidability, on the part of an astute modern consciousness, of various degrees of alienation from nature, society, and oneself; and the search for a pattern of meaning in the self's seemingly wasteful journey through time. Finally Eliot, like Proust, shows the culmination of his journey of self-discovery to be a vision of eternal reality, with the truth of that vision presented as a universally discernible fact. For each author, the self most truly finds itself—or finds the ground of its temporally accreting facets or constructions of self—when it explicitly recognizes and understands its relationship to a transcendent mystery that embraces and completes it.[75]

Eliot's vision, however, unlike that of Proust (but like that of Dickinson), presents transcendent reality as personal. For Eliot the ground and center of reality is not merely "Eternal Being," as it is for Proust; it is "God." Furthermore, the God Eliot pays witness to is the God of Christian faith and Trinitarian tradition. It would be a mistake, though, to regard Eliot's Christian vision of transcendent reality as constituting a retreat into some kind of premodern doctrinal parochialism. Although grounded in his association with the Anglo-Catholic Church, the Christian vision Eliot presents in *Four Quartets* is not in the least provincial; it is informed by, and in part articulates itself in terms of, mystical, philosophical, and religious symbolisms belonging to Hindu, Buddhist, and various cosmological traditions. The mystic vision of *Four Quartets* is confidently ecumenical, recognizing the mystical experiences that form the core of Christian self-understanding to be universally available and attested to across a range of world cultures.

As we shall see, the types of mystical experiences described by Proust in *In Search of Lost Time* have their counterpart in and find validation in *Four Quartets*. But Eliot describes additional varieties of access to transcendent mystery as well, thereby providing in his poem cycle a more comprehensive mystical phenomenology than that offered by Proust.

CHAPTER THREE

Unsought Revelations of the Eternal

T. S. Eliot's *Four Quartets* and Proust

MARCEL PROUST AND T. S. Eliot are roughly contemporaries but rarely compared with each other. This is understandable given the different natures of their literary genres, of their stylistic methods and accomplishments, and, in large measure, of their investigative concerns and themes. However, if one compares the vision of human existence presented in Eliot's late poetic masterpiece *Four Quartets* with that presented in *In Search of Lost Time*, three parallels become obvious. First, each work presents human existence (as Dickinson does as well) as life in the In-Between of time and eternal being, as participation simultaneously in the spatiotemporal world and in a timeless realm of meaning. Second, each work shows how an everyday sense experience can *suddenly and unexpectedly* become the occasion of an apprehension by human consciousness of its participation in the eternal. And third, both works indicate that these unsought experiences are the starting point of any person's advance toward the deliberate mysticism that each author portrays as humanly normative.

A careful examination of the second of these parallels—the two authors' descriptions of unsought revelations of the eternal—will enable us to examine what is in fact common to the visions in the two works of human participation in timeless meaning while creating a critical foundation for distinguishing Eliot's mysticism from that of Proust.[1] For Eliot's masterwork is the culminating poetic expression of a Christian mystic who understands the existential implications of unsought experiences of timelessness in terms, finally, of obligations to spiritual discipline and religious practice; while the mature Proust, as we have seen, regards as his primary duty the creation of the great cathedral of his novel, since for him it is above all in the creation and appreciation of art that the human quest for spiritual self-knowledge is best oriented, and through which the needs of the spirit are most dependably met.

Having already examined in the previous chapter Proust's portrayal of mystical illumination and his understanding of its metaphysical implications, we will begin our comparison with an overview of Eliot's *Four Quartets*, first describing its general nature and genesis, and then looking more closely at its content and its poetic form.

Four Quartets

Four Quartets, written when Eliot was in his late forties and early fifties, is his spiritual autobiography, the poetic testament of a Christian mystic whose topic is human existence in time and its relation to eternity.[2] The work is a sequence of four poems, totaling about 900 lines, first published as a whole in 1943. The title of each poem is the name of a place of personal significance to the poet: *Burnt Norton* identifies a mansion in Gloucestershire whose then-deserted house and garden Eliot visited in the summer of 1934; *East Coker* is the name of a village in Somerset from which Eliot's ancestors emigrated to America in the seventeenth century, to which Eliot made a brief pilgrimage in 1937, and where he chose to be buried; *The Dry Salvages* refers to a group of rocks off Cape Ann in Massachusetts, known to Eliot (a native of St. Louis) from many summers staying at his family's vacation home in Gloucester, northeast of Boston; and *Little Gidding* is the name of a small village in Huntingdonshire which was the location of an important Anglican community in the early seventeenth century, and which Eliot visited in 1936. These concrete places, though, serve in the four poems primarily as symbolic locales, "points of departure" for spiritual meditations, which cumulatively portray various dimensions of Eliot's consciousness as well as stages in his mystical journey.[3]

When Eliot wrote *Burnt Norton* it was not as the first of a series but as an isolated work, and it was published as such, "enigmatic and beautiful," as the last poem in his *Collected Poems 1909–1935* (1936).[4] He wrote it relatively quickly in 1935 following the completion of his verse drama about St. Thomas Becket, *Murder in the Cathedral*, and before starting work on his next play, *The Family Reunion*, first staged in 1939. Eliot later stated that had it not been for the outbreak of the Second World

War he would probably have continued to focus on writing for the stage, in which case *Burnt Norton* might have been his last major poetic composition. Instead he began composing, "in fits and starts," *East Coker*, an intentional companion to *Burnt Norton*, which repeated the former's five-part structure (which itself echoed the structure of Eliot's Modernist breakthrough *The Waste Land*).[5] It was during the composition of *East Coker* that the idea of a four-poem sequence emerged, in which each successive poem would introduce new scenes and situations but would continue to present and explore, while recontextualizing, important symbols, themes, phrases, and ideas.[6] The three later poems were first published as individual pamphlets under their respective titles in 1940, 1941, and 1942; but when the complete cycle of four poems appeared in 1943 as *Four Quartets*, the aptness of the musical title was obvious. Each individual quartet proceeds like a musical composition, introducing a number of distinct themes, developing variations on them in a range of poetical voices, and bringing them to a resolution in its concluding fifth part; while on a larger scale the four poems do the same, constantly looping back to retrieve motifs and play variations on them until, at the conclusion of *Little Gidding*, major ideas and symbols from all the poems are echoed and integrated.

In *Four Quartets*, Eliot employs all the skills he had developed in making himself the Modernist poet who initially established a significant place in literary London with the publication of his first book, *Prufrock and Other Observations* (1917), and then in 1922 altered the landscape of English poetry with *The Waste Land*. *Four Quartets* is a more accessible work than *The Waste Land*, written in a more straightforward style and welcoming set of idioms, although it is still Modernist in its reliance on a juxtaposition of diverse voices and disjunctive transitions, in its intellectual sophistication and constant literary referencing and borrowings, and in the often open-endedly allusive use of images and phrases in the manner of the Symbolists (a crucial inspiration for Eliot).[7] The poem combines a generalizing, inviting, traditionally meditative style of verse with the imagistic compression, conceptual density, and multidimensional suggestiveness of high Modernist poetry, enabling Eliot to endow it with a simultaneously up-to-date, summarizing, and valedictory feel. Eliot considered it to be his crowning achievement, and he wrote no further major poetry during the remaining twenty-two years of his life. As for the critics, it is not uncommon to see *Four Quartets* praised as the finest sequence of long poems written in the twentieth century.[8]

The outstanding theme structurally uniting *Four Quartets* is the many ways life in time is humanly experienced: as the cyclical rotations of the seasons, celestial phenomena, and fertility; as the linear time that advances from a partially known past toward an unknown future; as the temporal field of relationships and circumstances that situate each individual; and as the time of past generations that recede ultimately into the darkness of prehistory. Then there are the dimensions of interior time that structure personal consciousness: time remembered, sometimes regretfully, sometimes gratefully; time anticipated, with hope or dread; time experienced, at times, as enchainment in suffering or as purposeless repetition.

The theme of memory is central to these poetic meditations. Memory provides consciousness with narrative context, with a story, in light of which it experiences the "now" of existence, and through the presence of memory we search for meaningful patterns in our lives. Memory too is the platform for our envisioning of future choices, of the possibilities for new and better decisions that time will afford us (we trust). And always, human memory of the past and anticipation of the future bear with them an awareness of perishing: a recognition that time is the medium in which all things come into existence only to pass away, ourselves and our loved ones, cities and societies, political factions and countries, leading us to ask: What is time for? Does human existence finally mean anything?

Four Quartets presents the core human longing as the desire for existence to add up to something meaningful, despite the awareness of having wasted so much of our time, of having lived for long periods in dull-minded routine, of having made decisions intentionally harmful to others, and of having turned away from promising opportunities. We want to redeem the time we have misused, and to not waste the time remaining—to make of our lives, in sum, a *wholly* meaningful design. It is this desire that leads us to search for, and when receptive to find, convincing indications of a realm of meaning beyond time and perishing in which our existences participate. In the vision of *Four Quartets*, it is alone the revelation of essential, humanity-defining participation in transcendent being that liberates us—if only perhaps momentarily—from the anxiety that life has no meaning.

The vision of the relation of time to eternity in *Four Quartets* takes its ultimate orientation from Christian experiences and symbols. Beginning with *East Coker*'s evocation of the theological virtues of faith, hope, and love, its extended literary quoting of St. John of the Cross, and its fourth section's extended metaphor of Christ (though he is not named) as the "wounded surgeon" whose "sharp compassion" (*EC*, IV.147, 150) we may come to recognize, Eliot's commitment to the Christian vision of human existence becomes ever more prominent and resounding. But in the first quartet, this commitment is not yet clear. *Burnt Norton*'s descriptions of human life in time and tantalizing moments out of time would resonate with any reader whose religious or philosophical persuasion sees the field of human experience as including revelations of a realm of transcendence. It includes one obviously Buddhist symbol of enlightenment, a momentary vision of a lotus rising from water, and one obviously Christian symbol, "the Word in the desert" assailed by "voices of temptation" (*BN*, V.155–56).[9] And the religious ecumenicism of *Burnt Norton* persists in the symbolic allusions woven into the later three quartets, especially in *East Coker*'s unattributed adaptation of spiritual directives from St. John of the Cross that "[resonate] so profoundly with Buddhist insights into nothingness," and in the extended reflection in *The Dry Salvages* on Krishna's advice (as related in the *Bhagavad-Gita*) to nurture the habit of disinterested action.[10] This ecumenic mysticism, so important to the interspiritual resonances of the poem cycle, has its roots in Eliot's immersive study during his university years of Eastern religious traditions, especially Hinduism and Buddhism, which permanently shaped his religious personality.[11] *Four Quartets* reflects his abiding awareness (as he put it in 1951) of "how frequently contemplatives of religions and civilizations remote from each other are saying the same thing."[12] Although Eliot's conversion to Anglo-Catholicism in 1927 (which surprised most, and angered some, in the English and American literary world) formalized his embrace of what he called the one visionary "scheme" that seemed to him, in the end, the "only one that would work" because it found a place for all the values he felt he had to "maintain or perish," this declaration of commitment did not entail a repudiation of the authenticity of non-Christian religious experience.[13] *Four Quartets* is the testament of a Christian poet, but one for whom core mystical experiences correspond across numerous religious and philosophical traditions.

As a learned and multilingual mystic, Eliot was familiar with both the kataphatic and apophatic mystical literatures of Eastern and Western philosophies and religions.[14] Both modes of mystical experience and practice are repeatedly alluded to in *Four Quartets*, including through direct quotation from St. John of the Cross's *The Ascent of Mount Carmel*, the *Bhagavad-Gita*, and Dame Julian of Norwich's *Showings*. The kataphatic path toward communion with the ground of being—the way of light, of affirmations of transcendent presence, of beatific exaltations of sense and perception—is exemplified most fully in two episodes in the poem: in the visionary experience in the rose garden in the first section of *Burnt Norton*, to which we shall return below, and in *Little Gidding*'s opening passage in which the poet experiences, in midwinter, the sun's blazing on ice and frost as a revelation of "pentecostal fire" and an everlasting spring "not in time's covenant" (*LG*, I.10, 14). References to the apophatic path—the way of darkness, of the disciplined negating of the senses, passions, language, and thinking, in order to attain interior experiences of union with the "no-thing" of ineffable transcendence—recur through all four poems, but it is given extended description in both *Burnt Norton* and *East Coker*. Section three of *Burnt Norton*, for example, provides the apophatic directive:

> Descend lower, descend only
> Into the world of perpetual solitude,
> World not world, but that which is not world,
> Internal darkness, deprivation
> And destitution of all property,
> Dessication of the world of sense,
> Evacuation of the world of fancy,
> Inoperancy of the world of spirit . . . (*BN*, III.114–21)

Of such practice, the poet continues, "This is the one way, and the other / Is the same . . ." (*BN*, III.122–23). That is, the *via negativa* of apophasis is identical in spiritual purpose and outcome to kataphatic accesses of illumination of divine presence. The goal of both mystical paths are the same: a "further union" and "deeper communion" with transcendent being (*EC*, V.206).[15] Both paths are, of course, inexhaustible, since they lead always to *deepening* participation—to a fuller apprehension of sacred presence, or to a truer aligning of human to divine will—but never to an escape from temporality, from "the enchainment of past and future / Woven in the weakness of the changing body" (*BN*, II.79–80). That is why we must continue always to "fare forward" in our spiritual journeys (*DS*, III.162), and why in our quests to shape existence into meaningful stories, not just the young or middle-aged but even the old "ought to be explorers" (*EC*, V.202).

A few comments, finally, on the formal structure of *Four Quartets* will be relevant to understanding how its accounts of mystical experiences both parallel and differ from those in Proust's novel.

The five sections of each quartet follow the same pattern. The opening section presents some version of a "landscape meditation" in which the theme of the human situation between time and timelessness is presented and reflected upon.[16] The second section consists of, first, a compactly lyrical passage, and then a discursive reflection, which together focus on human entrapment in time but offer also images, or glimpses, of human existence as the intersecting of time with eternity. The third section develops some metaphor of journey while making explicit references to a form of mystical practice or quoting from a mystical text, as it concerns itself with the turning of the soul toward the divine—that is, with conversion, "where descent becomes ascent."[17] The fourth section is a brief lyric, meditative or prayerful, always pertaining to the desire or need for spiritual purgation. The fifth section, beginning in a colloquial idiom and ending in lyric, recapitulates, recontextualizes, and integrates its poem's principal themes and images.[18]

The key formal principle of the work is repetition: repetition of the five-part structure; repetition of the styles of verse and general topics or themes in the corresponding section of each poem; and above all repetition of symbols and phrases, of ideas and images, whose connotative suggestions are altered and deepened by reformulation and recontextualization. The work is built upon the continual development of what in music (since Wagner) are called leitmotifs—some of the most important involving symbols of rose, fire, sea, river, garden, birds (thrush, dove, and kingfisher), light, darkness, music, and journey—recapitulations which, as David Perkins writes, "bring with them suggestions and associations from former contexts [to] become progressively denser nodes of connotation and feeling."[19] Eliot uses these repetitions, too, to reflect the fact that in our search for meaning in existence we discover and create patterns, and that the stories we construct—personal, social, and historical—are designs made of what we have found to be important in remembered experiences, thoughts, and decisions: patterns that, if we are not to remain deluded, include acknowledgment and symbolization of the eternal basis of all patterns.

It may be noted, finally, that the overall tone of *Four Quartets* is one of impressive calm—of stillness and stability. The poetry is not jagged or high-pitched with emotion, although the profoundest human emotions are identified or described: suffering, ecstasy, terror, affection, regret, agony, love. Its stillness is achieved through great formal clarity of design, and impersonality of voice. (It is as though, as Hugh Kenner has remarked, we are overhearing someone speaking to himself, rather than feeling ourselves spoken to.)[20] Although *Four Quartets* is a spiritual autobiography, through the transformation of his idiosyncratic experiences into "the emotion of art" Eliot the man remains remarkably invisible.[21] As with Proust's novel, the highly wrought object of the artwork offers itself as the product of an alchemy of perceptual self-organization by which the author, functioning as a medium (not as a "subject" interesting in himself), hopes to inspire the reader to discover how the pattern of his or her own existence might reveal both a narrative coherence and a promise of involvement with enduring meaning.

Unsought Revelations and Mystical Reflection in *Four Quartets*

Among the mystical experiences with which the poet concerns himself in *Four Quartets*, one type is the "gift" of an unlooked-for moment of transport in which both self and surroundings feel charged with a timeless significance. This is the first type of mystical experience described in the work, in the opening section of *Burnt Norton*, where a visit to a rose garden becomes the occasion for an unexpected moment of revelatory illumination. In the poetic passage describing this epiphany, the mystical moment proper is preceded by unusual spiritual apprehensions: a sense of "dignified, invisible" personages (parental, or ancestral, or Edenic, or all three) with their "unseen eyebeam" crossing the box circle of the garden as they gaze upon the roses, and of "unheard music" to which birds are responding (*BN*, I.23–29). The mystical vision occurs while the poet is looking down into a drained pool:

> Dry the pool, dry concrete, brown edged,
> And the pool was filled with water out of sunlight,
> And the lotos rose, quietly, quietly,
> The surface glittered out of heart of light, (*BN*, I.34–37)

Then a cloud passes, the pool is empty again, and while the poet senses a mysterious presence of hidden children and their "contained" laughter, the vision's vanishing is accompanied by his hearing a bird say "Go, go, go," since "human kind / Cannot bear very much reality" (*BN*, I.38–43).

The rose-garden vision, in the words of Denis Donoghue, is an example of "the sublime moment" that gives human beings a "sample of the ultimate experience, beatitude, the Heaven of God's presence"—but is nothing more than a sample, a transient experience that leaves in its wake a sense of exile and sorrow over the passing of time and lost opportunities.[22] Its enticing revelation of "the mystery and the meaning lying behind the temporal order," however, resonates throughout the remainder of *Four Quartets*, which can be described not inaccurately (though with caveats, as explained below) as an extended meditation on the significance of the rose-garden moment, a sustained effort to grasp its meaning and pursue its implications in ever more differentiated contexts of spiritual insight.[23] Its symbols of roses and garden, water and sunlight, birds and music, children and ancestors, will be evoked in numerous later passages in *Four Quartets*, including the final lyrical passage of *Little Gidding* that concludes the four poems, each symbol growing richer in connotation. It will become clear that the rose-garden vision represents the revelation of transcendence to everyday consciousness: a spontaneous illumination and "instance of . . . given joy" involving a suddenly charged sense-experience which, the poet suggests, is a kind of mystical experience given to everyone, though it is typically ignored or misunderstood among the passing distractions of life in time.[24]

In the second section of *Burnt Norton*, after a compact lyric alluding to an ultimate reconciliation between earthly and heavenly patterns, the poet approaches the mystery of a temporal mind experiencing eternity in a very different way: in a meditation devoting close attention to the paradox presented to consciousness by the "dance" of experienced reality (*BN*, II.63, 67). If time and timelessness are somehow one, then the movement of things and the stillness of eternity are also one, an idea that gives rise in the poem to the image of a "still point" as the axis of the "turning world"—a still point that is not "fixity," but rather the mystery of conjoined contradictions (*BN*, II.62–67). The poet, focusing on his own mystical experiences and that of others as a conscious involvement in this paradox, reports, "I can only say, *there* we have been: but I cannot say where. / And I cannot say, how long, for that is to place it in time." (*BN*, II.68–69). Here we have a description not of an unlooked-for glimpse of beatitude, but of a mystical speculation, a speculation that has grown out of the moment in the rose garden, but which is quite different in character: its concerted reflections on the meaning of the still point "generalize [the rose garden's] strange concurrence of sensations, supply it with meaning not merely eerie, and unite its gravity with that of the meditative life."[25] The poet has advanced to a state of mystical appreciation that is specifically *spiritual in intention*, entailing a self-transcending focus that enables him, as the meditation continues, to envision a mysterious "completion" and "resolution" (*BN*, II.77–78) of the dance of the cosmos.[26] This in turn leads to the apophatic exercise described in the third section of *Burnt Norton*—"Descend lower, descend only" into "that which is not world" (*BN*, III.114, 116)—and to the reflective mystical discernment that the way down (the way of darkness, negation) is "the same" (*BN*, III.123) as the way up (the way of light, affirmation). The latter includes, to be sure, traditional spiritual disciplines of kataphatic mysticism but also, importantly, all unsought moments of revelation such as that in the rose garden.

In the lyric that concludes the final section of *Burnt Norton*, the moment in the rose garden and the memory of mystical concentration are linked together, in a vision that captures eloquently the conflicted feeling that, while every revelation of eternal being affords us (as Denis Donoghue writes) "an intuition of divine grace, given lest we despair," such revelations nevertheless make unillumined life in time seem pointless:[27]

> Sudden in a shaft of sunlight
> Even while the dust moves
> There rises the hidden laughter
> Of children in the foliage
> Quick now, here, now, always—
> Ridiculous the waste sad time
> Stretching before and after. (*BN*, V.169–75)

For the individual who recognizes experiences that are simultaneously in and out of time for what they are, the question becomes how one's existential journey, with all its "waste sad time," might be redeemed.

Burnt Norton does no more than barely suggest (by an elusive reference in its last section to "the Word in the desert") a Christian answer to this question. Beginning with *East Coker*, though, Eliot situates both the beatific and apophatic experiences presented in *Burnt Norton* within a Christian interpretation of mystical glimpses of and yearning for the eternal, with the later quartets showing how individual life and history itself might be understood as participation in a story of divine origins and purpose with a mystery of redemptive Love at its center. As they do so, the poet repeatedly suggests that any dedicated spiritual life is imbued with memories of unsought epiphanies of timelessness in time. For example, in the third section of *East Coker*, a reflection on mortality and perishing first leads the poet to an exercise of spiritual apophasis:

> I said to my soul, be still, and let the dark come upon you
> Which shall be the darkness of God . . .
> I said to my soul, be still, and wait without hope
> For hope would be hope for the wrong thing; wait without love
> For love would be love of the wrong thing . . .
> Wait without thought, for you are not ready for thought:

> So the darkness shall be the light, and the stillness the dancing.
> (*EC*, III.112–13, 123–25, 127–28)

And then immediately comes a reference to sublime moments, that of the rose garden together with others:

> Whisper of running streams, and winter lightning.
> The wild thyme unseen and the wild strawberry,
> The laughter in the garden . . . (*EC*, III.129–31)

The reference to illuminative experiences associated with sense-experiences of wild thyme and winter lightning will appear once again in the third quartet, *The Dry Salvages*, together with the "shaft of sunlight" from the end of *Burnt Norton*.

Why does Eliot place this emphasis on the importance of unlooked-for beatific moments, as *Four Quartets* explores ever deeper and more comprehensive understandings of the relation of existence to eternity?

There are three answers. First, there is no apprehension of timelessness, the poet relates, except within the conditions of time and embodiment; the gift or achievement of attention to transcendence always occurs in a specific time and place:

> . . . only in time can the moment in the rose-garden,
> The moment in the arbour where the rain beat,
> The moment in the draughty church at smokefall
> Be remembered; involved with past and future.
> Only through time time is conquered. (*BN*, II.86–90)

Second, these beatific moments are the *beginning* of every mystic journey of discovery; the initial apprehension of eternity is always by way of a glimpse, a drenching of the senses with a sense of the mystery of a sacred beyond, and the return of such images in the poems "highlights the necessity of transient moments in the achievement of transcendence."[28] And third, these kinds of moments are given to everyone: they are universally given, revealing to each consciousness its situation in the In-Between of immanence and transcendence.

It is in *The Dry Salvages* that the poet introduces the symbol that most richly integrates, for him, the meaning of all his mystical experiences and reflections: the symbol of *Incarnation*. The early parts of *The Dry Salvages* evoke how the rhythms of the natural world, represented by river and sea, are charged with destructive power and the threat of death, and of how the sufferings and perils of existence require that a convincing search for their meaningfulness look beyond earthly conditions. The symbol of Incarnation affirms that human suffering and death are not mere attrition and waste, but have a mysterious significance in the economy of human-eternal communion. The symbol also indicates that our unlooked-for sublime moments are "hints" of the presence of timelessness in human consciousness generally, and also of the *fullness* of divine presence in Christ, the singularly complete Incarnation that guarantees the redemptive meaningfulness of human participation in the eternal.[29] Of human-divine Incarnation, the poet declares:

> Here the impossible union
> Of spheres of existence is actual,
> Here the past and future
> Are conquered and reconciled, (*DS*, V.216–19)

The actualization of "the impossible union" of the "intersection of the timeless / With time" (*DS*, V.201–2) in human existence generally and in Christ supremely is for anyone, the poet stresses, difficult to contemplate. To give one's entire life to that contemplation, attempting to live out its implications in "a lifetime's death in love, / Ardour and selflessness and self-surrender," is "an occupation for the saint" (*DS*, V.202, 204–5). And few of us are saints.

It is less unusual for people to develop *some* degree of mystical understanding that a realm of eternal being manifests itself in human consciousness, whether that understanding occurs within a Western or an Eastern religious or philosophical context. But at the broadest level, for "most of us"—the poet says—the truth that conscious existence is an intersectional In-Between of temporal and eternal being is never clearly grasped or reflected upon, even though it is experienced by all in fleeting moments of illumination. "For most of us," he writes,

> . . . there is only the unattended
> Moment, the moment in and out of time,
> The distraction fit, lost in a shaft of sunlight,
> The wild thyme unseen, or the winter lightning
> Or the waterfall, or music heard so deeply
> That it is not heard at all, but you are the music
> While the music lasts. (*DS*, V.206–12)

In this passage the moment in a shaft of sunlight from *Burnt Norton*, with its children in the rose garden and laughter, and the epiphanic moments associated with the smelling of wild thyme, the sight of winter lightning, and the hearing of unseen water introduced in *East Coker*—now linked with experiences of immersion in music when one is transported to a kind of timelessness in time—are pointedly identified as "lost," "unattended," experienced only as a "distraction fit." Their significance as "moments in and out of time" have not borne reflective and spiritual fruit in their recipients: people "had the experience but missed the meaning" (*DS*, II.93). The allures, concerns, and distractions of life in time, combined with the difficulties of paying disciplined attention to what has been experienced, keep people from recognizing how unsought moments revealing eternal being point to the fact of universal incarnation in human consciousness, as well as to the message of perfected Incarnation in Christ.[30]

The reader is now prepared for the kataphatic experience described in the opening section of *Little Gidding*, with its wintertime flaring of sun on ice evoking "pentecostal fire," before the poet approaches the chapel in the village (once the site of the seventeenth-century Anglican community led by the religious charismatic Nicholas Ferrar) with its "dull façade," in order "to kneel / Where prayer has been valid" (*LG*, I.10, 29, 45–46). *Little Gidding*'s meditations on the conflicts and terrors of wartime; its haunting explorations of communion between the dead and the living; its urging of a disciplined life of spiritual detachment (as opposed to both attachment and deathlike indifference); and its affirmation that memory in service of love liberates the soul to live life in attunement with the divine Love that "devised" the order of the cosmos, lead ultimately to the Christian eschatological assertion that—in the comforting words of Julian of Norwich quoted three times in the poem—"all shall be well and / All manner of thing shall be well" (*LG*, III.196–97).[31] And finally, in the lyric that completes *Little Gidding* and concludes *Four Quartets*, an echo of the rose garden and other moments of illumination return one final time, but now with "The voice of the hidden waterfall / And the children in the apple-tree" as elements of a vision in which the reconciliation of time and eternity is anticipated in faithful expectation that "the end of all our exploring / Will be to arrive where we started / And know the place for the first time" (*LG*, V.241–42, 247–48). The unlooked-for moments of illumination that most of us fail to attend to are now recalled, in the poet's most comprehensive vision, as the original, compact indications of a future grace of divinely perfected meaning, a mystery of redemption that will be achieved when life in time, with its sufferings of desolation and purgation, and its timebound revelations of spirit, are reconciled with the eternal love humans yearn for,

> When the tongues of flame are in-folded
> Into the crowned knot of fire
> And the fire and the rose are one. (*LG*, V.257–59)[32]

Mystic vision has progressed in *Four Quartets* from the transient "intuition of divine grace" in the rose garden at the beginning of *Burnt Norton* to the complexly "Edenic moment" of transfigurative revelation that concludes *Little Gidding*, where children and garden, rose and waterfall, are re-envisioned in relation to the fire of human suffering and the loving self-sacrifice of Christ, to suggest a final reconciliation beyond earthly life, incomprehensible to the rational mind but figurable in the symbols of art.[33]

Four Quartets and Proust's *Impressions Bienheureuses*

With the foregoing analysis of *Four Quartets*, we are well-positioned to compare its descriptions of unsought revelations of the eternal with Proust's descriptions of *impressions bienheureuses* in *In Search of Lost Time*.

They have five obvious characteristics in common.

First, in *Four Quartets*, the rose-garden experience and its equivalents are involuntary—they come as unexpected gifts. This distinguishes such experiences from those of mystical communion arising from meditation, prayer, or engagements with works of art. The last of these may indeed come suddenly and unexpectedly, but in their context they are also sought after. By contrast, the rose-garden type of moment appears out of nowhere, as it were, to startled consciousness as an enhancement of certain sense-experiences whose catalytic function could not have been anticipated. In a similar way, the Narrator of Proust's novel describes the most profound of his *impressions bienheureuses* as mystical moments, triggered by sense-experiences, which are unsought and unexpected—"chance happening[s]" that take him by surprise. Explaining that "their *essential character* was that I was not free to choose them," he goes on to assert that there are no truths more important to a person than those that "life communicates to us against our will in an impression which is material because it enters us through the senses but yet has a spiritual meaning which it is possible for us to extract."[34]

Second, in *Four Quartets* these moments of unsought gift are associated with chance happenstances of personal biography. The episode in the rose garden, for instance, while rich with allusive overtones of both biblical and Buddhist character, is clearly intended to be read as autobiographical, as peculiar to the poet's life story. In a less elaborated way, later references to the aroma of wild thyme, to a flash of winter lightning, and to the whisper of a running stream or the sound of a distant waterfall are highly personal, even as they represent corresponding special sense-experiences in the lives of readers. Likewise in Proust's novel, every *impression bienheureux* arising from involuntary memory or triggered by some momentary perception of the natural or human world is pointedly personal, peculiar to the Narrator's situation and disposition. Tasting bits of madeleine in a spoonful of tea causes an epiphany in Marcel for wholly idiosyncratic reasons, and the same is true for each of his major and minor sensation-induced epiphanies: the mystical moment resulting from touching the top button of his boot as he begins undressing in the seaside hotel at Balbec, for example, or from standing on uneven paving stones in the courtyard of the Guermantes mansion, or from hearing the harsh noise of water in a pipe in the mansion's waiting room.[35] Whatever Proust the man may have experienced by way of such sense-triggers of epiphanies is irrelevant; as an author his point is that, as with his character Marcel, such catalysts are biographically accidental.

Third, in *Four Quartets* such catalysts are invariably trivial. The smell of an herb, an angled beam of sunlight, the sound of children laughing—these are everyday phenomena. But each can suddenly be filled with transcendent suggestiveness, through a coalescence of certain conditions—a fortunate inclination of psychological openness and readiness, elements of associated meaning in personal memory, felicitous timing. The triviality of the objects occasioning these revelations sharply distinguishes such experiences from epiphanies of the eternal that arise from encounters with artworks—the latter memorably exemplified by the description in *Burnt Norton* of a spiritual-aesthetic appreciation of how "a Chinese jar still / Moves perpetually in its stillness" (*BN*, V.142–43). The best works of art have been designed to evoke such a moment. But the scent of wild thyme or the sight of sunshine suddenly brightening a drained pool merely happen, despite their trivial natures, to become occasions of epiphany. In Proust's novel this is also the case with respect to the sense-objects that trigger both the *impressions bienheureuses* of involuntary memory and sudden mystery-laden perceptions (such as the sight of the twin steeples of Martinville "bathed in the setting sun").[36] Their triviality is underscored in the Narrator's account of his childhood intimations of eternal being, when as a boy Marcel would sense some "mystery that lay hidden in a shape or a perfume . . . the play of sunlight on a stone, a roof, the sound of a bell, the smell of fallen leaves"—inklings, the Narrator notes, of the wondrous unknown that he would later in life understand to be Eternal Being.[37]

Fourth, *Four Quartets* describes such experiences as producing a unique kind of happiness, as they fill the psyche with a sense of ultimate harmony by imbuing the temporal with the quality of timeless meaning. It is a happiness that liberates consciousness—momentarily—from feeling the burdens of living. In *The Dry Salvages*, Eliot suggests that this happiness is unlike all others, distinct from the pleasures of "[f]ruition, fulfilment, security or affection" or, as he drily asserts, "even a very good dinner" (*DS*, II.91–92). It is one that delivers, in fact, a brief taste of the joy that informs the spiritual promise made by Julian of Norwich that in the fullness of time "All manner of thing shall be well" (*LG*, V.256).

Likewise in Proust's novel, with one exception, the *impressions bienheureuses* induced by special sense-experiences evoke in Marcel a unique kind of joy, a "special pleasure," a "positive rapture," which because it entails a sense of participating in eternity he goes so far as to describe as an "extra-temporal joy" and a "supraterrestrial joy."[38]

Fifth and finally, in *Burnt Norton* Eliot evokes how these gifts of unlooked-for revelation allow consciousness to feel momentarily liberated from the sense of being bound to time, even as the locale of the experience—the rose garden, or "the arbour where the rain beat," or "the draughty church at smokefall" (*BN*, II.86–88)—is drenched with significance. The temporal world and the eternal are as one; and consciousness experiences itself, as mystic reflection may clarify later, as "the intersection of timelessness / With time" (*DS*, V.201–2). In Proust's novel, also, each *impression bienheureux* entails a feeling of being freed from the limitations and contingencies of temporal existence—we recall Marcel describing how, in tasting the tea-soaked crumbs of madeleine, for him "at once the vicissitudes of life [became] indifferent, its disasters innocuous, its brevity illusory" and he ceased to feel "contingent, mortal"—even as in each instance of such transport the worldly locale is lit up with momentary glory, and consciousness experiences itself as co-constituted by time and eternity.[39]

The parallels are striking. Equally striking, though, are the similarities in Eliot's and Proust's descriptions of the existential impact of such unsought moments on those with a mystic's temperament or inclination.

In the course of *Four Quartets*, Eliot elucidates that the moments of illumination are opportunities. We ought to pay attention to them: they are the primary existential clues which, if we consider them and understand their import correctly, can guide us to satisfying insights into our true metaphysical situation and provide assurance in our search for meaning and purpose. By using memory, in the words of Kenneth Paul Kramer, "as an agency for retrieving [these] redemptive moments . . . of vital reciprocity" between the ourselves and the eternal—using to whatever degree we are able the interpretive assistance made available in the teachings and texts and artworks of various cultural traditions—they can be recognized as crucial nodes of meaning in the pattern of a life.[40] This use of memory is not easy, nor does such remembrance bring with it the happiness the original experience brought, for

> . . . approach to the meaning restores the experience
> In a different form, beyond any meaning
> We can assign to happiness. (*DS*, II.94–96)

And yet we ought to engage in this effort of remembrance and reflection, this transfiguration in memory of the moment of illumination, because through this effort we can enable our love for transcendent reality to begin to expand over the whole field of temporal existence, and thus free ourselves from the pervasive fear of death and from a grim sense of entanglement in worldly desire and goals along the "metalled ways / Of time past and time future" (*BN*, III.125–26). Eliot writes that this, above all other functions,

> . . . is the use of memory:
> For liberation—not less of love but expanding
> Of love beyond desire, and so liberation
> From the future as well as the past. (*LG*, III.156–59)

For Eliot, this expansion of love is the dutiful human response to the revelation of the divine mystery apprehended in unexpected moments of revelation, which are the first signs to transcendence-aware consciousness of the "drawing" of divine Love (*LG*, V.238).

In Proust's novel, similarly, the responsibility to reflect on the meaning of unsought epiphanies is presented in terms of our duty to use *voluntary* memory to examine the implications of the *impressions bienheureuses* that arise from *involuntary* memory. And like Eliot, Proust's Narrator describes the consequences of such reflection (analyzed with formidable rigor in *Time Regained*) as, firstly, freedom from the burdens of temporal concerns, and secondly, as the "restoring" of our human love from its typically narrow range of objects to its original "generality," so that we may give our love "to all, to the universal spirit."[41] Despite the fact that, as every reader is aware, Marcel in the novel indicates little capacity to exhibit this giving of love "to all"—perhaps for reasons suggested in the prior chapter—Proust's declaration here clearly echoes Eliot's remark that the essential "use of memory" entails expanding the scope of love.

Next, for Eliot, it is precisely sustained reflection on the gifts of compact mystical moments of illumination that reveals what each individual human story truly is: a pattern whose ontological coherence and unity derive from its constant participation in transcendence. In the final lyric of *Little Gidding* the poet's story (having in the immediately preceding passage been linked to the entire community of dead and living, since all humans participate in transcendent meaning) is envisioned as a completeness, as having been a successful journey from beginning to end, by envisioning our spiritual starting point as identical with our spiritual destination:

> And the end of all our exploring
> Will be to arrive where we started
> And know the place for the first time. (*LG*, V.240–42)

Similarly, in *In Search of Lost Time*, it is reflection on the significance of the *impressions bienheureuses* that reveals to Marcel that his existence in time constitutes a finally meaningful story, rather than being just a congeries of disconnected chronological episodes. As Marcel states, the *impressions* that had, over many years, induced his initial apprehensions of eternity "at remote intervals" at last become, through meditation on their significance, "foundation-stones for the construction of a *true* life"—"true" because existentially embraced, on the basis of reconstitutive memory, as an ontologically unified story whose integrity is grounded in its continual participation in eternal being.[42] Through intense efforts of reflection, as detailed in *Time Regained*, Marcel is able to dispel the suspicion that has haunted him throughout his life: that his existence has had no more significance than a perishable dream.

Further, it is emphasized in *Four Quartets* that one condition, or cost, of this spiritual liberation and self-confirmation is the willingness to accept the fact that consciousness has a paradoxical structure, since it must be understood as being always simultaneously both in time and beyond time. The poem cycle recursively presents mystical moments that expose this basic fact, from the rose-garden epiphany to the moment of prayerful self-awareness in the chapel recounted at the close of *Little Gidding*'s first section: "Here, the intersection of the timeless moment / Is England and nowhere" (*LG*, I.52-53). Proust, too, as discussed in the previous chapter, describes consciousness as being essentially paradoxical, existing as it does at every moment both in spatiotemporal locatedness and in the "beyond" of Eternal Being. The *impressions bienheureuses* arising from involuntary memory bring this paradox to light by revealing a sensation that belongs to the past to be genuinely *present* as it merges with a corresponding present sensation. Consciousness, in being able to access the timeless "essence" that unites the two sensations, must be affirmed, paradoxically, to be simultaneously temporal and "extratemporal."[43]

And one final parallel is worth noting. Eliot and Proust agree that the unsought moments of illumination are given to everyone. The unfortunate fact is that few pay proper attention to them, explore their significance, and advance to the discoveries of deliberate mysticism (whether kataphatic or apophatic). Eliot writes, "For most of us, there is only the *unattended* / Moment, the moment in and out of time" (*DS*, V.206–7, emphasis added). And without attention and meditation proceeding to unlock and explore the significance held in such experiences, it is all too typical that in the search for life's meaning a person's unliberated "curiosity searches past and future / And clings to that dimension" (*DS*, V.199–200). In a 1948 interview, Eliot made clear his conviction that existential self-understanding, if led by sufficient rigor and openness, leads *always* to mystical vision: "[I]ntelligence pushed to its depths leads to mysticism. . . . All human faculties pushed to their depths end in mysticism."[44] But native capacities, and spiritual readiness and courage, must find and create the conditions in which this normative mysticism can be realized.

Proust's view on this is the same as Eliot's. His novel's Narrator states that knowledge of eternal reality is "all the time immanent in all men," and that everyone has "moments of perception" that constitute glimpses of transcendence which, if understood, would lead to a responsible mysticism. But "it is very easy for us to die without having known" the truth of transcendence, since most people fail to use attention, memory, and reflection in such a way that they proceed to explicitly mystical self-knowledge.[45]

Proust's Impersonal Eternity and Eliot's God of History

The commonalities reveal the agreement between Eliot and Proust about what might be called *existential starting points* for human awareness of transcendent mystery and for the development, in some, of a deliberate mysticism ranging from casual interest to the most absorbing and demanding of spiritual disciplines and vocations. The understandings the two authors share with regard to these existential starting points, though, as this and the previous chapter have made apparent, in the end serve two quite different spiritual visions: two fundamentally different symbolizations of transcendent reality; two different interpretations of the ultimate purpose of human existence; and, finally, two different appreciations of art's importance with respect to the cultivation of spiritual orientation. These differences may be summarized by saying that Eliot's spiritual perspective is properly described as religious, while Proust's is best identified as aesthetic.

The vision of the cosmos, existence, and human destiny in *Four Quartets* is a Christian vision. And in keeping with the Christian apprehension of transcendence in both mystical and doctrinal streams of tradition, *Four Quartets* insists that the timeless ground of being is divine Love: a reality beyond time and desiring that suffers itself to be manifested as desire in creaturely longing and love:

> Love is itself unmoving,
> Only the cause and end of movement,
> Timeless, and undesiring
> Except in the aspect of time
> Caught in the form of limitation
> Between un-being and being. (*BN*, V.163–68)

For Eliot, all creation is divine Love; but human consciousness, uniquely, is a created "form of limitation" that can participate *knowingly* in transcendent divine Love, a site in creation where immanent being is directly permeable by the revelation of the divine transcendence that, properly understood, is the unrestricted Act of Love that is the Christian God.

This means that for Eliot all mystical moments of illumination—whether occasioned surprisingly by suddenly charged sense-experiences, by a work of art, by prayer or meditation, or by any other catalyst—would, in their most advantageous and fulfilling conditions of spiritual insight, lead to the discovery that eternal reality is the divine Creator of world and self, and would guide a person thereby into a vital relationship to that Creator in a conscious reciprocity of seeking and being drawn. It means too that although *Four Quartets* repeatedly refers, in its representation of mystical or religious experience, to both the kataphatic way of light or affirmation (to which the unsought epiphanies belong) and the apophatic way of darkness or negation, it is the latter that Eliot regards—in agreement with Christian mystics going back to fifth-century Pseudo-Dionysius, who introduced the distinction between the two ways into Christian theology—as the superior avenue toward communion with the divine mystery.[46] This is because transcendent being in the Christian (as in the Jewish and Islamic) understanding is a divine reality radically "beyond" all images and concepts, all language, and all human knowing. Concepts or symbols in which the nature of transcendence is affirmatively described—all kataphatic language such as "being," "goodness," "light," "fire," and "love"—is in the view of most mystics of Western religions "very imperfect compared with the knowledge which is found by denying concepts and going to God by unknowing."[47] Eliot's continual references in *Four Quartets* to stillness, silence, and darkness, as well as his repeated use of the language of paradox to indicate that the truths of consciousness, world, and transcendence surpass the resources of language, reflect his appreciation that the apophatic way is the more profound way of mystical apprehension. Kataphatic experiences may, as in the rose garden, be gifted, and not only unsought but unappreciated; the way of darkness and negation, however, is a "chosen way,"[48] a way of purposeful existential descent into the darkness and stillness of interiority in order to seek, in the reaching out of love toward Love, a deeper communion with the divine ground which, for the practicing Christian mystic, is always "the darkness of God" (*EC*, III.113).

In Proust's portrayal of types of mystical experience, by contrast, there is no mention of the way of darkness or negation—of *chosen* practices of seeking communion with the eternal—which is commensurate with there being no descriptions in the novel of eternal reality as divine Creator, or of Marcel engaging in prayer, or of Marcel feeling himself drawn by a divine partner who is Love. All of this is consistent with Proust's metaphysics. He never symbolizes transcendence as "God," even though on a few occasions he uses adjectives such as "divine" and "supernatural" to refer to what he calls the "essential" reality of eternal being. Once, as we have noted, Proust refers to a "universal love" of which his own perennially disappointed efforts to love another person he knows to be a "tiny fragment"; and in another place he refers to a "universal spirit" to which, he says, "the portion of [his] mind more durable" than the part of the self that dies should "give [its] love [and] the understanding of this love."[49] But in the voluminous pages of the novel there is no expansion on these unique references to a "universal love" and "universal spirit," and no reference to a divine Lover.

One crucial consequence of Proust's view that eternal reality consists of impersonal essences is his conviction that there can be no higher human duty than to create artworks that evoke in others the mystical experiences that can serve to ground and integrate what is in each personal case a vast and unique world of perception. In Proust's outlook, his artistic calling and his spiritual calling are fulfilled through the same action: the writing of a novel (of unprecedented psychological acuity) whose climax describes, and elaborately explains the meaning of, experiences of "the bliss of the Beyond" and of freedom "from the order of time" that Proust himself enjoyed and that he seeks through his literary art to induce in responsive readers.[50] Proust's spiritual perspective is therefore best described as aesthetic rather than religious, not—as previously explained—because he worships art, but because for him the highest fulfillment of spiritual obligation is the creation of artworks that successfully convey both the meaningfulness of life in time and the reality of human participation in transcendence.

The Eliot of *Four Quartets* (and of the post-conversion poetry that preceded it, such as "Journey of the Magi" and "Ash-Wednesday"), by contrast, is a writer who views the creation and appreciation of art as the handmaiden of religious commitment and practice, his own religion being Anglo-Catholicism. After his conversion in 1927, he was "punctilious in attendance and duties," and allowed the language and rhythms of the Anglican liturgy he heard daily to enter into his poetry.[51] Poetry, Eliot declared in 1928, in his preface to the second edition of his volume of essays *The Sacred Wood*, is not to be taken as "religion or an equivalent of religion," but should be regarded rather as a "superior amusement" whose most valuable function, like that of all art, is to awaken us to, or remind us of, spiritual realities whose truths we can truly honor only by adopting a salubrious, character-forming religious practice.[52] In a somewhat startling line in *East Coker* the poet remarks that, with regard to what is most important in how we should live, "the poetry does not matter" (*EC*, II.71). What matters is progressing in a life of self-sacrificing love inspired and supported by a regular discipline of sacramental participation and communion. In 1951, in an essay on "Poetry and Drama," Eliot summarizes his view of the relation of art to religion: "It is ultimately the function of art," he writes, by ". . . eliciting some perception of an order *in* reality, to bring us to a condition of serenity, stillness, and reconciliation; and then leave us, as Virgil left Dante, to proceed toward a region where that guide can avail us no farther."[53]

Eliot's embrace of transcendent reality as the God of Christianity also requires him to interpret human existence *historically*, which sets him apart from both Proust and Dickinson. Dickinson's poetic investigations, for all their profundity, are concerned neither with political developments nor with the purposes of history. She lived and wrote during the Civil War, but this enormous social and political upheaval in the national life goes almost without notice in her poetry. Proust's novel, for its part, for all its minute and vivid descriptions of the altering customs, mores, political events, costumes, furnishings, and other cultural features of the successive epochs of its settings, is as little concerned as is Dickinson's poetry with the topic of the meaning and goal of history. His vision of Eternal Being and our human immersion in it no more demands a properly historical explanation of existence than do Plato's dialogues or the *Upanishads*. Eliot's experiences of the mystery of transcendence, however, make the issue of history and human historical meaning inescapable, because the Christian God is the God of history, of a *creatio ex nihilo* with an absolute beginning of time and universe, with divine intention issuing in the divine invention of history. The Christian vision of transcendence accentuates human historical transfiguration through time, and raises the question of the ultimate purpose of the unfolding of history toward its divinely intended end. *Four Quartets* is consequently a poem cycle not just about Eliot's lost time redeemed, but about the redemption of *all* human beings throughout all of time: and so not at all incidentally the three later quartets, among other themes, elucidate what historical "progress" does and does not mean, portray the life of the soul straining to discern historical purpose, and offer an eschatological vision of a fulfillment of history.

Besides Eliot there was one other major Modernist, also a poet, who wished to create a literature that witnessed to human involvement in a divinely eternal reality and for whom such a testimony would also be required to make sense of world history. This was Ezra Pound. The next chapter will compare the poetic visions of divine reality and history presented in Pound's voluminous masterwork, *The Cantos*, and Eliot's *Four Quartets*, examining how the works agree in affirming the priority of the sacred in any accurate understanding of the human situation but differ in their presentations of how divine reality, and the structure of human history, are properly to be understood.

CHAPTER FOUR

History and Transcendence in Ezra Pound's *Cantos* and T. S. Eliot's *Four Quartets*

THE RELATIONSHIP BETWEEN Ezra Pound and T. S. Eliot is legendary. Almost exactly Eliot's contemporary—he was his senior by three years—Pound was instrumental in launching Eliot's career and championing his early poetry, and famously edited Eliot's *The Waste Land* to about half the size of Eliot's original and transformed it, as is generally agreed, into the poetry-world-altering masterpiece that was published in 1922. Together in their respective work, the two men were the most important originators—along with William Carlos Williams, working in a different vein of colloquial American speech—of an English-language Modernist poetics.[1] Beyond their linked and profound stylistic innovations, however, there is a shared purpose of substance in their great mature works, Pound's *The Cantos* and Eliot's *Four Quartets*. Both works aim to illuminate through convincing symbolic evocation the reality of divinity in the cosmos and human affairs, and both also present a vision of history grounded in experiences of human-divine encounter—each poet convinced that, given the historical-mindedness of modern consciousness, a compelling cosmic or metaphysical portrayal of the human situation ought to address the issue of historical process and purpose.

As discussed in the last chapter, Eliot's *Four Quartets* explores experiences of divine transcendence in the context of Christian faith and situates such experiences in a God-based history, presenting the mystery of divinity as inseparable from the mystery of history. Pound's enormous poem *The Cantos*, written over the course of six decades, is likewise a work in which illuminating experiences of human-divine encounter, epiphanies of divine timelessness, are described in part for the purpose of giving shape and meaning to human history, thereby offering a response to modern anxiety about historical meaning. Both works, by grounding history in a reality of divine meaning, have a therapeutic intent. Each is meant to be a corrective to modern conceptions of history that understand it to be a purely secular or material process. Pound and Eliot were in agreement that modern materialism and what is now called secular humanism entail a disastrous eclipse of the divine reality that grounds and contextualizes human endeavors; and each decided to create a major poetry that re-embeds the human in the divine and by doing so corrects and clarifies historical meaning.

Like other major artists and thinkers of the early twentieth century, such as the novelist Thomas Mann, the psychologist Carl Jung, and the artists Wassily Kandinsky and Kazimir Malevich, both Pound and Eliot were appalled by the modern phenomenon of the radical disenchantment of the universe. All of them recognized that this was a consequence especially of the increasingly widespread acceptance of worldviews based on scientific reductionism: of images of the cosmos and human existence that insist that the methods of the modern natural sciences—developed to explain the physically observable universe—supply the criteria for *all* cogent ontological validations, and which consequently remove spiritual experiences from the realm of the real and true. Acceptance of the disenchanted universe gave rise, of course, to disenchanted conceptions of history. And what could historical purpose be, in the absence of divine grounding, divine meaning, and an economy of divine redemption? The answer was progress—and only progress. Accordingly, the two major secular conceptions of history that erupted into modern culture beginning in the eighteenth century were variants of progressivism: liberal progressivism, which envisioned a process of inevitable moral and social progress, leading perhaps (as for example Kant predicted) to a state of perpetual peace among nations, and utopianism, whose most famous version appears in Marx's "science" of historical advance-through-conflict culminating necessarily in a perfect worldwide communist society. The common theme of both variants is the *inevitability* of progress—for what could a purely secular history mean without progress as its purpose and goal?[2] But secular progressivist conceptions of history were anathema to Pound and Eliot, as in their view they are built on delusions that are destructive, first, of social and political wisdom, and second, of personal self-understanding.

First, political outlooks and policies are warped and corroded, Pound and Eliot held, by the belief that moral progress in human life is inevitable. That scientific and technological progress continues apace is indisputable; but the idea that human beings have been or will be more *moral* simply because they are born later in time and have more sophisticated tools, and that later political and cultural life will always be more enlightened than that of prior times, is not only nonsense, they agreed, but dangerous nonsense. If there had been any doubt that this is so, the calamitous extended slaughter and destruction of the First World War emphatically put paid to, as they saw it, complacent assumptions about the inevitability of moral and political "progress."

Second, with regard to personal self-understanding, they perceived that reductively materialist images of cosmos and existence resulted in people being unable to properly interpret their genuinely spiritual experiences, such as the "gifted" moments, discussed in the previous chapter, in which a sense of timeless meaning floods consciousness. The natural human surmise of a mystery of transcendent meaning; human questioning that out-questions the physical universe; experiences of the immaterial deeps of consciousness in which one finds, in Eliot's words, "the darkness of God"—all of these become *unintelligible* experiences without the interpretive structure and imaginal guidance of spiritual visions of human nature, history, and cosmos that account for the full range of human experience. To adopt a purely materialist view of existence and history, they insist, doesn't eliminate the feeling-based intimations and revelations of timeless being available to all persons; the experiences occur, but remain unrecognized for what they are. (Dickinson and Proust would of course concur.) It is typical of the modern condition, as Eliot writes in *Four Quartets*, to have compact, unexpected spiritual experiences but to miss their meaning (*DS*, II.93). A principal goal of *The Cantos* and *Four Quartets* is to offer their readers symbols, images, phrases, and visions that will help them to recognize their spiritual experiences for what they are—and by doing so to escape the prison of a reductively secular historical imagination. Only a realization that divine presence has constantly attended and inspired human consciousness, and that human history is most basically the history of human-divine encounter, would provide these corrections. A key aim of both *The Cantos* and *Four Quartets* is to assist in that realization.

While this is a goal of both poets, there is nevertheless a major difference between Pound's vision of divine reality as elaborated in *The Cantos* and that of Eliot as presented in *Four Quartets*. Pound was consistently resistant to Christianity (except in certain cases of Neoplatonist-infused Christian imagery), as well as to Buddhism, Taoism, and the Hindu Upanishadic notions that so appealed to Eliot. This aversion, combined with his strong attraction to the mythopoetic symbolisms of early Greek, Chinese, and other polytheistic cultures, led him to attempt to "recover" and pay witness to divinity while rejecting any religious tradition that described or portrayed a *singular* transcendent reality, whether personal or impersonal. His rejection of the Jewish-Christian-Islamic stream of tradition meant, of necessity, the elimination of a monotheistic Creator-God from his vision of the human-divine cosmos, and thus the elimination of the God of history. Pound's world history therefore, as presented in *The Cantos*, is not eschatological in the way that Eliot's is in *Four Quartets*. The human-divine inspirations and movements within history that head toward a human "perfecting" in Pound's *Cantos* are movements within a cyclical process, wherein human societies rise toward good order through communion with divine truth and goodness only to fall away again into disorder and decline, in a process that has no metaphysical conclusion.

The Cantos and *Four Quartets* are worth close attention as modern literary efforts to grapple with the problem of transcendent meaning and in so doing to critique and provide an alternative to materialist views of history. In exploring them we need to remember, of course, that a poetic exploration and evocation of the drama of history cannot be expected to have the discursive completeness, terminological rigor, and explanatory precision of a theoretical philosophy of history. With that in mind, let us look at each author's opus with a view to its concern with both divinity and history. Because of our focus on history, Eliot's poem cycle will be looked at from a rather different angle than in the previous chapter; and because Pound's is the more unfamiliar of the two poetic visions, offering a "pagan" spirituality in contrast with Eliot's Christian mysticism, it will be discussed first, and then brought into comparison with that of Eliot's *Four Quartets.*

Cosmic Divinity and History in Ezra Pound's *Cantos*

There is some irony in the fact that Ezra Pound, who is well known as a pivotal figure in the creation of Modernism in English poetry and prose—not only through his poetry and criticism, but also through his championing of the work of T. S. Eliot, James Joyce, Wyndham Lewis, Robert Frost, William Carlos Williams, and others—had no allegiance to the idea that history is a story of inevitable cultural and moral progress. New and daringly experimental forms of literary expression were needed, in his view, not because novelty was required in order to keep up with a march of ever-ascending cultural progress, but for a very different, and indeed contrary, reason: Pound perceived early twentieth-century Western culture to be hollow at the core, in moral disarray, and thus as calling for a strenuous effort on the part of writers, artists, and educators to diagnose modern cultural decadence, teach society about its predicament, and provide restorative civilizational insights in language and images reflective of contemporary life. Pound was unusually sensitive to what was stagnant and enervated in social and cultural life, and his sense that Western civilization had lost its bearings—was being "botched"—was confirmed for him by the pointless and devastating waste of the First World War.[3] From early in his career his work reflects his conviction that civilization is no steady march of progress but rather that history, apart from scientific advance and technological invention, is a tale of oscillating progress and decline—or rather of multitudes of overlapping oscillations of progress and decline, among both persons and societies.

Pound held that constructive civilizational and societal order always derive from the efficacious influence of insightful, energetic, well-ordered individuals, and he viewed artists as having a special role among these, due to their power to produce culturally compelling images, guiding visions, and persuasive myths. His overriding desire was to assist in the *renewal* of the Western civilization he lived in. To that end he set out to discover, to the best of his abilities, what the highest and permanent values are; how good order is established, and reestablished, in self and society; and what is inconsequential or leads to disorder in human living.

As he put it, to have maximum positive impact as an artist, he needed "to find out what sort of things endure, and what sort of things are transient; what sort of things recur; . . . to learn upon what the forces, constructive and dispersive, of social order move; to learn what rules and axioms hold firm, and what sort fade, and what sort are durable but permutable . . ."[4] As a poet, he ultimately chose as his vehicle of cultural instruction and elucidation the writing of an epic poem, *The Cantos*, running in its final edition to over 800 pages, to which he devoted his poetic powers for nearly sixty years (roughly 1910 to 1967), into which he tried to pour all he had learned and that he hoped would contribute toward the emergence of a civilization "*as good* as the best that has been."[5]

With regard to the poem helping to usher in a vast twentieth-century Western civilizational renaissance, Pound's ambitions for *The Cantos* obviously went unfulfilled, although *The Cantos* had a major impact on the world of English-language poetry, especially with regard to the creation of an idiomatically fresh and formally powerful modern poetic style. Still, this isn't our concern. Our focus is the results of the fact that, to satisfy Pound's concerns, *The Cantos* had to address basic questions about the nature and meaning of history. His intent was to show in poetic form what world history—in major moments both ancient and modern—could tell us about good and bad civilizations, and about their respective causes. Its scope, as Hugh Kenner writes, "was to be nothing less than a vast historical demonstration."[6] Consequently, it presents to its readers "a theory of history" in general.[7] Our question is: In what manner did Pound's *Cantos*, in providing an alternative to modern materialist and progressivist views of history, affirm human experiences of a divine "beyond" and envision a divinely grounded human drama?

Perhaps the most striking feature of the portrayal of human history in *The Cantos* is its insistence on the reality of the divine. As has often been noted, Pound is "essentially a religious poet," convinced that order, goodness, truth, and beauty flow into society only through human participatory attunement to divine being or "light."[8] *The Cantos* abound both with theophanies—appearances of the divine, usually in the symbolic form of gods drawn from Greek, Roman, and Chinese mythology, or from Neoplatonic imagery, including some of its Christian formulations—and with epiphanies—human experiences of mystical exaltation, in which persons experience visions of supernatural or timeless being. In a typical lyric passage from canto 3, gods of ancient Greece and Rome are evoked, with a compelling sense of the truth of numinous experience:

> Gods float in the azure air,
> Bright gods and Tuscan, back before dew was shed.
> Light: and the first light, before ever dew was fallen.
> Panisks, and from the oak, dryas,
> And from the apple, mælid,
> Through all the wood, and the leaves are full of voices,
> A-whisper, and the clouds bowe over the lake,
> And there are gods upon them, (3/11)[9]

A strand of Neoplatonist religiosity in the Christian tradition is also welcomed by Pound—insofar as it centers on light symbolism—to convey his devotion to the divine source and measure of the real, the true, and the good:

> in the light of light is the *virtù*
> "sunt lumina" said Erigena Scotus
> [. . .]
> Light tensile immaculata
> the sun's cord unspotted
> "sunt lumina" said the Oirishman to King Carolus,
> "OMNIA,
> all things that are are lights"[10] (74/429)

Such evocations, which continually recur in the poem's most lyric passages, are not, as Hugh Kenner points out, mere literary conceits.[11] They reflect Pound's deep conviction that the "enduring constants" of good order in self and society are grounded in the permanence of divine reality, and that cultural creativity and beneficial productivity are dependent on a lively, reverent spiritual sensibility. "Without gods," he states emphatically, "no culture."[12]

As Pound makes clear, this means that all historical periods are ontologically interconnected in their meanings—that they are, in a sense, contemporaneous through human participation in timeless being; and therefore that the great achievements of the past should not be thought of as irretrievably behind us, or irrelevant to modern times, but rather as "here, now," and profoundly instructive, if only we welcome their presence and immediacy to our minds, pay attention to them, and recover and reactivate their lessons and wisdom.[13]

A deep respect for tradition therefore permeates *The Cantos*, as it presents us with historical "paradigm after paradigm" of good and bad government, virtuous and destructive individuals, beneficial appreciation of beauty and order, and human betrayal of what is noble and fine.[14] This respect for tradition is built into the poem's conceptual structure in that its "narrative" pays homage to the masterpiece of Pound's predecessor Dante, *The Divine Comedy*, by dividing the human drama into the three categories of *inferno*, *purgatorio*, and *paradiso*. But while for Dante these divisions both provide the directional "plot" to the poem that relates the human drama and grounds this drama in an eschatological vision based on Christian teaching, for Pound they do neither of these things. Pound transfigures the three categories into descriptions of worldly existential states: "I was not following the three divisions of the *Divine Comedy* exactly," he wrote, "[b]ut I have made the division between people dominated by emotion [hell], people struggling upward [purgatory], and those who have some part of the divine vision [paradise]."[15] The point that *The Cantos* is intended to make is that all three types of people, as well as the communities reflective of them, *continually recur in history*. The history in which they recur is not headed toward a divine end, a Last Judgment, or a Second Coming, as in the Christian vision of a transfigurative act of God at the end of time and world; rather for Pound, human "perfecting," such as is attainable, is a recurrent possibility of personal and social ordering grounded in especial receptivity to divine beauty, goodness, and truth. Thus the vision of history conveyed in *The Cantos* is fundamentally "cosmological"—that is, it reflects experiences in which divinity has not receded from the cosmos into *radical* transcendence—and so is, in a qualified sense, *cyclical* rather than eschatological.

Which brings us to a critical insight into Pound's understanding of the nature of divine reality and the design of history. If one follows the various threads of divine symbols and theophanies in *The Cantos*, despite the occasional references to "God" and to Neoplatonic light imagery of the kind quoted above, one finds oneself in what is essentially a polytheistic world. The radically transcendent God of Hebrew-Judaic, Christian, and Islamic faith is almost totally absent. In part this is because Pound viewed as civilizationally destructive the Hebrew and Christian condemnation of the gods of polytheistic myth—destructive, because such teachings (along with their iconoclastic elements) have, in his view, undermined the human ability to perceive the divine in nature and to trust in personal ecstatic experiences. Thus, as a guide to human intercourse with divine reality Pound will "substitute for the Moses of the Old Testament the Ovid of the *Metamorphoses*, with his recognition of the vivifying personal immediacy of supernatural forces and the constant penetration of the supernatural into the natural, producing change."[16] Hebraic and Christian religious exclusivism was an affront to Pound's tolerant polytheistic religious sensibility, and remained, in his view, an obstacle to civilizational renewal, which depends on continual access to "'magic moments,' visions of the light, divine energies, paradisal states of mind" through numinous encounters that fall within the field of positive *imagination*.[17] As Pound states, it is "*images of the gods* [that] move the soul to contemplation and preserve the tradition of the undivided light" as this informs a well-ordered soul or populace. "Tradition inheres [in] the images of the gods," not in iconoclastic religion or apophatic theology.[18]

The basis, then, for Pound's rejection of the Christian conception of the divine (Jesus does not figure in *The Cantos*, and among Western paradigmatic sources of ordering vision, one will find Voltaire and Thomas Jefferson, but not Augustine or Aquinas) is his distrust of what he views as "transcendent otherworldliness." Pound takes no stock in a radically unknown Beyond, a God who does not and *cannot* appear, or in any ultimate reality that is considered improperly construed or debased if imagistically represented. For this reason, too, he disdains Buddhist and Taoist teachings on nirvana or transcendence. Instead he lauds Confucianism, with its powerful emphasis on social responsibility and its focus on the politically practical and realizable. *The Cantos* dismiss Buddhism ("the Bhud rot") as degenerately passive, and Taoists ("Taosers") as irresponsibly fascinated with "otherworldliness" and magic:

And of Taosers, Chu says:
                concerned neither with heaven, earth
                or with anything on the square
but wholly subjective, for the Dragon moaning,
the screaming tiger, mercury, pills, pharmacopia,

And the Bhud rot: that floaters eat
                without maintaining their homesteads
   (99/696–97)

Confucian teaching, by contrast, is praised as a guide to an appropriately energetic commitment to religious, personal, and civic responsibility, a commitment from which grows true social and civilizational order. Confucius (K'ung-Fu-tzu) is described most vividly in canto 13:

          And Kung said
"Respect a child's faculties
"From the moment it inhales the clear air,
"But a man of fifty who knows nothing
          Is worthy of no respect."
And "When the prince has gathered about him
"All the savants and artists, his riches will be fully employed."
And Kung said, and wrote on the bo leaves:
          If a man have not order within him
He can not spread order around him;
And if a man have not order within him
His family will not act with due order;
          And if the prince have not order within him
He can not put order in his dominions.
And Kung gave the words "order"
and "brotherly deference"
And said nothing of the "life after death." (13/59)

In line with these allegiances and distrusts, Pound—as an artist whose faith rests on the ordering, civilizing power of images, symbols, myths, and the rhythms of language—has little patience for religious wisdom in the forms of abstract doctrinal formulations, abstruse mystical speculations, or explanatory theologies with their systematic and apologetic arguments. Theological disputes, for him, are a sure sign of decline, for they replace the lived, experienced vision. “Disputation,” he writes, “destroys faith. . . . Suspect anyone who destroys an image.”[19]

So Pound, while energetically affirming divine, eternal reality and the recurrent presence of real, society-ordering theophanies in history, refuses any validation of a radically transcendent divine ground of reality, and thus not only disdains the Creator-God of Christian vision but also ignores Christian eschatological vision and sensibility. Likewise the “Eternal Being” of Proust (or Plato’s Idea of the Good) would be too abstract and non-imaginal for Pound—too completely transcendent. Worldly time is related to divine timelessness in *The Cantos* only in the form of cyclical recurrences *within the cosmos*: there is no end of time, no linear direction to the overall story of history—no *telos*, no climax. Pound’s resistance to progressivism together with his recovery of divine reality as the basis of historical meaning and order lead him to envision in *The Cantos* something like the cyclical experience of time in ancient cosmological societies, where the “good order” of human-divine harmony is strongly associated with the “cosmic rhythms of nature.”[20]

The result is that *The Cantos*, an epic poem *about* history and *including* history that offers an alternative to the secular-progressivist idea of history, excludes from its vast visionary compass all religious experiences or symbols that suggest that history has a teleological “direction” or culmination. At the level of the individual, there is no indication of a personal eschatological orientation: no symbols that suggest that every person lives in a tension of relatedness to a God of history promising a mysterious, transfigurative fulfillment. At the same time, at the level of social and political life, Pound decisively rejects the secular-progressivist idea that history is an inexorable process of civilizational advance or is heading toward some kind of utopia, a perfected condition of society in this world. *The Cantos* offers as ideals of historical “culmination” only images of a *paradiso terrestre*—sublime and excellent civilizational orders that are always temporary in their realization, attainable through the right combination of political, economic, and cultural wisdom, strong leadership, and reverence for the divine realities revealed in the rhythms and orders of nature and the cosmos. Therefore, despite the fact that in reading *The Cantos* we find ourselves, as William Carlos Williams once commented, standing "continually in the presence of history" as participants in the unfolding of a human-divine drama, the poem arcs unavoidably toward a kind of "immanentism"—a strange (to most of us) polytheistic, pantheistic immanentism, in which *paradiso* is not a symbol of a transfigured "beyond" but a symbol for the best of personal moments and civilizational actualizations.[21] Both secularism and progressivism are discredited, while divine reality and history as a process of human-divine relationship are affirmed. But images of history heading toward eschatological fulfillment, images central to traditions that understand divinity to be a radically transcendent Creator-God, are not to be found in *The Cantos*.

God and History in T. S. Eliot's *Four Quartets*

The only other poetic work in twentieth-century literature that offers a vision of the drama of history as a whole and contains an implicit philosophy of history is T. S. Eliot's poem cycle *Four Quartets*. In proportion to such an ambition *Four Quartets* is extremely compact, running as it does to just under 900 lines. Just like *The Cantos*, however, it is vigorously ecumenic and world-historical in scope and reference, making symbolic reference to traditions, events, and personages from cultures ancient and modern, Eastern and Western. Also like *The Cantos*, it constitutes a reaction against and rejection of Western philosophical materialism and secular-progressivist views of history, having as one of its principal aims a poetic illumination and symbolic evocation of timeless divine being as the source of order and meaning in history. Its vision of divine being, however, differs significantly from the vision of Pound's poem, with profound implications for its portrayal of the drama of history and of the ultimate aims of both personal and social existence. We will see how the idea of history offered by *Four Quartets* complements and expands on its portrayal of unsought moments of illumination and mystical reflection discussed in the last chapter.

A first point to note is that Eliot links each of the four poems with symbols related to each of four basic dimensions in our experience of reality—the individual person, society, the natural world, and divine being—so that as a whole they explore human existence in its relation to the cosmos in its completeness.[22] *Burnt Norton* focuses on the individual person; *East Coker* on the social world of community and heritage; *The Dry Salvages* on nature, and its rhythms and powers; and *Little Gidding* on the ultimate reconciliation of finite being and history with a timeless divine ground. Also, the four poems are successively dominated by images of air, earth, water, and fire, again together symbolizing the totality of the cosmos, and further, each of the four poems is associated with one of the four seasons.[23] In these ways, and others, Eliot places his poetic meditations on existence in the context of the fullness of reality, grounding its vision of history in multiple symbolizations of cosmic wholeness.

A second point is that Eliot, like Pound, decisively rejects all secular progressivist and "social evolutionary" views of history. Not, as David Tracy points out, that he fails to appreciate the genuine achievements of modernity "in science and technology, in democratic politics and cultural pluralism"—but that he recognizes such developments, again like Pound, as occurring within a larger cultural process that in the early twentieth century glaringly evidenced moral and spiritual exhaustion and cultural sterility and decadence.[24] The poem cycle repeatedly emphasizes—as Eliot did in *The Waste Land*—that a loss of contact with spiritual reality is characteristic of his time; and also that progressivist ideas and ideals that envision earthly utopias are culturally disastrous, in that they undermine political realism and divert our spiritual potential while at the same time keeping us from paying proper attention to the guiding wisdom of heritages and traditions of the past. Thus he describes progressivism in *The Dry Salvages* as

> a partial fallacy
> Encouraged by superficial notions of evolution,
> Which becomes, in the popular mind, a means of disowning the
> past. (*DS*, II.87–89)

Such "superficial notions" of evolution permeate modern reflections about history in which human "curiosity searches past and future / And clings to that dimension" (*DS*, V.199–200), not only for the general reason that openness to timeless reality is unsettling and demanding, but also specifically because of the widespread influence in modernity of reductively materialist views of history that eclipse the timeless dimension of reality.

Like Pound, Eliot identifies the elemental conceptual error underlying all liberal progressivist and utopian views of history as being a failure to appreciate that the ultimate source of personal life, society, history, and the natural world is a timeless divine ground. Once this reality is properly taken into account, the line of historical meaning "that runs from time into eternity" (in Eric Voegelin's phrase) may be seen to constitute the most significant line of meaning in history, and all historical periods can then be recognized, as they were by Pound, as being in a sense contemporaneous through the essential participation of all human beings in the eternal ground.[25] Eliot's portrayal of human consciousness throughout *Four Quartets* in terms of the "intersection of the timeless / With time" (*DS*, V.201–202) leads him to summarily describe history—the cumulative meaning of all human existences—as "a pattern / Of timeless moments" (*LG*, V.234–35).[26]

But this sense of what history is goes widely unappreciated in modernity. And consequently, if the promises of progressivism come to lose their allure, for some, through realistic assessments of moral and political conditions, while history is still regarded as a purely material process, the result is existentially disastrous. More perhaps than any other major Modernist poet, Eliot is sensitive to what history *feels like* when it is drained both of apprehensions of timeless divine meaning, and of faith in the inevitability of progress. *Four Quartets* continually returns to evocations of the fear of meaninglessness and the quiet desperation of those who experience time as a "mere sequence" (*DS*, II.86). Eliot describes the

> strained time-ridden faces
> Distracted from distraction by distraction
> Filled with fancies and empty of meaning (*BN*, III.100–102)

of modern commuters and consumers; the "mental emptiness" and "the growing terror of nothing to think about" that haunt the imaginationally time-bound (*EC*, III.120–21); and fear of a pointless human struggle and suffering that has "no end" (*DS*, II.79) but only further repetitions in time. The therapy for such existences, Eliot advocates, lies in access to experiences of the divine: at a minimum, in granting gifted moments of illumination—beatific flashes of eternity—their full suggestiveness as hints of a realm of timeless meaning; or more fully, in engaging in disciplined efforts to reflect on mystical surmises and to join one's personal will with the divine will through some of the many modes of observance, prayer, meditation, or spiritual practice. Eliot, offering *Four Quartets* as a therapeutic vision of the true nature both of history and of human possibilities within history, affirms in it again and again the reality of divine being while alluding to various manners in which persons can access the presence of divine reality.

It is when we consider how divine being is symbolized in *Four Quartets* that we see most clearly where Eliot and Pound, as envisioners of a divinely grounded history, and as cultural recoverers of a timeless reality for modernity, part ways. Not that the two poets do not evidence some commonalities in their approaches to affirming the divine. Both of them, for example, are insistently ecumenical, employing images and symbols from an intentionally global range of religious mythologies, theologies, and philosophies. In *Four Quartets*, as we have seen, Eliot's "use of specifically religious words and symbols shows a scrupulous care"[27] in indicating how a multitude of religious traditions testify, in diverse ways, to universally available experiences of divine reality, embedding in the poems Buddhist ("the lotos rose quietly, quietly"); Hindu ("I sometimes wonder if that is what Krishna meant"); mystical-philosophical ("the still point of the turning world"); cosmological ("I think that the river / Is a strong brown god"); and Christian ("the Word in the desert"; "Figlia del tuo figlio / Queen of Heaven") languages and symbols (*BN*, I.36, II.62, V.155; *EC*, III.24; *DS*, I.1-2, IV.77-78). David Tracy sums up the result: "Eliot, as both poet and religious thinker, went as far as any twentieth-century poet in the English-speaking world has ever done to evoke and provoke both ancient and new, both Eastern and Western religious spiritual thinking."[28] Eliot also parallels Pound in identifying the essence of divine reality as Love; but where in *The Cantos* it is Aphrodite, under various names, who most frequently symbolizes the theophany of divine being as Love, in *Four Quartets* Eliot's allusions and symbols guide the reader firmly toward a Christian (and at times explicitly Dantesque) God of love. Indicating how the poem cycle enacts this guidance will show how far Eliot diverges from Pound in his understanding of the nature of divine reality, personal existence in history, and the overall structure of history.

Despite the ecumenicism of *Four Quartets*, its Christian understanding of personal existence and historical meaning is brought home to the reader in many ways, some of them mentioned in the previous chapter. There is Eliot's use of direct quotations from the Christian mystics St. John of the Cross and Julian of Norwich (*EC*, III.136–46; *LG*, III.166–68, V.255–56); his direct references to Good Friday, Pentecost, and the Incarnation (*EC*, IV.171; *LG*, IV.200–206; *DS*, V.215); his crafting of the fourth movement in each poem as a brief lyric that successively evokes the divine in the four aspects of God the Creator (or Unmoved Mover), the Redeemer Son, the Lady, and the Holy Spirit;[29] and the work's concluding with a reiteration of Dante's portrayal of the metaphysical consummation of the human drama as a transfigured participation, beyond worldly history, in a divine union and harmony represented as a "knot" of flames constituting the celestial "rose" of divine Love (*LG*, V.255–59).[30] The vision of history in *Four Quartets* is correspondingly an *eschatological* vision—not a vision of recurrent periods of human-divine attunement in a cosmos without culmination, as in *The Cantos*.

We can further elucidate this difference from Pound's vision, as well as the nature of Eliot's eschatological view of existence and history, by turning to some of the thematic concepts and symbols that recur throughout *Four Quartets*, in particular those that convey Eliot's understanding of the radically transcendent nature of divine reality.

First, Eliot's evocations of divine being continually present the ultimate divine ground as radically "beyond" all that can be imagined of existence and world. Where Pound's symbols of the timeless and the divine find their highest expression in metaphors of illumination and manifestations of light, Eliot persistently turns the reader's attention to the absolute unknowability of the timeless ground. For Eliot, the divine ground is finally a God whose being is, for humans, an abyss of mystery, which to our understanding is darkness:

> I said to my soul, be still, and let the dark come upon you
> Which shall be the darkness of God. (*EC*, III.112–13)

The profoundest way to divine union—the apophatic way—is through accepting the darkness that is "the world's end" (*LG*, I.36), learning how to put off "sense and notion" (*LG*, I.43) in order to approach

a deeper communion
Through the dark cold and the empty desolation (*EC*, V.206–7)

Beyond our experiences of divine light lies the divine mystery for which even the language of "time and timelessness" are inadequate. Eliot's vision of reality is far from Pound's pantheism and cosmologicism.

Next, as the work of a Christian mystic, it is no surprise that one of the key themes in *Four Quartets* is death—death as reality, and death as symbol. The Christian vision of human participation in eternal reality centers upon the recognition that one must "die" to this life and the world in order to "live" in union with a divine that is a beyond of existence and world. *Four Quartets* repeatedly indicates that *fulfilled* human communion with the divine involves, ultimately, a transfigurative process that is "perfected in death" (*LG*, III.195). But because the divine mystery is Love, and our union with it can only be *through* love, our dying to the world and to the time-bound dimension of our lives cannot be a mere renunciation or condemnation of the world, but a "practice of dying" (to borrow a phrase of Plato's) which takes the specific form of a love that unites one *both* with the transcendent divine Love *and* the world whose essence is created Love. As a Christian, Eliot views the finite world as created by the Word of God; it is thus divine Word and Love

in the aspect of time
Caught in the form of limitation
Between un-being and being. (*BN*, V.166–68)

So to love the world as Word and Love, and at the same time to move toward union with a divine Love that is not to be simply identified with the world, one must "die" to the world and to one's present self in a distinct way: through a self-surrendering and world-surrendering loving (the "detachment" of *Little Gidding* III) that unrestrictedly loves the world even as it wills and loves that which radically transcends experience and world. This is a movement of the willing self that is, as Eliot phrases it, a "death in love" (*DS*, V.204), and those who are able to engage in such spiritual movement in a profound and habitual way are "saints," who manifest in their existences

> a *lifetime's* death in love,
> Ardour and selflessness and self-surrender.
> (*DS*, V.204–5, emphasis added)

The saint's existence is impossible for all but the few; but those few are nevertheless the measure of well-oriented and well-ordered spirituality.

Because of Pound's existential resistance to an Unknown God, to a radically mysterious *Urgrund*, death has no function as a positive image in his work, and certainly not as a symbol for transfigured life. In canto 29, in a passage possibly prompted by an encounter with Eliot,[31] Pound writes of Christian mystics and their like:

> And I, "But this beats me,
> "Beats me, I mean that I do not understand it;
> "This love of death that is in them." (29/145)

Pound's lyrical evocations of the divine, and of the "magic moments" of its apprehension, move always within the light-and-nature imagery of the mythopoeic traditions that avoid what he derides as "otherworldliness." For Eliot, however, there is no deepening movement into what is *ultimately* divine except through death: death of the clinging-to-world self and death of the world itself, which, however, as a process of "death *in love*," point eschatologically toward an ultimate paradoxical accord between existence and world, on the one hand, and a divine beyond, on the other, in which the former will find fulfillment in a mysterious transfiguration—an accord that Eliot strangely and beautifully symbolizes in the affirmation that

> The moment of the rose and the moment of the yew-tree
> Are of equal duration. (*LG*, V.232–33)

That is, the rose (life, beauty, love) and the yew tree (traditional symbol of death) will finally, in the end, be united as one meaningful reality—in the being of God.

In light of this vision, it becomes clear why the theme of conversion is central to *Four Quartets*, with the third section of each of the four poems concerned with the soul's turning, "where descent becomes ascent"—where immersion in tedium, the strain of unillumined existence, and the burden of the time-bound self's accumulation of guilt give way to a dying-to-self-and-world that is simultaneously a loving ascent to a true communion with God.[32] This movement of "turning" is described in the poem cycle as involving the self's humble recognition of all its moral and spiritual imperfections: errors of desiring and clinging, and waywardness in choosing and acting. Committing oneself and one's hopes to a vision of ultimate fulfillment in perfect divine Love entails acknowledging, and feeling, one's existential failures in loving; one's misplaced pride; one's many modes of self-deception: in Christian language, one's sins. Following Christian tradition, *Four Quartets* symbolizes the painful awareness of one's sinfulness—intensely experienced in the process of conversion—as a purgatorial "fire," a "torment" that is nevertheless the sole means of "refining" and "redeeming" wayward spirits. Without undergoing such torment ("devised" by Love), the soul cannot recognize either what God truly is (a perfection of transcendent Love) or what human beings are (inherently imperfect, prideful, sinful, and in need of redemptive grace) (*LG*, II.145, IV.206, 207). And without these insights into God and human nature, a civilization, Eliot contends, has lost its bearings. "To do away with a sense of sin," Eliot wrote in a letter from September 1939, "is to do away with civilisation."[33] The contrast with Pound is here at its most acute. For Pound human nature, even with all its propensities for aberration and destructiveness, is not *inherently and irreparably* wayward and thus in need of divine redemption. "Original Sin," George Kearns writes, is "a term not in Pound's vocabulary."[34]

We can see then why, for Pound, the Christian invitation to recognize and embrace Christ's passion and crucifixion as the saving event initiated by divine Love to reconcile fallen humankind with divine perfection, through redemption of human sin, is unmoving and alien; while for the Eliot of *Four Quartets*, it is an invitation that crucially orients our consciousness of sin, capacity for love, spiritual need for humility and repentance, and desire for redemptive grace:

> The dripping blood our only drink,
> The bloody flesh our only food . . . (*EC*, IV.167–68)

The nature and meaning of the soul's journey toward its proper end is essentially eschatological for the Eliot of *Four Quartets*, portrayed as it is as a journey whose destination is a mystery of transfiguration beyond anything we can presently understand of the intersecting of time and timelessness. We cannot say that our understanding penetrates the mystery of this fulfillment; but we can accept it in faith and humility as journey's end for the soul, a *telos* where "All manner of thing shall be well" (*LG*, V.256). And of course, it is not only the "past and future" of a *person's* existence that shall be reconciled, it is the past and future of *all people* of all times and places; it is history itself. History, as the "pattern of timeless moments" of all human participation in reality, in the vision of *Four Quartets* has an eschatological, not cyclical and unending, structure—a structure revealed in the mystic's journey through love toward God, and witnessed to by the signal historical events of the "one Annunciation" and the supreme "Incarnation" of Christ (*DS*, II.84, V.215).

Two facts at this point should again be stressed. The first is that Eliot's "beyond" of eschatological fulfillment is not any kind of spatial divine "elsewhere," ontotheologically conceived in terms of an *abandonment* of existence and world. Eschatological fulfillment is the goal of history as a transfigurative *completing* of its past, present, and future meanings, through which persons and world are envisioned as redeemed and renewed through the fulfillment of their present modes of being in a manner mysterious to human consciousness,

> When the tongues of flame are in-folded
> Into the crowned knot of fire
> And the fire and the rose are one. (*LG*, V.257–59)

The second is that the Christian faith of the author of *Four Quartets* does not presume to be able to comprehend what is incomprehensible. Eliot remained all his life acutely aware that the human intellect is incapable of penetrating the mystery of Incarnation, or the reconciliation of matter and spirit, or the justification of evil in relation to a God of love.[35] Eliot's Christian faith is that of a person for whom all these are truly mysteries, but who embraces the "scheme" of the Christian vision because it is the one religion or philosophy that accords best, in his view, with the experienced facts and values of existence. The work's concluding symbolism of ultimate oneness, therefore, is not an assertion of knowledge, but an artistic figuration arising from faith, hope, and love.

Both the Eliot of *Four Quartets* and the Pound of *The Cantos*, in the end, created poetically expressed visions of history that broke with progressivism and attempted to reclaim, for civilizational instruction, therapeutic insight into the divine basis of existence, order, and history. But while Pound's vision insists on the real presence of "the gods" in the world, his aversion to radically transcendent divinity, and thus the Christian view of history, means there is no place in his poem for a vision of ultimate transfigurative fulfillment such as Eliot's. Eliot, on the other hand, challenges modern secularism and progressivism by re-envisioning the Christian view of existence and history in a Modernist idiom for a modern readership—an audience whose global, multicultural awareness and historical-mindedness are addressed by Eliot's careful use of both traditional and contemporary, and Western and Eastern, symbols, allusions, and language. What is common to both poets is insistence that modern existence need not be experienced as merely a doubtful struggle for progress and satisfaction in a desacralized, purely material universe, because eternal, divine meaning as witnessed to throughout human history is real, intermittently accessible through loving openness, and the ultimate source of both social and personal order. Modern life need not, they indicate, be wedded to delusions about inevitable progress or, undeluded, reduced to stoic, anxious existence in a disenchanted world. Experiences of eternal being can be, the two poets insist, a source of succor, and even sensed as redemptive—as they were for Proust, and at times for Dickinson.

Transcendence Inaccessible, History Unredeemed: Samuel Beckett

The confidence of Pound and Eliot in the accessibility of human recovery, through love, of experiences of timeless meaning are not typical of existential visions in major Modernist literature. Neither pantheist "cosmologicism" nor Christian eschatology is a convincing answer to questions about the meaning of history and existence for writers such as Joyce, Woolf, Kafka, Yeats, William Carlos Williams, or Wallace Stevens. The *search* for transcendent meaning can easily be recognized in the works of these and other pivotal figures; it has not disappeared as motive or theme. But *access* to a transcendent dimension of meaning appears closed off, having been obstructed by modern suspicion of religious dogmas and symbols resulting in part from religious warfare, in part from scientific advances, and in part from Enlightenment teachings; by sophisticated complexities of psychological explanation (e.g., Nietzsche and Freud); by an exhausted distaste for grand metaphysical systems and solutions; and by the appalling irrationalities manifest in twentieth-century politics and warfare. The ability of human consciousness to out-question the physical universe does not fade, but a frustrated inconclusiveness about what this ability might mean becomes the hallmark of much Modernist literature. And no author manifests this frustration more painfully and indelibly than Samuel Beckett.

In Beckett the longing for transcendence is continually present, even as a dismayed suspicion about its truth suffuses every novel, play, and short story. Rather than ignoring the question of transcendence, as is often supposed, Beckett's vision of existence is cursed by it. The question both obsesses and oppresses Beckett because, like Pound and Eliot, he sees the notion of divine being as central to human thinking and feeling, but unlike Pound and Eliot he accepts no possibility of genuine human *encounter* with the divine. For in Beckett's universe, human existence is sealed within finite being; it has no metaphysical access to infinite and timeless reality. Therefore in his view people are incapable of knowing whether the ideas of divine reality that haunt human consciousness correspond to anything real, and must remain existentially bereft of the solace of any true human-divine interaction.

For Beckett, this inability to experience divine timelessness completely drains history of meaning, since Beckett agrees with Pound and Eliot that history could only be known to be meaningful, could only be "redeemed," through the revelation or intervention of a supernatural power of presence and grace, and his anthropology and metaphysics exclude any possibility of such a revelation. The popular modern alternative answer, that history is meaningful because of progress in worldly affairs, because of human achievements alone, is no more intelligible to Beckett than it is to Dickinson, Proust, Pound, or Eliot. Humanist confidence that history will be justified by its own progress is for Beckett a risible delusion, since humans to him are obviously incapable of fundamental moral improvement, much less of justifying or redeeming the vast human history of struggle, blundering, and undeserved suffering.

With Beckett, then, twentieth-century literature arrives at a total breakdown of confidence in historical meaning. Withdrawn from faith in both God and human progress, Beckett is led to a startling vision of history as nothing more than the accumulation of time, moment adding to moment, amassing without seeming significance.[36] Yet still, this horrified experience of pointless temporality—substituting for Proust's indifference to the overall meaning of history a pointedly scornful dismissal of the idea of progress—is not Beckett's final word on the human condition, because he stays intensely focused on the fact that human consciousness could have no appreciation of its own condition as time-bound and finite at all unless it also had an innate apprehension of the notion of timelessness, of an absolute divine reality. Since for Beckett there can be no *encounter* with divinity, however, the consequences of this innate notion consist principally of (1) every person's yearning for access to timeless being or meaning; (2) frustration over the satisfaction of this yearning being forever denied; and (3) disappointment with everything worldly that might appear to promise, or pretends to provide, what only absolute and perfect reality (i.e., God) *could* provide. Beckett's vision of human existence is thus essentially one of unappeased longing for transcendent meaning. That vision will be the focus of the next chapter.

CHAPTER FIVE

Mystic Without Faith

Samuel Beckett and the Ghost of Love in *Krapp's Last Tape*

SAMUEL BECKETT IS most widely known for his play *Waiting for Godot*, which brought him international renown not long after its first productions in the mid-1950s. He remains best known as a playwright—other major plays include *Endgame*, *Happy Days*, and *Krapp's Last Tape*, the last of which will be discussed below—although his novels and short fiction are as original and profound as his plays and were an equal basis for his being awarded the Nobel Prize in Literature in 1969. Since through his plays and fiction together Beckett is credited with expressing the bleakest existential vision of all major Modernist writers (with the possible exception of Kafka), he would appear to be an unusual candidate for inclusion in a study of authors whose work importantly grapples with the issue of transcendent reality. But in fact, among the great Modernists of fiction and drama, Beckett is the author whose work is most centrally concerned with the problem of transcendent meaning. That this concern primarily takes the form of a furious attack on complacent presumptions about life's meaningfulness doesn't make it less of an informing concern. Beckett's mature work, in fact, shimmers throughout with an obsession with the question of God—a fact not always appreciated.

Beckett is frequently, and wrongly, considered an "absurdist," and his dramas labeled examples of "theater of the absurd," the supposition being that his works portray human existence as a pointless nullity, denying it all meaning and purpose. This is a mistake. Beckett's view of the human condition is far more ambiguous and troubling than would be the case if he were a nihilist or absurdist. What Beckett's characters and narrators suffer from is the malady, not of knowing that life is meaningless, but of *anxiously fearing* that their lives are without meaning or value. Beckett presents the condition of human life as slippery with existential uncertainty in every regard, although his characters try endlessly to find fixed points of meaning, along with assurances of purpose and identity, which always elude them. These unsuccessful searches for stabilities of truth and repose are sometimes portrayed as desperate and agonized, but at other times—true to how we often appear to each other and ourselves—as amusing, sometimes even hilarious in the mode of existential or intellectual slapstick. Beckett is expert at portraying both the tragic and comic aspects of lives that struggle to keep their balance in a climate of perpetual existential unknowns. And foremost among these unknowns, haunting every Beckett character, is the question of whether—against all evidence, as Beckett presents the case—a transcendent meaning might exist that could somehow justify and redeem the travails and sufferings of existence. Human distress over the impossibility of ever attaining an answer to this question, and the fretful supposition that all we will ever know is a life permanently crippled by longing for communion with an inaccessible transcendence, are conditions of consciousness so important to Beckett's vision of existence as to be the foundation from which all his work arises.

This places him in continuity with the four authors already discussed, for all of whom the meaning of human existence can only be brought into clarity by examining its negotiations with eternal being. The difference with Beckett is that this negotiation is in his view permanently one-sided: the adventures, sufferings, pratfalls, and internal monologues portrayed by Beckett are the actions of beings yearning for but denied any communion at all with transcendent attention, comfort, or promise. But still a divine transcendence, an absolute and perfect being, remains in the vision of his works always the measure against which worldly things and experiences are evaluated. His writings from early to late show him to be a "God-haunted man," whose mouthpieces—the heroes and heroines in his works—scorn all worldly realities, including themselves, as disappointing and ridiculous precisely because they are not timelessly divine.[1] Indeed, as Michael Robinson has pointed out, the frustration, rage, and contempt so often expressed by the Beckett protagonist echoes "the turning from the world in anger and disgust of the Old Testament prophets or the early Fathers of the Church, a renunciation which originates in the conviction that 'whatsoever is not God is nothing.'"[2]

Beckett's disgust with the world, therefore, is not the disengaged dismissal of the absurdist, but rather that of a certain type of mystic, the most intransigent and austere type. But in Beckett's case, the divinity that establishes mystical orientation and perspective is not an *experienced presence*. It exists only as a mental notion of perfect being and soteriological possibility that terrorizes consciousness due to the impossibility of its validation under worldly conditions. The offstage "character" of Godot in the tragicomic *Waiting for Godot* is the most straightforward symbol of this notion in Beckett's works, a person whose appearance would constitute "salvation" if he appeared, but who does not appear.[3] The play encapsulates the mystic impulse paralyzed by ignorance.

It is important to emphasize here by way of contrast that the four authors discussed in previous chapters would argue, each in his or her way, that the notion of absolute being is present in every human consciousness because this being is *experienced* in some way—or "participated in," to use the classical philosophical and theological language. The origin of Beckett's disagreement on this point is his strict metaphysical dualism. For Beckett, the gap between the finite and the infinite cannot be bridged; the two cannot "touch." What is finite and temporal, including human nature in its entirety, cannot in any way participate in the infinite and eternal. The two are incompatible. Humans long to establish themselves, somehow, in enduring and redemptive being, but this is a longing that cannot, in Beckett's view, be experientially fulfilled.

Yet humans are not merely physical or material beings, for Beckett, because a second dualism, equally strict, informs his anthropology: the ontological separateness of mind and matter. A perfect Cartesian in this respect, Beckett views mind, human consciousness, as a substance separate from and irreducible to bodily or physical reality; mind is "spirit," the anti-physical. The dilemmas and ambitions of Beckett's protagonists frequently are founded in an existential struggle with the fact of consciousness being yoked to the opposite and alien substance of the body. For example, it is the mind's ontological alienness from the body that allows Beckett characters such as Murphy and Molloy, in their respective eponymous novels, to strive toward and attain a fleeting "bliss" achievable only by "the ability to live in one's mind by pure contemplation," a state that—extremely brief as it always is, the body having its demands—yields "the momentary peace of suspended action."[4]

Beckett's adherence to these two dualisms—mind/matter and finite/infinite—is thoroughly modern; one or both of them informs much of modern self-understanding. The philosophical suppositions informing Beckett's vision may be seen as a matter of taking the two dualisms in tandem to their logical conclusion in narrative or dramatic portrayal. His lifelong allegiance to them showed itself also in his philosophical tastes, which are attested to in his letters, and explicitly alluded to occasionally in his literary works. It will be useful to consider these briefly—but before doing so, it should be stressed that Beckett is a literary artist, not a philosopher, and his works ought never to be construed as mere literary vehicles intended for the didactic conveyance of philosophical or moral ideas, along the lines of, say, Diderot's *Rameau's Nephew* or Camus's *The Plague*. As Beckett once stated regarding his writings, "If the subject of my [works] could be expressed in philosophical terms, I wouldn't have had any reason to write them. I am not an intellectual. All I am is *feeling*."[5] As artworks, Beckett's fiction and plays invite us to surrender to them emotionally, so that we can experience them as human possibilities of being, feeling, and thinking. Still, when we *are* moved by Beckett's art, it is because their vision of reality presents itself as an emotional and imaginative unity, a vision not only artistically compelling but consistent within itself; and this coherence invites us to an examination of the metaphysical convictions that inform them, an inspection of the *logos* within the *mythos*, as it were. And the structure of this *logos*, in Beckett's case, is well indicated by his philosophical interests and influences.

Beckett read philosophers from early in his life, and never stopped; he even took upon himself a systematic study of the history of philosophy. The philosophers he studied with particular attention included the pre-Socratics (Democritus making a notable impression), Pascal, Descartes, Descartes's disciple Arnold Geulincx (whose *Ethics* he worked through diligently in Latin, taking extensive notes), Malebranche, Spinoza, Berkeley, Kant (and Cassirer on Kant), Schopenhauer, the turn-of-the-twentieth-century skeptic Fritz Mauthner, Wittgenstein, Bachelard, and Sartre.[6] Perhaps most fundamental to the consolidation of Beckett's philosophical vision was the impact of Descartes, who was the subject of

Beckett's first major publication, the poem "Whoroscope."[7] Beckett embraced wholeheartedly Descartes's dualism between mind and body, but rejected Descartes's proof of the existence of God. Likewise, in his appreciation of the Cartesian and Occasionalist philosopher Malebranche, Beckett agreed with his Cartesian dualism and his insistence that there is an unbridgeable gulf between man and God, but rejected the comforting elements of his insistence on God's mercy and an afterlife.[8] The pattern continues with other philosophers. Beckett agrees with every affirmation that the body and the mind are radically separate substances, but also with every philosophical argument that the mind, although innately and necessarily possessing the idea of a transcendent reality, can never attain an understanding of the nature of, or experience a personal communion with, this reality. As John Pilling has summarized, "The whole of Beckett's . . . philosophical thinking is determined by his acceptance of Descartes's methods [of universal doubt and orderly analysis of problems, leading to his mind-body dualism] and rejection of Descartes's consolations."[9]

As with Descartes, though, for Beckett the presence in the mind of an idea of perfect and non-contingent being does make one conscious of the *givenness* of one's contingent existence; and this awareness of givenness imposes, as Beckett sees it, an obligation, an inescapable responsibility, to persevere in existence. Every human being, mysteriously given to itself from whatever the ground of being might be, has, as he puts it, an obligation to "go on."[10] Suicide is not morally acceptable to Beckett. One has been granted one's existence, and must struggle to one's natural end, because the gift is *obliged* to the giver, even if the reality of the "giver" cannot be humanly encountered nor the purpose of the gift understood.

What does it mean, though, for a human being to "go on"? It means more than mere continued physical existence with the problem-solving appurtenances of consciousness, since humans for Beckett are not just physical creatures but *minds* attached to bodies, minds whose principal concern is self-understanding and self-expression. Most elementally for Beckett, to "go on" for a person means to keep telling one's story, to continue interpreting and expressing the narrative of oneself, told to self and others, using language inherited from tradition (which Beckett frequently mocks and despairs of) and then shaped by personal memory, imagination, and reflection. In this telling, each of us naturally wants our story to have a genuine purpose, a real, not illusory, meaning ("Tell him . . . that you saw me," Vladimir pleads to the Boy, Godot's messenger), a desire that could be fulfilled only if the story of the self has a meaning that is lasting, non-erasable—only, that is, if it is lodged in the eternal. But just as our bodies are finite and perishing, so are thoughts and words. The story of a life, the story that each of us is, told in contingent, incomplete, fragile language, must always in Beckett's view fail to tell the true (enduring) story of a true (enduring) self, which, as we are always at least implicitly aware, would have to consist of a *timeless* self. Faithfulness to the imperative to "go on" is to continue taking up the impossible task of finding the words about oneself and one's situation "that count," that is, that would tell the truth of the eternal soul that, alas, we are not.[11] Under the conditions of existence we cannot achieve what we most desire, but nevertheless we are obliged to go on striving to find truer narratives for our stories, ones that better shed untruths and illusions about ourselves and our situations, even if we cannot attain to timeless truth. Human authenticity lies in our recurrent willingness to "Fail again. Fail better."[12]

Given the finitude, ignorance, and suffering that condition our yearning for transcendence, it is tempting to try to allay the anxieties it entails by simply declaring the existence of God an illusion and so relaxing from the tension of hope. But intellectual honesty prevents Beckett from making such a judgment. What we know is that we are existentially ignorant: our ignorance with regard to God's non-being is no less a fact than our ignorance about His being. This is why Beckett's vision of existence, as the Beckett actor Jack MacGowran once remarked, is one of *distress*, but not of *despair*.[13] *Waiting for Godot* is again a touchstone here. Godot does not come, but his reality—whatever that is—cannot be ruled out. Godot's boy messenger arrives each evening, and so offers a kind of hope. And the spirit of this play runs through all the other plays, however bleak their characters and conditions. "The key word in my plays," Beckett once said, "is 'perhaps'"[14]—although, to be sure, Beckett frequently stated in various ways that he saw no "system" at work in the cosmos, which is why the attitude of the not-knowing self toward its mysterious origins in Beckett's stories and plays is usually harsh and accusatory, and not infrequently enraged. There is one major work of Beckett's, however, in which this dissonance is softened into something more benign: his one-act play

Krapp's Last Tape. This is due to Beckett placing the experience of love—the longing love entails, and the longing for love lost—at the heart of its drama. The frustration with timeless meaning that saturates Beckett's vision of existence is adjusted here in a unique way, and this makes *Krapp's Last Tape* worth special attention in a study of Beckett's posture toward transcendence.

Krapp's Last Tape

Krapp's Last Tape, written in 1958, has often been described as Samuel Beckett's most perfect work for the theater. Also, uniquely among Beckett's major plays, it was immediately recognized by drama critics and the literary world as a masterpiece.[15] To some degree this was due to its accessibility. Compared with Beckett's other plays, *Krapp's Last Tape*, despite its theatrical innovations, is almost old-fashioned in presenting a dramatic situation that is not abstract or metaphorical, and in exploring familiar human themes. The most important of these themes is that of lost love—or rather love abandoned. And this brings us to another exceptional characteristic of the play. *Krapp's Last Tape* holds a singular place in Beckett's canon, both in drama and fiction, in being the one major work in which the experience of love is not undercut by irony, rendered grotesque through vicious comedy, or reduced to vulgarity. It alone, among the central works, lets the emphasis of Beckett's compassion fall on the tenderness of love rather than on its comic or distressing futilities.[16] Even more remarkably for Beckett, the dramatic power of *Krapp's Last Tape* is built on the question as to whether love might not be the most significant of life's experiences, even indirectly suggesting that love might have a meaning that, since it transcends alterations in the self, might transcend the vicissitudes of time.

Since this chapter explores Beckett's portrayal of love's meaningfulness in *Krapp's Last Tape* and how this portrayal can be understood in the context of Beckett's overall vision of the human condition, a synopsis of the play is necessary.

The setting and structure of the play could not be simpler. The scene is "a late evening in the future" in the den of an old man, a failed writer it turns out, named Krapp—in German a common name, but in the play's original English the pun on dung of course intentional. The set consists of a desk and chair, in strong light with darkness surrounding, and on the desk a reel-to-reel tape-recorder, a microphone, and boxes that contain spools of tape. Krapp is seated at the table—he is old, described by Beckett as "wearish," unkempt, with grey hair and a nose purple from drinking.[17] The first thing he does is to raise himself laboriously to take out from a desk drawer a banana, unpeeling and eating it while musing and shuffling in a circle around the desk. He repeats this with a second banana, and naturally—this being Beckett—slips and almost falls on the first discarded banana peel. He then produces a huge ledger from the dark back of the den, drops it on the desk, looks in it to identify a certain tape that he wants to hear, and locates it: "Box three, spool five."[18]

What the ensuing action discloses is that Krapp has made a tape recording each year on his birthday, and has done for forty-odd years, wherein he records what seems most memorable and worth recording of the previous year's experiences. And each year he precedes making this *new* recording by listening to one selected from a prior year. This is his sixty-ninth birthday, and the tape he specifically wants to hear before making this year's is the tape he made on his thirty-ninth birthday. Before listening to it this evening, he reads from the ledger, in a cracked and weak voice, its themes: "Mother at rest at last . . . The black ball . . . The dark nurse . . . Slight improvement in bowel condition . . . Memorable equinox . . . Farewell to—(*he turns the page*)—love."[19]

He threads the tape, switches on, and we hear the thirty-nine-year-old Krapp, recognizably the voice of the same man but strong with youth, speaking in confident sentences. This Krapp recalls having just listened to a recording from ten or twelve years earlier—so, the twenty-seven- or twenty-nine-year-old Krapp—describing him as "that young whelp" he can hardly believe having been. *That* earlier Krapp, listened to by the thirty-nine-year-old Krapp, had mentioned an unhappy love affair with a girl named Bianca living on Kedar Street, summing it up as a "[h]opeless business," but also including a tribute to her "[i]ncomparable" eyes. The thirty-nine-year-old we are listening to on tape sneers at this younger self's ambitions and resolutions (especially to drink less), notes his reports of "[u]nattainable laxation," of his father's last illness, of his shadowy sense of the opus magnum he hopes to write—and then the thirty-nine-year-old concludes his review of the self of the earlier tape: "What remains of all that misery? A girl in a shabby green coat, on a railway-station platform? No?"[20]

The thirty-nine-year-old self on tape—to whom the onstage Krapp continues to listen after first switching off the machine and shuffling backstage into the darkness to have a drink—then proceeds to recount the memorable events of *his* recent year. He describes sitting in a park by a canal outside of the nursing home where his mother is dying, after her long "viduity." Krapp looks up, stops the tape, gets up and brings back from the darkness a huge dictionary, and, looking up the word *viduity*, reads aloud: "State—or condition of being—or remaining—a widow—or widower." Krapp lovingly pronounces the word "viduity," just as earlier he had delighted in repeating the word "spool": "Spoooooooool." He has always, it is clear, been in love with words. He turns the tape back on: his thirty-nine-year-old self describes waiting in the park by the canal to see the window blind pulled down that will signify his mother's death, and while doing so tossing a little black ball repeatedly to a white dog; he also recalls a beautiful nursemaid in the park dressed in white pushing a black perambulator, whom he offends merely by speaking to her. But what he best remembers about the nurse are her eyes. From the tape: "The face she had! The eyes! Like . . . (*hesitates*) . . . chrysolite!" The shade goes down; and he gives the ball to the dog, "gently, gently."[21]

The thirty-nine-year-old on tape then goes on to recount what he has "chiefly to record this evening," what he calls "[t]he vision, at last." It is his great revelation of what the nature of his literary work should be, the vision coming to him on the spring equinox, as he is standing out on a jetty at night in a storm in howling wind and crashing waves; he describes his vision as a "miracle" and a "fire" that has set his mind alight with creative understanding . . . and we would hear more about this if the Krapp on stage didn't angrily wind the tape forward to skip the rest of the passage; it makes him furious to hear it.[22] Because, as we learn, Krapp's literary efforts have come to nothing; what he thought to be grand vision was false fire; he has disgust for these ambitions, now, and for what he has become. He fast-forwards the tape until he arrives at what he has, all along it appears, been longing to listen to—the passage notated in the ledger as "Farewell to love."

When he stops fast-forwarding the tape he finds he has arrived at the end of this "farewell"; we hear a few lyrical, closing sentences, followed by the thirty-nine-year-old starting to close on his year's reminiscences, but then Krapp rewinds the tape to hear the "Farewell to love" more fully. What follows is a passage that, in its lyrical beauty, emotional evocativeness, and symbolic eloquence, is comparable to Shakespeare, Keats, or Joyce.[23] Lying together with a woman in a punt on a lake, drifting, Krapp calmly and sadly ends their affair—which will be his last—telling her it is "hopeless and no good going on"; she agrees; he leans over her to get her eyes in shadow, and she opens them to "let [him] in" one last time; then he lies across her with his face in her breasts; the punt drifts into the rushes and sticks there; he and she remain silent and unmoving, while the water moves them slowly up and down, and from side to side.[24]

After a long pause, the voice on the tape resumes: "Past midnight. Never knew—." Krapp switches off; goes into the shadows again for a drink; returns to take the old tape off the recorder and spool up a virgin tape. Having taken from his pocket an envelope with a few notes for this year's reminiscence, he begins his tape by calling his thirty-nine-year-old self a "stupid bastard" and thanking God he's past all that. But he suddenly exclaims: "The eyes she had! . . . Everything there, everything on this old muckball, all the light and dark and famine and feasting of . . . (*hesitates*) . . . the ages!" Then he reflects: "Maybe he was right"—that is, to bid love farewell. He then starts to describe his past year: too many bananas; a few occasions of meager sex; going to church and falling asleep off the pew; finding that seventeen copies of his magnum opus have been sold; noting that he has again been reading Theodor Fontane's novel *Effi Briest*, one page a day, "with tears again." But Krapp soon tires of this reporting and, unthinkingly still recording, wanders aloud into memories of his past, as a child with his father, out in the hills on a Christmas morning with the dog, among the berries, listening to church bells. He mutters, "Be again, be again. (*Pause*). All that old misery. (*Pause*). Once wasn't enough for you. (*Pause*). Lie down across her."[25]

Suddenly he tears the new tape off the machine and replaces it with the other one, rewinds, and listens again to the punt scene. This time, after his farewell to love, he allows his thirty-nine-year-old self to speak on to the end of his tape. "Here I end this reel . . . Perhaps my best years are gone . . . But I wouldn't want them back. Not with the fire in me now. No, I wouldn't want them back." The tape then continues to run on in silence, as old Krapp sits upright and motionless at the table, staring straight ahead at nothing, and after a while the stage lights fade out.[26]

This synopsis has, unavoidably, omitted much of the play's dialogue on the part of both the Krapp on tape and the onstage Krapp, and significant stage action—and almost completely ignored its comedic dimension—in order to present only the dialogue and development directly relevant to understanding how the drama unfolds and some of its key themes. Before exploring these themes, however, a few of the play's details should be noted, as well as what Beckett achieved through its dramatic architecture.

First, the name Krapp suggests that the protagonist is detritus, refuse, and what we discover is that Krapp sees himself as just that. Ruination is a theme of the drama. *We* know from the play's title that Krapp will not record after this. When Beckett first came to direct the play, in Germany (in his own German translation) in 1969, he told the actor Martin Held that Krapp senses death "standing behind him," and the next year, directing the play in Paris (in his French translation) he instructed the actor Jean Martin to look round into the darkness a few times, Beckett telling him, "It is death who is waiting for him there . . . Next day[,] he is found dead at his table."[27] Second, Krapp, a writer in love with words, manifests the human need for ritual in a peculiar but coherent way by making his recordings each birthday. The ritualistic element is emphasized by Krapp looking at his watch to make sure the time is exactly correct to begin the proceedings each year.[28] Third, he has a clownish element to his features and dress (not to mention the bananas), although Beckett played this down in his own direction, since he wanted the comedic and the tragic dimensions to blend as thoroughly as possible (in a manner Chekhovian).[29] Fourth, when Krapp attends to his boxes, spools, and tape-recorder, it is clear that his capacity for human affection has transferred itself largely to inanimate things; as the "farewell to love" passage plays in full, Krapp (in Beckett's direction) lays his head on the table and wraps one arm around the machine tenderly as if it were the woman he is remembering.[30] And fifth, Krapp is profoundly alone. Words, books, and drink are his principal companions.

The Krapp whom we encounter dramatically is not, however, one man alone. His former selves also inhabit the stage. Not only is the sixty-nine-year-old Krapp present, so is the thirty-nine-year-old Krapp; we listen to him while we watch and hear the older Krapp responding to him. And through *his* tape, we also find "present" the Krapp of twenty-seven or twenty-nine. And these three personae are supplemented, implicitly, by all the selves mutely present in the other spools in the boxes on stage. In this way Beckett achieves something remarkable: by way of a technology new in the late 1950s (the personal tape recorder), he supplies the back-story needed to appreciate character and development in a drama, while still keeping the drama to one character. Monologue becomes dialogue between multiple stages of a self, and the *changing* of a self through time is made audible and palpable. The Proustian inwardness of memory of past selves has been eerily transformed into audible externality.[31] In addition, the tapes and multiple selves show us vividly how our identities and self-understanding are constructed through language and narrative, and that these narratives are always changing—which raises the issue of the paradox, central to Modernist literature, that we are both one person and many persons as we develop through time. Our sense of identity *is* our apprehension of our own story, the play reminds us. But as personality develops, our self-interpretation of our identity not only expands but alters in unexpected and, at times, self-contradictory or self-erasing ways. What was once of utmost importance now is forgotten; who we are now serves as ironic, or comic, or tragic comment on selves we have been before; meanings we have staked our worth on can crumble; and experiences we once dismissed as either irrelevant or alien can come back, against our will, to permeate our consciousness and show how deeply they have defined us.

Bearing these factors in mind will be useful in considering the play's main themes and imagery. Foremost among themes is Krapp's choice of solitude, made at age thirty-nine. This was a decision against social life, romantic relationships, friendships, intimacy of any kind—for the sake of his intellectual life and the writing of his "opus magnum." Beckett, in his director's notes for an actor in the play (Rick Cluchey, in 1977), described Krapp as "an absolute being, he chooses either black or white," and stated that Krapp's decision for "the life of the mind," made under the influence of his vision on the jetty, is comprehensively against "the life of the body," sensuality, human interaction, and nature, with his "farewell to love" its poignant epitome.[32] But the choice has been a disaster. It has led Krapp, as we see, to failure upon failure. His intellectual work has come to little or nothing; whatever ambition, energy, and happiness he once experienced have vanished; he is at sixty-nine a husk of a man. Worst of all, he has not been able to stay true, in his mind, to his "farewell to love," to his rejection of the beauty of women, of their romantic and existential allure: Krapp has not been able to renounce love, despite his farewell, and the play is, above all, about *this* failure. The continued importance of love to Krapp is symbolized strikingly by his permanent fascination with the eyes of women he has loved. And it is the eyes of the woman in the punt that are, as James Knowlson (Beckett's authorized biographer) remarks, "the touchstone for all the others"—since in them Krapp finds the entire world, all of history, all meaning.[33] As Krapp exclaims, "*Everything* there . . . all the light and dark and famine and feasting of . . . the ages!"[34]

But the theme of Krapp's failed renunciation of love spreads beyond the central image of romantic intimacy and women's beauty to include other dimensions of love. There are two more principal varieties of love in the play, each important: Krapp's love for his mother (and thus familial love); and the love of beauty in nature, so poignantly evoked in the old Krapp's final words as he remembers his childhood, his memory leading him back to "Be again in the dingle on a Christmas Eve, gathering holly, the red-berried," and to "Be again on Croghan on a Sunday morning, in the haze, with the bitch, stop and listen to the bells."[35] It is not only love of, and with, women that the play is about, but love in all the forms that unite us with what is beyond our selves.[36] Krapp's failed farewell to love is in fact his failed attempt to reject communion with the rest of reality itself—leaving Krapp as we see him onstage: lonely, weary, dissipated, and depressed, filled with longing and regret. The point Beckett drives home in the course of the play is that Krapp has *never* been able to cleave his mind from devotions to the world of sensuality, nature, and beauty, and to live for his intellect alone.

Imagistically, Beckett conveys this in two important ways, one obvious and one more subtle. At the level of the explicit, there is Krapp's repeated emotional returning to sense-drenched memories. Most significant, of course, are his memories of the women presented to us through the tapes: Bianca of Kedar Street; the girl on the railway-station platform; his dying mother; the nursemaid with eyes like chrysolite; and above all, the woman in the punt. Also important, though, are his memories of childhood walks in the hills with his father and their dog, and of the hills, early morning haze, berries, church bells. To all of these, in turn, he attempts to deny meaning; but he finds them, and their meaningfulness, always resurging.

At a subtler level, there is Beckett's use in the play of symbols of black and white, and of light and dark, to indicate both the nature of Krapp's renunciation and his failure to carry it through. The "system" underlying this symbolization is Manichaean in principle, though it is unclear whether Beckett had Manichaeism in mind when he first wrote the play; certainly, however, in his directing of the work, as one discovers through Beckett's *Director's Notebooks*, he relied on research into Manichaean symbols, vows, and rituals to organize these imagistic elements.[37] In Manichaean teaching, darkness or blackness is equated with the senses and the physical world, all forms of sensual pleasures (including indulgence in alcohol, to which we can see Krapp has stayed addicted), and worldly vocations. Light and whiteness, in contrast, are identified with the world of mind: with intellect, spirit, and the processes of reason. Krapp's "absoluteness" of temperament has led him to try to live solely the life of intellect—the life, as it were, of "light," as if he were attempting to be true to Manichaean principles (which Krapp as a character is certainly unaware of). What the play reveals is that Krapp has never been able to successfully effect a Manichaean-type renunciation of the worldly and sensual; he has, despite his decision, remained desirous of involvement with women, with beauty, and with nature.

Krapp's betrayal of the Manichaean directive to separate himself from the world and the senses (black, darkness) and live for intellect alone (white, light) is indicated through a constant blending, or intertwining, of black and white and of light and dark in the play's visual components, and in Krapp's memories and stories.[38] Krapp's clothes are "grey ex black, grey ex white" (in the original text, Krapp is wearing a black waistcoat and trousers along with oversized clownish white boots, but Beckett amended these to grey for later productions).[39] The remembered nursemaid by the canal is dressed in white and wheels a large black perambulator. Krapp, in the park by the canal, throws a black ball for a white dog, and finally gives it into his mouth, gently, thus *blending* it with him.[40] Eyes, windows into souls, are both bright like "chrysolite" or, in the punt, the darkness that "lets him in." Bianca—whose name means "white"—lives on Kedar Street, which is both an anagram of "dark" (as Beckett once explained), and also means dusky, or dark-skinned, in Hebrew.[41] Krapp's epiphany occurs on the spring equinox, a day when daylight and nighttime are equally balanced, on a jetty near a lighthouse in the night. The thirty-nine-year-old Krapp refers to the singing of "Old Miss McGlome"—suggestive of *gloaming*, i.e., dusk. The young Krapp's intimations of his "opus magnum" is described as "shadows."[42] Krapp in the play moves back and forth between the bright light over the table and the darkness around it. And so on. The point of the symbolisms is that Krapp cannot escape, and cannot escape desiring, the intertwinement, the enmeshing, of black and white, light and dark—that is, the *mixture* of spirit and matter, mind and body, intellect and world. And Krapp's fate, with his memories and regret, suggest that this mixture and conjoining *cannot* be escaped, because a human being is *just that* conjoining, as the cosmos is *just that* conjoining ("as shown by the aeons," as Beckett comments in his *Director's Notebook*).[43] Thus Krapp, in trying to renounce the world and love, has attempted the impossible: to exist as a human being without humanness, and to escape the cosmos while remaining in and of it.

Krapp's attempted renunciation of love is thus shown to have been, unintentionally on his part but inevitably, an attempt to reject existence itself—which means that Krapp has betrayed his authentic being. Three images in the play underscore this self-betrayal with simplicity and poignancy.

First, there is the moment in the punt, after Krapp and his lover have agreed that it's hopeless to go on, when he leans over her to get her eyes in his shadow so that she can open them, which she does in order to—as Krapp's voice intones—"Let me in." The phrase in context means that his lover allowed his soul for a final time into her soul—Krapp's last experience of existential communion. But the phrase, spoken by Krapp after a pause and in a "low" tone and volume, as per Beckett's stage directions,[44] also carries the overtone of a plea: "Let me in." That overtone resonates throughout the rest of the play, underscoring the fact that Krapp has for decades denied his deeper self's continual longing for love. Second, there is Krapp's one-word description of the nursemaid's eyes: they are "[l]ike . . . (*hesitates*) . . . chrysolite!"—a word used so rarely in literature that it instantly calls up its one famous usage, in Shakespeare's *Othello*.[45] In that play's final scene, the hero says of his wife, Desdemona, whom he has just killed in a deluded and self-destroying passion of jealousy, "Nay, had she been true, / If heaven would make me such another world / Of one entire and perfect chrysolite, / I'd not have sold her for it." (5.2.142–45). The word "chrysolite" thus reverberates with connotations of self-betrayal through "the exchange of love for other values"[46]—in Othello's case for the value of honor, in Krapp's for the value of an idealized pure intellectuality. And third, when Krapp's memories of childhood invade his last recording and he repeats, "Be again, be again," Beckett directed that this should be spoken to sound like the church bells that Krapp longs, despite himself, to hear again: the word "be" to be held in a vibrato, like bells ringing.[47] The theme of self-betrayal resonates in all these motifs.

By the play's end we understand how deeply Krapp wants love back, in all of its dimensions, because he wants his self-betrayed self back, wants back the meaningfulness of love he has experienced in the human world as it is: the spirituality of intellect or mind united with material being. This invests with cruel irony the final words we hear in the play, the voice of the robust and confident thirty-nine-year-old Krapp who has just made his farewell to love, and who finishes his tape by concluding, "Perhaps my best years are gone . . . But I wouldn't want them back. Not with the fire in me now. No, I wouldn't want them back."[48]

What we watch Krapp suffering, in his last evening, is a classically structured moment of tragic self-recognition: he is suffused with remorse and regret for love wasted and rejected, realizing he has been guilty of a "selfish detachment" from the world.[49] And it is Krapp's acceptance of this fact that leads, in the play's last minutes, to his abandonment of the long-endured conflict between his desire to renounce the world and his longing for loving involvement in it—which means, to his abandonment of all interest in living. He is finished with everything: love, work, religion.[50] Beckett portrayed this when directing the play by having Krapp—once he has put spool five back on, to hear again his farewell to love—sit upright and completely still, staring ahead of him vacantly into space, no longer invested in the lyrical reminiscence or the recording's ironic final words. Krapp is ready for death. Now he knows, as do we from the play's title, that there will be no more tapes.

Krapp and the Ghost of Love

At the play's conclusion, the most important question Krapp's fate presents to the audience or reader is the question of the meaningfulness of love. We can examine this question first from the side of the subject, in terms of Krapp's psyche and his struggle, and then "objectively," as a metaphysical question.

In Krapp's consciousness, the meaningfulness of love has endured. It has endured across the decades, through all of his decisions and actions, from childhood experiences through to the present. On the evening the play takes place, we observe Krapp emotionally coming to terms, at last, with the wrongness of his choice for solitude by confronting the ghost of love, an encounter that tragically forces him to recognize that, beyond all other experiences and values, it is his experiences of love that have given his life meaning. As Michael Robinson summarizes, love seems to Krapp to have been the one factor in his life "which was not an illusion" in the sense that it is the one dimension "where a meaning endures."[51] Love's meaningfulness has transcended all the alterations in his character, all the multiplicities of Krapp's selves unfolding through time. Time—which Beckett once called "the indubitable villain" of the play—has not conquered love, although at play's end Krapp has certainly abandoned both love and life.[52]

This brings us to the metaphysical, or objective side of the question. If love has constituted not only the central, but also a *transtemporal* meaning in Krapp's existence, might it not also be the case that love's meaningfulness endures beyond even the transitoriness of his existence in time—that it has a *supratemporal* meaning? This question does not have the ring of the usual type of question raised by Beckett's work. But as the sorrow, regret, and final resignation of Krapp impresses itself upon the viewer, *Krapp's Last Tape* makes two questions inescapable: (1) Is love the central human experience? and (2) Does the meaningfulness of love perdure beyond existence itself?

Beckett's play, of course, provides no answers to these questions. The play shows the trajectory of Krapp's existence; and Beckett the artist is concerned only with the showing. Krapp's existence through time, his decisions and conflicts, his failures and final self-abandonment and resignation, are all suffered without Krapp being able to know if the memories and experiences of love that pull him into his deeper self like a whirlpool indicate that true existence, existential dignity, and fullness of meaning would have been found in living a life of loving communion with a woman or women, with others, and with the world. Neither could he know whether love has some sort of transcendent significance, a question he has likely dismissed long before we see him. If Krapp cannot know these things it is because, Beckett would say, none of us can. As in all his works, Beckett reveals to us through Krapp's existence the horizon of ignorance and mystery that surrounds our most pressing existential questions. Just as Beckett denied knowing who or what Godot means in *Waiting for Godot*, any question about the possibility of love's enduring metaphysical significance, as raised by *Krapp's Last Tape*, is for Beckett unknowable. But that means that no answer, *including an affirmative one*, is foreclosed upon—a point that Beckett's audience and readers tend to overlook.

Perhaps, in other words, despite Krapp's concluding resigned despair, the significance of love was not an illusion. Perhaps love is meaningful through time, and even beyond time; perhaps in our deepest experiences of love the mystery of transcendence flickers. An agnostic mysticism such as Beckett's, even as it produces dramatic portrayals of characters who, like Krapp, are completely lacking in faith, allows for that possibility. Krapp's recognition that his authentic being was what he had turned away from in abandoning love suggests that it is through the body that the soul attains its true life, that the body is the soul's proper vehicle for fashioning a personal story that counts—which reverses the direction of the typical Beckettian vector relating mind to world. Beckett can despise and ridicule the world of bodies and things with the opprobrium of the austere mystic so long as he can regard it from the apparent isolation of pure mind. But when the physical basis of all loving encounters forces his antihero Krapp to confess to himself that there is a value greater than the flame of pure intellect, Beckett's Cartesian duality of mind and matter, soul and body, is pressed into a union of need, emotion, meaning, and value.

And this in turn alters the tonality, in this work, of the question that human existence inherently, by way of its givenness, raises about transcendence. By suggesting that the communion that love entails, in all its forms, is the dominant value within existence, the play invokes the possibility that the seeking of communion in the human longing for transcendence is not solely, perhaps, a curse of despicable and risible frustration, but rather an unfulfillment, or interruption, between values—the value of the human and (possible) transcendent value. Recognition of the genuine value of human persons, grounded in profound sympathy for the human plight, is after all a major feature in Beckett's work, as shown for example by the characters of the tramps in *Waiting for Godot*, the character of Winnie in *Happy Days*, and the silent protagonist in Beckett's short play *Catastrophe*. And if humans genuinely have value, then awareness of human givenness inevitably resonates with the question of transcendent value. It is through its presentation of the overwhelming meaningfulness of love in human existence, and therefore of love as the substance of the possible transcendent value longed for, that this question is moderated in such a way that, in *Krapp's Last Tape*, the tenor of Beckett's agnostic mysticism is, for once among his major works, made somewhat more benign. Krapp's failure to attain Manichaean division due to the fact that his loving is his true being in the end is harmonious with a *potentially* benevolent (if still far from comforting) mysticism. Certainly, the bleakness of the play's ending, with the audience invited to empathize with Krapp's surrender to a sense of irredeemable loss and despair, and the extinction in him of the will to continue living, is suggestive of metaphysical hopelessness. Nevertheless, the question of the ultimate ontological meaningfulness of experiences of love and tenderness cannot simply be dismissed as nonsense when interpreting the comprehensive "perhaps" of the play.

With all this in mind, let us take a closer look at those aspects of *Krapp's Last Tape* that make it singular among Beckett's writings.

Not only is *Krapp's Last Tape* the one major work of Beckett's in which experiences of love and tender longing are portrayed and described without ironic or sneering subversion, it is also commonly recognized as his "most lyrical" work, written in an "unashamedly poetic idiom."[53] These characteristics, accompanied by the Irish cadences of Krapp's speech and the Irish landscape that informs the play's imagery, make its evocation of lost love feel unusually personal; and this sense is made more intriguing by learning of Beckett's special fondness for the play, which is certainly related to the autobiographical elements to be found in it.

Soon after the play's completion, Beckett wrote to Barney Rosset, his publisher in the United States, "I feel—to a disturbing degree—the strangest of solicitudes for this little work." "I feel as clucky and beady and one-legged and bare-footed about this little text as an old hen with her last chick."[54] There is little doubt these feelings were due in part to how much of himself Beckett had put into the play. As the actor Jean Martin (who played Krapp in the 1970 French production directed by Beckett) avowed, the drama is "very autobiographical," containing many "personal links" between Beckett and Krapp.[55] Without attempting to be exhaustive with regard to the issue, it will be helpful to mention some of the most important parallels between elements in the drama and Beckett's personal life.

To begin with, Beckett himself had had a "vision," a moment of profound inspiration and self-understanding, like Krapp at age thirty-nine, which altered permanently the nature of his work and gave it its unique themes, perspectives, and styles—and the content of that vision is closely matched by what is intimated about Krapp's vision, the precise details of which we are prevented from hearing by his angrily fast-forwarding the tape to get past its narration.[56] (Needless to say, the consequence of Beckett's vision, opposite to that of Krapp, was literary fame.) Beckett too sat by a canal, in a park outside a nursing home where his mother lay dying.[57] Scholars have enjoyed tracking down the details of Beckett's romances that correspond to those remembered by Krapp, down to the green coat of the girl on the railway-station platform.[58] And Beckett was always, James Knowlson writes, "hypersensitive to eyes."[59] Behind Krapp's childhood memories of walking with his father in winter among the hills lay Beckett's fond memories of exactly such occasions: "At night, when I can't sleep," Beckett once wrote to a friend, "I do the old walks again and stand beside [my father] again one Xmas morning in the fields near Glencullen, listening to the chapel bells."[60] Even minor details conform. Like Krapp, Beckett loved and often reread, and was moved to tears by, Fontane's novel *Effi Briest*.[61] Once, in directing the play, Beckett couldn't find a pair of shoes for the actor that created the shuffling sound of Krapp's walk the way he heard it in his mind; at last, he brought in an old pair of his own black slippers, which produced precisely the sound he wanted.[62] Finally, one actor in the role, Martin Held, even dared (with self-conscious temerity) to crook his little finger in imitation of Beckett's right hand, which showed the effects of Dupuytren's contracture, a disease that causes a gradual inward closing of the fingers usually beginning with the little finger. Remarking Held's hand, Beckett said, "Good."[63]

None of this of course means that Beckett—who was fifty when he wrote the play—envisaged his basic character as being like Krapp's, or, especially, that Beckett himself had made or would make any kind of "farewell to love" or renunciation of friendships, intimacy, marriage, taking pleasure in the beauties of the natural world, or involvement in worldly matters. On the contrary, Beckett was renowned for his many close friendships and his loving concern for (and financial generosity to) innumerable relatives, friends, fellow artists, students of his work, stage and business associates, and even the sons and daughters and nephews and nieces of his many acquaintances, not to mention his partner and wife of over fifty years, Suzanne Deschevaux-Dumesnil. But both Beckett's special fondness for the play and the tellingly close autobiographical elements in it inevitably suggest questions about Beckett's own view of the significance of love in human existence—questions that intensify as one becomes acquainted with accounts of his character from those who knew him well, which often emphasize his extreme sensitivity to suffering and "a visceral compassion" for those in need. His close friend Anne Atik remarks succinctly, "No one . . . who had anything to do with Sam, even for five minutes, could fail to be struck by his sheer goodness. It came to him as naturally and unselfconsciously as blinking, as swallowing. . . . Anecdotes about his goodness border on hagiography."[64]

The anguish of the onstage Krapp in *Krapp's Last Tape*, as he is torn by his longing for lost love and regret for love rejected, and the play's prompting of our compassion for Krapp's distress, are of a piece with Beckett's overall work, with its continual longing for transcendent meaning permanently unaffirmable. But what is exceptional about the work is that here the unanswerable question of transcendent meaning is presented specifically and poignantly in terms of love, love that Krapp cannot deny has given his life its most profound and enduring meaning. Krapp's reliving of his experiences of love, as Michael Robinson notes, "is the nearest any of Beckett's characters come to the end they search for."[65] Given its richly autobiographical elements; Beckett's special solicitude for the play; his reputation for compassion, benevolence, friendship, and generosity; and his constant directorial efforts to keep its performance from appearing "sentimental,"[66] it seems warranted to conclude that it might well be the work that most closely reflects the emotional center around which Beckett's doubt about transcendence revolves: that it is the experience of love, together with the religious promise of the God of love, that is the existential core in relation to which his doubt about transcendence discharges its disappointment, in his other mature works, in expression after expression of alienation, disgust, satirical humor, cruelty, and indifference. It would appear that the uniquely tender presentation of love in the play constitutes a uniquely unguarded revelation of the meaning that Beckett himself valued above all, and of the character of the transcendent reality that in his view would redeem—if any could—the anguish and the tragicomic "continuing on" that define and obligate his characters.

CHAPTER SIX

Bob Dylan's Evocations of Mystery

BOB DYLAN IS renowned for elevating popular song into an art form charged with high literary significance and seriousness, in part by introducing into lyric writing a complexity echoing that of Symbolist, Surrealist, and other genres of Modernist poetry. Dylan's reception of the Nobel Prize for Literature in 2016, after decades of increasing critical attention and a crescendo of honors, is a clear sign that Dylan's art is as worthy of careful literary attention as works of Dickinson, Proust, Eliot, Pound, and Beckett. That Dylan is a songwriter and not a poet, novelist, or playwright should not be a hindrance to an appreciation of his accomplishment. Lyrics of the finest of the medieval troubadours (such as those championed by Ezra Pound and Dante), the works of Sappho, and the choruses of Greek tragedy also belong to the category of "song." In Dylan's case, it is important not to let the technology-based immediacies of electronic recording for mass listenership, or the media-driven phenomenon of superstardom, confuse the core issue: that of literary achievement.

Dylan's best lyrics have often been lauded as striking examples of Modernist literary composition. In the songwriting and recordings for which he is best known and where he has been most poetically powerful and original—for example, in the triad of albums *Bringing It All Back Home* (1965), *Highway 61 Revisited* (1965), and *Blonde on Blonde* (1966)—all of the key features of Modernist literature are present: a self-conscious break with traditional forms of the genre; the juxtaposition of images linked by emotional association in place of narrative logic; a focus on social hypocrisy and the absurdities generated by modern technological and bureaucratic life; displaced subjectivity and humorous detachment; and a liberal use of borrowed phrases and symbols. Dylan's employment of these techniques in his lyric writing has identifiable sources, his literary influences having been well documented. In his early development these included the French Symbolist poets Rimbaud, Baudelaire, and Verlaine; T. S. Eliot; the Beat writers Allen Ginsberg, Jack Kerouac, William S. Burroughs, and Gregory Corso; and classic writers such as François Villon, Whitman, Poe, Melville, Keats, Byron, Shakespeare, and—underlying everything—the Bible. Not that he engaged in systematic study. Dylan was a magpie, looking for inspiration, absorbing examples quickly, and using them to stretch the boundaries of what songwriting might be. But he himself has made clear that such reading served his aim, from early in his career, to create lyrics that didn't get "thrown into the grave" and to write songs that could stand alongside enduring artworks.[1] Achieving that goal entailed the creation of a body of significant Modernist literature in a genre where no one could have guessed it would appear.

The real difficulty with accepting Dylan's work as significant literature, though, lies in its musical and performative dimension. Song lyrics are not poetry, whatever "poetic" qualities they may possess. They are not written for the page, nor for unadorned oral recitation. They are written to be *sung*, and especially in Dylan's case, to be sung by *him*. Their literary impact is inseparable from the melodic structures with which the lyrics are interwoven, and also from their performative delivery: phrasings, inflections, pace, emphases, all the expressive strategies of vocal song. But while it is impossible to convey the felt impact of Dylan's songs by writing about them, his lyric writing nevertheless constitutes a body of work that deserves analysis in a book such as this.

The concern of this chapter is to examine Dylan as a Modernist writer who notably and successfully takes up the challenge of expressing an awareness of genuine mysteries and of transcendent, divine meaning. In Dylan's songs, the human psyche is consistently presented as a locale where finite being encounters the presence of divine reality, and like all of the previously discussed authors, Dylan never takes his eye off the transcendent goal of human aspiration. Like Dickinson, he writes of distressed separation from the divine ground, but also of gratified communion with divine reality; like Eliot, Dylan is adept at portraying "timeless moments" of divine presence in consciousness and at suggesting that the movement of history morally requires an eschatological fulfillment. Although his lyrics, which serve a remarkably diverse range of compositions musically categorizable as folk, blues, country, gospel, rock, and American "standards," have no philosophical consistency—being expressions of temporary feelings and insights in the manner of most "lyric poetry," and also often articulating the experiences and viewpoints of a fictional persona who should not be confused with Dylan the author—their artistic revelations of encounters with mystery and transcendence are plentiful, and illuminate powerfully how the human-divine In-Between can articulate itself in a late Modernist cultural context.

The Picasso of Song

Dylan's most well-known revolutions in songwriting, beginning in 1964/65, have their counterparts in (and to an extent were inspired by) other Modernist breakthroughs in both literature and other art forms. In poetry, one finds parallels especially in Symbolist and Expressionist verse that employs fragmented narrative, obscure symbolic allusiveness, and borrowed phrases, as in the work of Pound and Eliot. In film, the often-obscure symbolism and breaking up of narrative structure in the works of directors such as Fellini, Resnais, and Antonioni have their analogues in Dylan's most ambitious experiments. And in painting, Picasso's and Braque's explorations of a confusing simultaneity of multiple perspectives in cubism have an exact counterpart in some of Dylan's songs.

The Dylan-Picasso comparison is, indeed, one that has proven irresistible to Dylan scholars and admirers, including fellow songwriter Leonard Cohen who in the mid-1980s described Dylan as "the Picasso of song."[2] The comparison is apt for several reasons. First, both artists, in periods of intense experimentation early in their careers, dramatically and shockingly expanded the formal possibilities of their respective art forms. Second, more than any other artists of the twentieth century these two warrant the epithet "protean," both of them continually changing styles and mastering new modes over decades, while manifesting the facility to create successful artworks across an astonishing spectrum of genres. Third, both artists notoriously acted as thieves and magpies in incorporating materials from past art into their own works while transforming them to serve new and original purposes. And fourth, most specifically, just as Picasso famously communicated new forms of vision and feeling in painting (and sculpture) through disassemblage and rearrangement of parts, use of overlapping planes of perspective, and juxtaposition of figurative elements from different periods and styles for unsettling allusive effect, so Dylan enacted similar experiments of fragmented narrative, use of rhetoric echoing both past and present times and high and low cultures, simultaneous seriousness and humor, and juxtapositions of borrowings from earlier styles of song, in order to invent lyrical "stories" that conveyed powerful originalities of vision and feeling.[3]

It is somewhat difficult for anyone not having lived through both eras of artistic invention to properly appreciate the types of paradigm shifts enacted by Picasso and Dylan and to recognize their parallels. The visual lexicons of cubism, collage, and abstraction have by now become familiar; and popular songwriting has long since absorbed and programmatically reproduced—almost always in far inferior manners—Dylan's innovations. But with some exercise of historical imagination, it is possible to appreciate how the newness and strangeness of Picasso's *Les Demoiselles d'Avignon* (1907; first exhibited 1916) is strikingly comparable to that of, say, the Dylan songs "Desolation Row" (1965) and "Visions of Johanna" (1965–66).[4] Both the painting and the two songs are powerful works that were experienced as outrageous and fascinating—especially to other artists in their respective fields—and also as aesthetically uncategorizable within accepted notions of their respective arts; both "gave a new rule" to their media, to use Kant's phrase.[5] In both cases the viewer or listener is presented, to use Bernard Lonergan's description of significant art, with something exceptionally "other, different, novel, strange, new, remote, intimate" that effects a radical opening of one's horizon and a transformation of one's perceptual world.[6] All three works are transfixingly rich and strange, fully realized in their communication of a bewildering variety of emotions, and suggestive of mysterious depths of meaning while conveying the "inevitability of form" that is a key feature of deeply satisfying art.

These comments indicate why some of Dylan's best work illustrates art's capacity for evoking what Lonergan calls "ulterior significance": hidden depths of meaning, true mysteries, that we surmise to lie beyond our comprehension.[7] Our lives are rich with mysteries, reaching from those we surmise in quotidian encounters with the beautiful or the uncanny to the ultimate mystery of divine transcendence. When works of art are important enough they remind us of these undefinable surpluses of meaning; and this remembrance can imbue existence with a sense of import and adventure, even of grandeur, especially when the artwork intimates not merely an ulterior but an *ultimate* significance—that is, when it awakens our wonder not just in a general way to suspected depths of meaning in the world of events and things, but specifically to participation in sacred or transcendent being.

Before proceeding to show how Dylan is, at his best, a master of evoking experiences of ulterior significance, including those that suggest a divine transcendence, it will be helpful, first, to consider in a general way Dylan's gifts as a lyricist and as a master of empathic communication, and second, to look at samples of two songs in which Dylan has used the symbolic elements of song to suggest both surfeits of meaning and the presence of the uncanny.

Formal Mastery, Empathic Mimicry, Symbolic Power

Dylan first gained notice as a singer-songwriter of so-called folk music, and became at a very young age a central star of the "folk revival" of the early 1960s. He was soon recognized to have a talent for composing and performing songs that simultaneously sounded deeply traditional and yet utterly fresh, and certain early works were felt to express with clarity and intelligence many of the cultural and political concerns—including concerns about civil rights—that were "in the air" at the time. Few people in the early years of his fame, however, realized just how deep and wide were the sources upon which Dylan drew for the power in his "folk" and "protest" songs. As would become clear later, both during the years before he arrived in New York at age nineteen and in his early time there, Dylan was a musical sponge, acquainting himself with and absorbing the influences of a huge variety of American popular (and not so popular) song forms available to him both through live performances and recordings.[8]

It is well known that his first hero and inspiration as a songwriter was Woody Guthrie. No less of an influence on his early sense of himself as a songwriter and on his compositions, however, was the 1930s Delta bluesman Robert Johnson.[9] But these two names barely scratch the surface in indicating the range of material Dylan was striving to absorb and creatively make his own. First, it entailed "folk music" in its entirety—a category that includes British folk ballads, Appalachian mountain music, bluegrass, white gospel, black gospel, country and western, rural acoustic blues, electric urban blues, union songs, Irish and Australian outlaw ballads, Tex-Mex borderlands music, hobo music, and hokum. In the first years of his songwriting and performing Dylan drew from all of these idioms—and quickly added those of rock 'n' roll (an early love and practice well before his immersion in folk music), Tin Pan Alley, Chicago R&B, southern soul, and the kind of Brecht/Weill compositions typified by "Pirate Jenny" from *The Threepenny Opera.*[10] As Mike Marqusee writes, "Recorded music enabled Dylan to ransack the American musical heritage like Ezra Pound at loose in a library of medieval manuscripts";[11] and his genius for imitation and creativity enabled him, in the years 1962 to 1964, first, to write new compositions that showed a remarkably adept mastery of traditional forms (e.g., "Bob Dylan's Dream," "John Brown," "Percy's Song," "Boots of Spanish Leather," "Seven Curses," "North Country Blues"), and second, to expand the possibilities of those forms, in terms of both content and structure, in ways that astonished his growing audience ("A Hard Rain's A-Gonna Fall," "The Lonesome Death of Hattie Carroll," "Only a Pawn in Their Game").

In part, what allowed for this early mastery in the composition of "folk songs" was a striking poetic talent. Dylan showed from his beginnings a rare gift for handling the core elements of strong lyricality in poetry and song: alliteration, assonance, metrical sensitivity, and rhyme (Christopher Ricks has acclaimed Dylan as "one of the great rhymesters of all time") in the service of an effective use of compelling imagery to tell a story or convey a mood.[12] Also, Dylan possessed an uncanny ability to experience an imaginative empathy with the figures in both inherited songs and those of his own invention—to inhabit personae and communicate feelingly their passions and perspectives, whether they were fictional characters of legend, historical persons told of in ballads, archetypal hoboes, outlaws, disillusioned lovers, or persons of the present whose stories Dylan had read about in the newspapers.[13] In his own songs, this imaginative empathy found expression in his lyrics, but in both traditional and original compositions, it was also apparent in his singing, in his talents for phrasing and delivery.

Much attention has been devoted to Dylan's singing voice. Depending in part on whether or not one looks for "attractiveness" and conventional sounds, textures, and phrasings in vocal music, one tends to be either put off or fascinated by it. For those receptive to it, from the start of his career Dylan was recognized to have an almost preternatural gift for what might be called empathic mimicry, relying on a combination of precision in timing, control of emotional tone, and inventive and surprising phrasing to serve lyrical meaning. The result—a very intentional result—was an ability to sound as if he were from any historical time and place in America; and, when singing from the perspective of aged or roughed-up characters, to sound as if he were channeling a singer four times his age.[14] Tim Riley writes that the early Dylan had a voice "as strange and arresting as those of [certain] backwoods white blues [performers] . . . a barbed yawp that made him sound like he was born an old-timer."[15] Greil Marcus makes the same point in a more elaborate way: "The way Bob Dylan sang on his early records," he writes, "he could have been born in Virginia in the seventeen hundreds, turned up for the Gold Rush in California in 1849, headed up to Alaska in the 1890s, made it down to Mexico in 1910 . . ." On through his albums of the mid and late 1960s, Marcus writes, Dylan "caught fifty states, four hundred years, and four seasons in his voice." He explains further:

> Empathy has always been the genie of [Dylan's] work, of the tones of his voice, his sense of rhythm, his feel for how to fill up a line or leave it half empty, his sense of when to ride a melody and when to bury it, so that it might dissolve all of a listener's defenses—and this is what allowed Dylan, in 1962 at the Gaslight Café in Greenwich Village, at home in that secret community of tradition and mystery, to become not only the pining lover in the old ballad "Handsome Molly," but also Handsome Molly herself.[16]

This capacity for empathic mimicry had two major consequences with regard to our concern with art's capacity to suggest mysteries. First, it allowed Dylan, through a reliance on unpredictability and emotional freshness in phrasing and delivery, to produce in the listener a constant awareness, line by line as a song was being sung, of the unbounded possibilities in human experience. And second, it enabled him to, in Sean Wilentz's words, "make the present and the past feel like each other," to sound like he was singing "in more than one era at once," and thus to evoke with peculiar efficacy the timelessness of truths about the human condition.[17]

Once these empathic capacities began to serve songs of Dylan's own making, they helped to make obvious his unusual talent for using the language of symbols. Before examining a few examples of Dylan's ability to charge symbols with a sense of uncanny significance, however, it will be useful to look briefly at how symbolic meaning functions generally in the art of song.

Symbols, although they may have a conceptual dimension (obviously so in the case of literary art), are essentially images; and all images employed skillfully by an artist become symbols that, first, invite us to undergo certain experiences by conveying meanings at a preconceptual level with emotional immediacy, and second, are able to evoke the richness of human experience by communicating or suggesting many meanings simultaneously. An artistic symbol, in any medium—in a painting, a symphony, a poem—is an image intentionally "overdetermined" with meaning; one symbol might even carry contradictory meanings, not being bound by the principle of noncontradiction.[18] And since the principal purpose of art is to communicate *emotional meanings*—meanings embodied concretely in the artwork, that we in turn concretely experience and as it were feelingly enact—a careful artistic creation of groups of symbols rich with meanings, composed into a compelling unity of form, can awaken in us feeling-laden apprehensions of depths of significance in a way that non-symbolic languages (such as those of commonsense description or science) cannot.

The symbolic languages of each art form—including music, painting, sculpture, architecture, dance, film, photography, fiction, drama, poetry and song—have distinctive powers of communicating meaning, certain privileges belonging to each medium that allow it best to evoke certain types of feeling and experience. The pure nonconceptuality and emotional immediacy of music have led some to argue that it, of all artistic media, has the greatest power to evoke not only complexities of human emotion but also the mysteries of meaning that we know to lie beyond the boundaries of human understanding and that enthrall us, or frighten us, or beckon to us as realities that complete the meanings we partially comprehend.[19] The verbal arts, on the other hand, are capable of the most *specific* symbolic evocations both of human experiences and of realities that lie beyond our full understanding, since words allow for the most exact communication of both apprehensions and intimations of meaning. Words have the unique symbolic virtue of being capable of carrying extreme conceptual precision along with profound emotional resonance, and what the talented verbal artist does is exploit the "retinues of associations" words can convey so that they attain a maximum of resonance, evoking multiplicities of concrete experiences and feelings in the consciousness of the listener or reader. Their purpose is to provoke a "dynamic situation," or a series of dynamic situations, in the consciousness of the recipient so that one concretely reenacts the scene, the dramatic moment, the intense feeling, the compelling or disturbing vision, that the verbal artist has succeeded in "objectifying" in the artwork.[20]

What we find in the artistic medium of song—whether classical *lieder*, operatic arias, church hymns, parlor ballads, folk songs, rock 'n' roll, Gregorian chant, or the songs of tribal peoples—is the uniting of *musical* symbols and *verbal* symbols in works that draw upon the powers of both media at once. When the combination of music and words creates a particularly satisfying unity of form—when the melody, rhythm, tempo, instrumentation, etc., of the music carries meanings that complement and intensify the meanings of the words (including through mimicry, counterpoint, adding of nuance, and other means), and when the feeling-laden meanings of the sung words are felt to have found their "inevitable form" in their actual musical setting—songs can take on an exceptional, sometimes mystical, significance for the listener or singer.

One of the factors that allows this union to be so powerful is that words themselves have a musicality: each evokes certain meanings due to the way it sounds to the ear, and words can be linked and arranged together in ways that create modes of musicality between themselves (such as rhyme, alliteration, and assonance). This musicality of words, which is central to the communication of felt meaning in poetry (and the best prose) can be exploited and enhanced in song through a multitude of means, including melody, pace, volume, the abbreviating and extending of words, and various intricacies of phrasing.

As already mentioned, there is an inescapable limitation to writing about the significance of Dylan's art insofar as one concerns oneself with his lyrics without considering their melodies and musical settings and, in Dylan's case, with his recorded (and live) performances. But imagining how they might gain additional meaning from apt musical setting and expert phrasing, let us consider the allusive and existential reach of symbolic meaning—a reach that touches on mystery—in two of Dylan's songs.

Written when he was twenty-two and released on his fourth album, *Another Side of Bob Dylan*, "Chimes of Freedom" (1964) is a song whose situational premise is that of two lovers taking shelter from a night storm in the doorway of a cathedral. Dylan presents the experience as an occasion of epiphany, in which lightning and thunder synesthetically become one with church bells tolling out a promise of freedom and redemption for all who suffer. The fourth of its six verses conveys a sense of the whole:

> In the wild cathedral evening the rain unraveled tales
> For the disrobed faceless forms of no position
> Tolling for the tongues with no place to bring their thoughts
> All down in taken-for-granted situations
> Tolling for the deaf and blind, tolling for the mute
> For the mistreated mateless mother, the mistitled prostitute
> For the misdemeanor outlaw, chained and cheated by pursuit
> And we gazed upon the chimes of freedom flashing[21]

There are two "dynamic situations" being evoked here. First, there is the hallucinatory transformation of rain, storm, and lightning into bells chiming out tales and circumstances, which toll as a witness, and as a moral and spiritual promise, to those who suffer. Second, there is the awareness and identifying of the chimed-for, the witnessed-to. For the effective communication of the first, Dylan relies on imagery and syntax that merge different types of sensory experiences into one another while at the same time compressing narrative, moral, and spiritual meanings into elemental images of nature ("the rain unraveled tales," "chimes of freedom flashing"). For conveying the second, Dylan lists—as he does in each verse—a sequence of human types in vivid images: "disrobed faceless forms of no position," a phrase conveying the feelings of humiliation, helplessness, and anonymity in victims of social and political oppression; "the misdemeanor outlaw," a concise image for those hounded to the margins of society and denied opportunity for the sake of petty trespasses. Overall there is a luxuriance of symbolic meaning—within lines, within verses, and in the lyric as a whole. And the song's symbolic meanings revolve around three themes that appear consistently in Dylan's work: indignation at man's inhumanity to man; the permanence and depths of suffering in human history; and intimations of an ultimate and mysterious moral and spiritual redemption.[22]

A second example shows another side of Dylan's art in its power to evoke the mysterious: less concerned with social than with personal experience, more fragmented and unkempt in its allusiveness, mordant and ironic rather than unguardedly sincere, and using its condensations of imagery to convey coherencies of mood rather than coherent narrative. Here is the first verse of the six-verse "Just Like Tom Thumb's Blues" (1965):

> When you're lost in the rain in Juarez
>   And it's Eastertime too
> And your gravity fails
>   And negativity don't pull you through
> Don't put on any airs
>   When you're down on Rue Morgue Avenue
> They got some hungry women there
>   And they really make a mess out o' you

The images come thick and fast, some of them specific ("lost in the rain," "Juarez," "Eastertime"), some of them general but with familiar meanings ("Don't put on any airs," "hungry women"), some of them obscure but pointedly suggestive ("When your gravity fails / And negativity don't pull you through"), all adding up to a litany of warning, evoking a miserable and possibly dangerous situation. There is narrative here, but only barely—just enough to give imaginative and emotional unity to the sequence of images, whose purpose is clearly to convey, not a description of social or worldly events, but a mood—a feeling. "The point," Dylan said in 1965 about this song and its companions on the album *Highway 61 Revisited*, "is not understanding what I write, but *feeling* it." Of course, this is the concern of every artist—successfully communicating emotionally significant experience. But when the artistic medium is a verbal one, words must be used in a symbolically charged and original way if ready-made conceptual understanding—what Proust inveighed against as "habit"—is to be pierced by fresh experiences of emotional possibility. In this type of song, Dylan is doing what Symbolist, Expressionist, and Surrealist poets had done before him in the medium of poetry: using feeling-laden verbal images to evoke in the psyche, not a unity of *understood* experience, but a unity of *felt* experience whose distinctive emotional character includes the psychological dislocation of *not being able to clearly understand the experience*. It is one way of provoking a sense of mystery—a sense of there being more to what is happening in and to oneself, and in the world, than one can figure out. This sense of mystery, which at times articulates itself as an awareness of genuinely transcendent meaning, has been a motivating concern and communicative goal of Dylan's songs throughout his recording career.

Ulterior Significance

Dylan's love of the open-endedly allusive, the mysterious, the indefinable "more" inhabiting experiences and things, and his mastery in evoking it, has enabled him repeatedly to fulfill what the Russian filmmaker Andrey Tarkovsky proclaimed to be the principal duty of the artist, which is to create images that communicate the human "aspiration towards the infinite"—to invest artworks with ulterior significance in such a way as to put us imaginatively in touch with the highest hidden meanings with which our lives are involved, spiritual meanings that are too rich for human comprehension.[23] In the most charged and revelatory modalities of art's suggestiveness, that presence is experienced as the timeless or divine presence in whom all lines of existential concern and meaning meet. It is this sense of presence that is the basis of art's capacity not only to fascinate but also to induce spiritual insight, a piercing awareness of the numinous, or even awe and worship—and thus, at its most inspiring, to lead us to consider changing our lives.

During Dylan's burst of invention in 1964 to 1966, when he did most to redefine the contours of what popular song could be, he was concerned to evoke mysterious and not-fully-knowable realities primarily in the dimension of worldly adventures and human encounters, which was often accomplished through the Surrealist techniques of fragmentation, jarring juxtaposition, and allusion without resolution. Sometimes this resulted in songs recognized to be original and evocative but, for some, unsatisfying in their lack of conceptual coherence or narrative structure. (Critics have leveled such complaints against, for example, the major compositions "Gates of Eden" (1964) and "Sad-Eyed Lady of the Lowlands" (1966), the latter an eleven-minute "baroque extravagance" of allusive romantic images that expresses a tapestry of feelings but tells no story.)[24] But Dylan succeeded frequently, in most songs of this period, in using a combination of symbolic allusiveness and disjointed events to create works that did feel narratively complete and also conveyed a sense of ulterior significance—"unities of vision" that suggested that personal and local dramas of modern life were somehow bound up with real mysteries of meaning beyond our ken. "Mr. Tambourine Man" (1964), "It's Alright Ma (I'm Only Bleeding)" (1964), "Like a Rolling Stone" (1965), "Highway 61 Revisited" (1965), "Ballad of a Thin Man" (1965), "Desolation Row" (1965), and "Visions of Johanna" (1965–66) are all songs that fascinated listeners in part because of the ways in which they evoked everyday life as immersed in mysteriously consequential, if not clearly graspable, depths of existential significance.

But Dylan also early expressed an overt concern (as in "Chimes of Freedom") with expressly spiritual mysteries—meanings not just hidden from our full understanding but mysteries entailing the *ultimate* meanings of human suffering and freedom; of moral failure, struggle, and hope; of mortality and intimations of sacred timelessness; of redemption and salvation. And if one focuses not on one period of Dylan's songs but on his almost sixty years of work as a whole, it is apparent not only that he has regularly shown a concern to evoke a sense of the mysterious and the uncanny but that this concern has consistently been associated with an explicit sense of a divine reality more permanent than the worldly, to which human hopes and fears are ultimately oriented, and in relation to which human actions and decisions take their final meaning. To put it simply, Dylan as an artist has constantly evinced a religious sensibility.

This helps to explain why for a few years Dylan embraced the assurances of an evangelical form of Christianity, releasing three albums—*Slow Train Coming* (1979), *Saved* (1980), and *Shot of Love* (1981)—containing songs expressing gospel truths, sung with the fervor of a new convert, a good handful of them rooted in musical forms of the African-American church. (These albums are invariably grouped together as Dylan's "gospel" albums, which is roughly accurate with regard to their expressions of Christian commitment, but only *Saved* sounds predominantly like "gospel music," and *Shot of Love* is a mixture of secular and Christian songs.) The albums shocked Dylan's fan base and divided critics, but these so-called Christian albums can be seen, in a broad view, to be thematically and emotionally consistent with Dylan's repeated concern with matters ultimate and divine, and more specifically with three mysteries to which his songs have always paid attention: human sinfulness (and the mystery of iniquity); the spiritual outcome of personal destiny; and the mystery of end times and divine judgment.[25] Dylan's overtly Christian songs, alternately pleading, castigating, grateful, or filled with apocalyptic rage, channeled his fascination with these themes into what were often message songs barbed with evangelical decisiveness.

But soon—beginning with a few of the songs on *Shot of Love*, including the calmly providentialist "Every Grain of Sand"—the elemental mysteriousness of transcendent reality returned to the fore in Dylan's imagery, along with evocations of the confounding and the elusive in everyday existence. Dylan never renounced the songs of his "gospel period"; indeed, Christian symbolism continued to be woven into the lyrics of many subsequent songs. But then, such symbolism had permeated his songwriting from the beginning. In the long view, it is the continuity between the Christian albums and those that came before and after that stands out more than the degree to which their Christian-evangelical witnessing, preachifying, and scriptural quoting and paraphrasing sets them apart: first, because of Dylan's abiding concern with mysteries of iniquity, spiritual destiny, and ultimate judgment; and second, because

Dylan's appreciation of spiritual truths—including the truth of transcendent being—had always been informed and shaped by the Bible.

The impact of biblical language and symbolism on Dylan's songwriting, and his reliance on biblical themes and imagery to express his deepest apprehensions and concerns, was obvious from the beginning of his career. "I have always read the Bible," he stated in 1968, and scholars who have devoted research to identifying biblical sources of specific phrases, words, images, storytelling structures, and types of diction in Dylan's work leave no doubt that the practice was continuous throughout his life and career.[26] But many statements of Dylan have made clear that his initial receptiveness to biblical texts and symbolisms was itself grounded in existential openness to the most important mysteries of the human condition: mortality, suffering, the enchantments and confusions of erotic love, epiphanies of timelessness, sinfulness and complicity in evil, the longing for innocence and redemption, the promise and fear of divine judgment, and the question of historical direction and purpose. Indeed, as he tells it, what first attracted Dylan to "folk music" (or "traditional music," as he has more encompassingly called long-handed-down ballads, "spirituals," "old-time" music, blues, shanties, and all their kin) was that "the main body of it is just based on myth and the Bible and plague and famine and all kinds of things like that which are nothing but mystery and you can see it in all the songs."[27] "All these songs about roses growing out of people's brains and lovers who are really geese and swans that turn into angels. . . . I mean, you'd think that the traditional-music people could gather from their songs that mystery—just plain simple mystery—is a fact, a traditional fact."[28] It would seem that Dylan's fascination with and insistence on attesting to the basic mysteries of existence, in all their disquieting character, was the source of his responsiveness to biblical symbolism in the first place, as well as of the generally "spiritual" flavor—whether muted or glaringly obvious—of so many of his songs.[29]

Given his lifelong attraction to the mysterious and to evocations of sacred reality, it is not surprising that Dylan's lyrics so often address questions of the relation of historical, worldly time to transcendent truth and being. There are two principal ways this manifests itself. One involves what might be called the interweaving of historical time with transhistorical significance. From very early on, his songs—especially those in which he relied on the form of traditional ballads—aimed to create in the listener a sense of living in multiple eras at once, and thus a timeless sense of human solidarity and universality. Eventually, beginning in the mid-1970s, one of Dylan's deliberate artistic concerns became the creation of songs having "to do with the break-up of time," where a song's symbolic allusions, diction, and narrative (or quasinarrative) locate the singer and listener in what could be either biblical times or the present, or perhaps in very specific historical epochs simultaneously—say, the Civil War era *and* the southern United States in the early twentieth century *and* modern times.[30] About such compositions—notable examples would be "Shelter from the Storm" (1974), "Isis" (1975), "Changing of the Guards" (1978), and "Blind Willie McTell" (1983)—Dylan himself once stated, "You've got yesterday, today and tomorrow all in the same room, and there's very little that you can't imagine happening."[31] The imagination is opened up because a sense of the full scope of the human drama is suddenly present, while at the same time the listener is led to feel how human existence of all times and places is shot through with timeless meaning. At their most successful, such songs carry the feeling of myth, of *mythos*, because they remind us experientially that human existence is lived always in the intersection of timelessness and time, in the In-Between of world and transcendent reality.

The second way is more direct and obvious. Because Dylan's sense of transcendence is so strong, because he is a Westerner with a spiritual imagination primarily shaped by the Bible, and finally because he has persistently been drawn by temperament to "the border experience of the examination of conscience" (Voegelin) where questions of ultimate moral judgment and history's meaning converge, an eschatological bent characterizes songs from throughout his career.[32] The ultimate significance evoked is frequently that of the fulfillment of human meanings in an historical end beyond time—the mystery of a divinely intended conclusion of all temporal human wanderings and hopes, the last goal of the trajectory of what Martin Luther King Jr. called "the arc of the moral universe."[33] In Dylan's songs, we find ourselves again in the orbit of T. S. Eliot's Christian insistence that human history only makes sense if it is leading toward a transfigurative human-divine fulfillment. An eschatological sensibility is already present in Dylan's first genuinely outstanding composition, "A Hard Rain's A-Gonna Fall" (1962), based on the form and melody of Child Ballad #12, "Lord Randall," which finds Dylan evoking repeatedly a sense of "end times" through symbol-laden answers to questions put to the song's narrator about where he has been, what he has seen and heard, and whom he has met—

> I've been out in front of a dozen dead oceans
> I've been ten thousand miles in the mouth of a graveyard
>
> I saw a roomful of men with their hammers a-bleedin'
> I saw a white ladder all covered with water
>
> I heard the sound of a thunder that roared out a warnin'
> I heard the roar of a wave that could drown the whole world

—each stanza concluding with the melodically scale-ascending, frighteningly prophetic refrain:

> And it's a hard, it's a hard, it's a hard, it's a hard
> It's a hard rain's a-gonna fall.

An eschatological tension is also vivid in other songs of Dylan's "folk" period—for example, "Whatcha Gonna Do?" (1962), "When the Ship Comes In" (1963), "Chimes of Freedom" (1964), and "Farewell, Angelina" (1964–65)—and becomes even more common thereafter.[34]

Apocalypticism, which unsurprisingly drives a number of Dylan's Christian evangelizing songs, infuses many others as well, whether by way of intimations or straight-out declarations of a universal, inescapable divine judgment that will reveal all that has been hidden and pay all moral and spiritual accounts, their apocalyptic imagery revealing Dylan's special attraction to the book of Revelation.[35] And the most dire of these songs convey a feeling of imminent crisis and destruction, of being on the edge of final judgment and doom right here and now.[36] It is a feeling clearly communicated in "All Along the Watchtower" (1967), widely known through the version recorded by Jimi Hendrix, with its ominous conclusion:

All along the watchtower, princes kept the view
While all the women came and went, barefoot servants, too
  Outside in the distance a wildcat did growl
  Two riders were approaching, the wind began to howl

and by this couplet from "Jokerman" (1983):

False-hearted judges dying in the webs that they spin
Only a matter of time till night comes stepping in

as well as by the opening lines of "Blind Willie McTell" (1983):

Seen the arrow on the doorpost
Saying, "This land is condemned
All the way from New Orleans
To Jerusalem"[37]

and by vivid lines in less well-known songs such as "Angelina" (1981):

I see pieces of men marching, trying to take Heaven by force
I can see the unknown rider, I can see the pale white horse

In Dylan's Christian evangelical songs, symbolic allusiveness and allegorical suggestiveness were briefly replaced by unambiguous scripture-based prophesizing,[38] but for most of his career his apocalyptic foreboding—from "Blowin' in the Wind" (1962) to "Series of Dreams" (1989) to "Ain't Talkin'" (2006)—has tended to be expressed through passing biblical allusions, open-ended symbolism, and the multilayered, mythic imagery of visions, dreams, parables, and allegories, usually suffused with a mood of unresolved questioning.

Some of Dylan's finest songs express, at once, an acute sensitivity to the eschatological tension in human existence; a sense of the inescapability of divine judgment; awareness that the outcome of human spiritual longing remains a mystery; hope—frail or confident—in some kind of ultimate redemption; and a careful use of imagery to "make the present and the past feel like each other," thus evoking both the concrete sweep of history and a constant "flux of divine presence" in human affairs.[39] "Chimes of Freedom" (1964), already looked at, is one such song; another is 1983's "Blind Willie McTell," often referred to as one of Dylan's masterpieces;[40] and a third is "I Dreamed I Saw St. Augustine" (1967). A close look at the latter will indicate how the themes just mentioned can be united to evoke mysteries of ulterior significance and divine presence in a not-untypical Dylan song-parable.

"I Dreamed I Saw St. Augustine" appeared on Dylan's 1968 album *John Wesley Harding*, an album largely composed of stripped-down, three-verse parables and allegorical stories. Some of its songs are evocative of the American western frontier, while others are overtly biblical in tone and symbolism.[41] Its simplicity of musical instrumentation complements the landscape of legend, and the cycles of suffering, heroism, guilt, and yearning for deliverance, that its combined stories bring into view. The St. Augustine who figures in this song about a dream is not the famous St. Augustine of Hippo, since in the singer's dream the saint is portrayed as a martyr. The less well-known St. Augustine of Canterbury was not martyred either; and although the even less well-known St. Augustine Webster, an English Catholic of the sixteenth century, *was* martyred, he wasn't canonized until a few years after Dylan wrote his song. None of this really matters. The subject of Dylan's song is not historical, but allegorical, in keeping with the allegorical character of many of the album's songs. The singer sings of a dream-vision in which a saint appears who symbolizes human-divine mediation—and whose name, not so incidentally, fits the meter. The song also links the religious and the political through Dylan's explicitly basing both the words and melody of its first lines on "Joe Hill," a protest song about a union organizer for the Industrial Workers of the World (IWW) executed in 1915, which portrays Hill as a martyr.[42] Dylan's overtly spiritual song thus carries an echo of the hopes for social justice that energized the folk song community.[43]

The first verse establishes the spiritually haunted mood of the song (enhanced by its somber, delicate melody) in which an unusual mixture of formal and everyday language and symbolism, within a compressed narrative, creates the kind of timeless ambience Dylan is so fond of, where the here-and-now is permeated by ultimate questions:

I dreamed I saw St. Augustine
  Alive as you or me
Tearing through these quarters
  In the utmost misery
With a blanket underneath his arm
    And a coat of solid gold
Searching for the very souls
    Whom already have been sold

In a dream-vision, the singer sees the saint from earlier times as not dead after all, but alive in the present as a frantic and suffering seeker, searching for souls to save, or for souls capable of being saved, but discovering that in these times such souls "already have been sold"—with the word *sold* suggesting both the bondage of sin and modern absorption in the world of secular and commercial concerns. The saint's blanket conveys lowliness and solidarity with all persons; the coat of gold suggests his spiritual nobility; together they create a figure with simultaneously ancient and modern features who bridges the humbly human and the graciously divine.

The second verse delivers the saint's message to the singer as well as to us, his contemporaries:

"Arise, arise," he cried so loud
  With a voice without restraint
"Come out, ye gifted kings and queens
  And hear my sad complaint
No martyr is among ye now
    Whom you can call your own
But go on your way accordingly
    And know you're not alone"

We are called to arise—we who see ourselves, now, as "gifted kings and queens," that is, as imbued with exceptionality and privilege—and to come out from our immersions in worldly concerns and listen to the words of spiritual authority, which are a complaint, though a sympathetic rather than a damning one. There are, we are told, no "martyrs" in present times—no one living a life of such spiritual commitment that he or she is in danger of being "nailed to the cross of [the] world."[44] Nevertheless, the saint tells us, we have not been abandoned by divine presence, even as we ignore spiritual matters and the question of salvation. For this we are not condemned, but adjured to "go on [our] way accordingly," that is, in the way we must given our proclivities and the circumstances of modern life, but still knowing that we are "not alone"—that saintly and divine presence have not abandoned us, and that spiritual redemption remains a possibility, even in such a dissolute and desolate era.

The final verse begins by expanding the dream-vision, briefly and with the weirdness of allegory, and then concludes with a description of its impact on the singer:

> I dreamed I saw St. Augustine
> Alive with fiery breath
> And I dreamed I was amongst the ones
> That put him out to death
> Oh, I awoke in anger
> So alone and terrified
> I put my fingers against the glass
> And bowed my head and cried

The figure of St. Augustine now represents not only divine compassion for sinful humanity but also the fire of divine judgment. And the dream's conclusion sees the singer as one of a group that martyrs the saint—that is, as someone sinfully complicit in the modern turning away from spiritual awareness and responsibility, in the modern killing of the spirit. The singer wakes up angry, with a loneliness that derives both from his sense of separation from divine presence and from his alienation from a derelict society. The dream has induced a border experience of conscience, inducing anger that gives way to grief, as the singer—awakened in both a literal and a spiritual sense—bows his head and cries, putting his fingers against the coolness of the window glass to assure himself that his dream is indeed over, the window symbolizing his feeling of invisible separation both from other people and from God.

"I Dreamed I Saw St. Augustine" has features often found in the best literary art: self-transcending vision; the suggestion of time intersecting with the timeless; an admission of complicity in spiritual forgetfulness; and recognition of the pressures of existence in between hope and despair. It is a song of perfect structure and coruscating vision portraying human beings as actors in a drama with transcendent significance. In this, it represents well Dylan's many songs and lyrical moments that, in his distinctively Modernist manner, direct the attention of listeners to a transcendent mystery of divine presence, power, and promise.

CONCLUSION

THE TRAJECTORY OF discovery and illumination in Modernist literature stretching from Emily Dickinson to Bob Dylan traced in the prior chapters—from the proto-Modernist originalities of discovery and expression in Dickinson's poetry to the late Modernist assemblages of Dylan's song lyrics—ends at the edge of our own literary time with its postmodern figurations. But though we live in a post-Modernist literary era, the great Modernists remain at the center (insofar as a center exists) of contemporary literary life, as evidenced by the current, and in most cases increasing, popularity of the authors examined here. While Eliot and Pound do not, of course, dominate literary discussions of poetry as they once did, their impact is everywhere, and the scholarly industries devoted to their works remain robust, while Dickinson, Proust, Beckett, and Dylan are each more vitally present in the world of literature than ever before. Fascination with and admiration of Dickinson's poetry has never been greater. Twentieth- and twenty-first-century literature, as Eric Karpeles writes, "is unthinkable without Proust."[1] Beckett's plays opened up radically new possibilities in drama that have "given a new rule" to the art, and either inform or hover over all later theatrical innovation. Modern popular songwriting was single-handedly altered by Dylan; suddenly songwriting could aspire to, and attain, serious literary significance—though as yet no other songwriter commands the literary respect accorded him. All six authors discussed inhabit the highest literary tier as innovators and influencers.

Numerous factors led to my choice to write on these artists, the most important being (with the exception of Proust) my fascination with them from teenage years. Accidents of temperament and home and learning environments brought me into their orbits; and the "plainly-lit excellence" of their best work has resulted in my trying for many decades to allow each of them to expand the range of my imagination and thought.[2] That only one of the authors discussed here is a woman, and none are authors of color, is not intended to be any kind of a statement regarding cultural or literary canons. My selection is the consequence of my owing each of these particular figures a profound existential debt.

We read literature in order to grow, to expand the range and depth of our experience. Like all art, literature invites us to discover what lies beyond our current horizons of thought and feeling, beyond the already-understood, the familiar, the domesticated, the stale. This expansion occurs in two ways. First, literature introduces us to what we would never have encountered or become on our own, what would have otherwise remained inaccessible: the foreign, the historically distant, tragic or ecstatic extremes of human experience, characters and circumstances only knowable through their presences in literary art, emotions we otherwise would not have felt, behavior we could not have enacted, insights of a sophistication and complexity that our unaided curiosity would never have brought to light.

But second, literature reveals to us what we *have* experienced or undergone but haven't adequately attended to or understood. Neglected feelings are brought into focus; vague memories are clarified; repressed images or insights come to light. Over and over, artists draw our attention to aspects of our lives we need to know about in order to understand ourselves accurately. This yields the oddly paradoxical experience of remembering, at times, aspects of who and what we are for the first time. But after all, it is a commonplace, as Eliot indicates in *Four Quartets*, to have experiences of import and miss their meanings.

When we read (or listen to) these six authors to learn what they have discovered and recorded with respect to possibilities of human experiences, so that we can know our own selves better, we find at the core of their testimonies a metaphysical affirmation central, in their shared view, to authentic human self-understanding. Each of them insists on the priority, first, of remembering that conscious existence is granted, or gifted, from a "ground" of being beyond itself, and second, of recognizing that this ground must be timeless, or eternal, if existence and history are to be meaningful in any moral or lasting sense. They also recognize that such a timeless, transcendent ground is essentially mysterious: that it is (speaking epistemologically) a *mysterious* ground of all reality; and that it is (speaking ontologically) a *real* mystery of transcendence. And they all envision their own consciousnesses as sites where transcendent reality reveals itself, either as *presence* or (in the case of Beckett) as *idea*—for the consternation and wonder, the torturing or comforting, of the searching soul. As a result, each author's vision of the human is characterized by humility, shaped as it is by recognition that the human drama is a story being told not only by persons struggling to make sense of existence and history but also, more primordially, by the mysterious "beyond" from which consciousness, along with the rest of the universe, has arisen in its trajectory of revelatory emergence.

Importantly, in all of these literary visions the transcendent mystery is never portrayed as experienced by persons in its purity, as if somehow the bodily conditions of existence were not involved. If it is true that transcendence only appears in the "within" of consciousness, this "within" is nevertheless a site in which spatiotemporally conditioned being is the medium, the element, in which the ontological presence or inescapable idea of an infinite "other" reveals itself. Explicitly in the writings of Dickinson, Proust, Eliot, and Pound, consciousness itself is described as the *unity of an interwovenness of time and timelessness*, of worldly and eternal meaning: it is a distinctive mode of reality constituted by the tension of the interpenetration of immanent and transcendent (or divine) being, an in-between reality neither reducible to the worldly nor ever removed from time.

None of the six, though, ever confuse the beyond with consciousness or world itself; none of them collapse the Lover, Eternal Being, God, or the Eschaton into interiority, time, or history. Even Pound, who comes closest to envisioning the two dimensions of meaning as one in his imaginings of a *paradiso terrestre* (although he renounces this symbol and its connotations, in the end, as a blunder), did not make the error of believing in a permanent fusion of world and perfected meaning in the manner of liberal progressivism and utopianism.[3] Their imaginations, in other words, remain uncorrupted by sentiments demanding the tangible fulfillment of the perfection and absoluteness of meaning that belongs to the beyond. None are persuaded by ersatz images of the worldly completion of meaning, any more than they are by the idea that meaning is a radically human invention. The revealings of a transcendent meaning—or, in Beckett's case, the presence in the mind of the idea of God—are appearances beyond human invention, will, and complete comprehension, and as such are crucial to human self-understanding since they establish a founding principle of what it means to be human: that our desire and our questioning continually reach for and (except in Beckett's case) discover that we *ontologically participate in* a reality timelessly beyond finite universe and consciousness itself, all the while recognizing that if there were no such timeless meaning then human striving, moral effort, suffering, and accomplishment would be ultimately pointless. Only transcendence, they all (including Beckett) affirm, can guarantee the meaning of meaning and the value of value.[4]

Transcendence anchors each of the visions of reality treated here, but it is symbolized in a variety of ways, reflecting differing *experiences* of transcendence. For Dickinson it is a personal divinity, a "God"; but this is variably the Judeo-Christian God or some less benign and more ambiguous, more confusing divine power. It is perhaps [God] in brackets, with Dickinson hesitating to judge, not that her intense encounters are real, but with whom in fact they occur. As such, Dickinson's portrayal of transcendent being represents the widespread diffraction of Western religious faith into idiosyncratic visions, as well as the modern rejection of religious dogma in favor of a sometimes-groping mysticism. Proust affirms an impersonal, Platonic type of transcendence, recognized as Eternal Being—without, however, any intimations of Platonic (much less Hindu or Buddhist) reincarnation. Eliot's transcendent reality in *Four Quartets* is the God of Christianity, but ecumenicized, in that the work grants genuineness and authority to both Western and Eastern mystical traditions while affirming that the profoundest non-Christian spiritual experiences are compatible with the Christian epiphanies. Pound recalls and recovers transcendence as the gods who infuse the natural world with beauty and glory and whose inspiration is the "divine light" from which radiate order, creative insight, good government, harmony, and joy; this is, in his experience, the true source of historical meaning and success, which waxes and wanes as humans are more and less receptive to divine influence. Beckett's transcendence is that of the authentic and consistent agnostic: it is the reality of God that, if it exists, would give meaning to human life, but which in his view is inaccessible because of the limitations of both nature and spirit in human existence. Finally, Dylan's transcendence—less thought-through than the others, since even less than Dickinson is he concerned, as a song lyricist, with analysis or consistency—is the biblical God of history, love, and judgment, whose mysterious reality and power give the measure to moral meaning, confound earthly efforts, and promise both retribution and consolation.

These are visions in Modernist literature that testify, then, to mystical apprehensions of transcendence as—in some mode or another—normative and needful in contemporary life. Each vision invites persons to apprehend within themselves the ontological presence, or at the very least the commanding idea, of timeless and sacred being—however foreign to our self-understanding such apprehension might be, given the present popularity of abjurations of transcendent reality and the dismissal of its symbolizations as irrelevant. Indeed, each of the six visions discussed here would be viewed by its author as a corrective to a habit of forgetfulness about transcendence that runs broadly through modern culture. Each aims to disrupt modern imaginative oblivion about the mystery of the ground of being, constituting an act of remembrance—in the Platonic sense of *anamnesis*—in which transcendent reality is paid witness.[5] "Through art alone," Proust reminds us, "are we able to emerge from ourselves, to know what another person sees of a universe which is not the same as our own"; and the universe an artist sees, and which we explore, may be a more rich cosmos than what we have hitherto imagined, a cosmos in which a genuinely transcendent mystery is the beginning and end of human questioning, knowing, and loving.[6]

ACKNOWLEDGMENTS

PERHAPS THERE ARE many people who enjoy, as I do, reading the acknowledgments pages that often start books, where friends, colleagues, and family members who have helped the author in different ways are identified. I invariably read all the names and circumstances mentioned, letting them conjure worlds of relationship and community I will never know as I glimpse a few details of the author's life. Together with gratitude, authors often convey a sense of humility, since book writing is usually found to be a daunting and effortful enterprise.

But obviously not always. Read enough and one finds that, as the poet James Wright once said, "there are authors in this world who work with great facility." He continued, "May I offer them my respectful envy. I myself am one of those people who, granted the choice between writing the opening sentence and being hanged by the neck until I am dead, would cheerfully prefer the latter." I sympathize, since I find writing to be as unfacile an activity as any I have attempted. But the presence and encouragement of a blessed array of friends has helped me to keep at it. They have provided not only requisite insight and encouragement but, in the words of Clive James, "the infinite liberation of knowing that one is not alone."

There are friends whose love, intelligence, and humor have had a direct impact on the making of this book. They include my dear friend Henrik Syse, forever gracious and loyal; James Greenaway, who incarnates the openness in genuine dialogue; Tom McPartland, who understands everything and forgives everything; Paul Caringella; Mary Pope Osborne; Pat Brown; and Paulette Kidder. Julian Bull and Gene Solis have patiently encouraged me as I sounded out its ideas with them.

The Eliot scholar Jewel Spears Brooker brought me into the company of the International Association of University Professors of English (IAUPE), for whose 2013 and 2016 conferences I developed the talks that matured into chapters 1 and 5. Through Jewel also I had the opportunity to give a talk on T. S. Eliot and Proust at a 2015 symposium on "T. S. Eliot and His Contemporaries" in Florence, which was the basis of the comparative work presented in chapter 3. I am deeply in her debt. At the first IAUPE conference I attended, in Beijing, I was privileged to meet the poet and scholar Dana Gioia, who directed me toward the journal *Renascence*, where the Dickinson work which became chapter 1 first appeared. His poetry and friendship have been an inspiration.

Charlie Embry's organization of a panel on Marcel Proust for the 2014 meeting of the Eric Voegelin Society with the American Political Science Association was the impetus for initial work on what would become chapter 2, and from his vision and energy came our co-edited volume *The Timelessness of Proust*, in which early drafts of chapters 2 and 3 were published. I am thankful for his invitations to join all the APSA panels on Voegelin and Literature that he enthusiastically created over a number of years. Wayne Cristaudo and Paul Caringella organized two conferences on philosophy and history at the University of Hong Kong in February and March 2010, in which I was invited to participate; for the first of them I began the comparative study of Eliot and Pound that became the nucleus of chapter 4. And finally, the late Mike Shute, scholar and musician, encouraged me to write about Bob Dylan and art for his co-edited online *Journal of Macrodynamic Analysis*; an early version of chapter 6 was published there in 2011.

For more than fifty years I have depended on Joe Vinikow's intellectual curiosity and his exhortations (in French) of *courage!* as together, The Sibling Brothers, we inspire and conspire. Over the same period, adventures with the indefatigable and hilarious Marie McCaffrey have produced a thousand tales to tell. And for equally long, Libby Burke has been a partner in life, music-making, love of song and film, and shared astonishment at Bob Dylan's artistry.

Friends in scholarship who have given me wonderful encouragement and advice over the years include David Walsh, Brendan Purcell, Tilo

Schabert, Martin Palouš, Barry Cooper, Pat Byrne, and Bill Petropulos. The enthusiastic embrace by Jamie and Vieve Price of my efforts to understand how poetry, philosophy, and theater might speak to each other raised my spirits in difficult times. Fred Lawrence and Mark Morelli have kept faith in the value of my work for decades, and due to each of them opportunities to present research have never been lacking. My departmental colleagues Robert Skipper, Steve Calogero, and Conrad Kaczkowski have provided constant support.

I am indebted to Gene Webb both for the forty-plus years of teaching and friendship that helped lay the groundwork of many of my studies, and for his responses to the manuscript of this book. The encouragement of Rodney Kilcup has been a blessing since my first years of graduate study, long ago.

For broadening my horizons of appreciation in the realms of poetry and art, I bow to my friend the poet Tim McNulty and give thanks to my colleague the artist Brian St. John for our passionate, always-enlightening conversations.

Norwegian friends who have provided experiences of delightful comity include Greg Reichberg, of the Peace Research Institute of Oslo (PRIO), and Asbjørn Bjornes, Dante scholar and translator; and my thanks go, too, to the gracious and incisive Dylan writer Johnny Borgan, and to the master of the Dylan website *Expecting Rain*, Karl Erik Andersen.

The anonymous reviewer of this manuscript for University of Missouri Press who made numerous critical recommendations, which were invariably on point, was of great assistance.

My administrative superiors over the course of thirty years at St. Mary's University have made funds available for me to present work at every conference that I wished to attend. As laborers in the vineyards of academe know, this is an extraordinary level of support, and I am happy to acknowledge it here.

Others whose loving friendship indirectly nourished this book's creation include Larry Spaulding and Nancy Zugschwerdt, Beth Hailey, Barb Hathaway, Julie Sakahara, Luke Celt, Liz Illg, Paul Romero, Terri Boggess and John Moder, Carey Tremaine, Kurt Johnson and Robin Gray, Jeff Hillock and Harold Bravo, Trish Johnson, Sarah and Jan

Watson, Jef and Lisa Waltman, Brad Robison, Raina and Dean Ballard, Jude Gervais and Bob Luby, the late Richard Dyksterhuis, Randy Courts and Jenny Laird, and the resilient Tova Wein.

Gary Kass, Acquisitions Editor at the Press, has been a model of thoughtfulness, clarity, and attention to detail. It is rare to receive such prolonged and good-humored assistance in this kind of professional relationship; I thank him for his true friendship. I am also grateful to Mary Conley at University of Missouri Press for her courtesy and professional expertise, to Drew Griffith for his patience and guidance, and to Barbara Smith-Mandell for copyediting.

NOTES

Introduction

1. Pound, *ABC of Reading*, 14.

2. Kiberd, Ulysses *and Us*, 21, 30–31, 62–63, 348.

3. Riasanovsky, *Emergence of Romanticism*, 99. Coleridge, in a telling moment, expresses his desire to make "the whole one Self! Self, that no alien knows!" Quoted in Abrams, *Natural Supernaturalism*, 296.

4. On the literary Modernists as counter-Romantics, along with a treatment of continuities and discontinuities between Romanticism and Modernism, see Quinones, *Mapping Literary Modernism*, esp. 120–36. On the disjunction between Romanticism and Modernism with regard to the understanding of self and the relationship of self to world: "If one were to follow a line of continuous development from Romanticism one could arrive at Tennyson or Thomas Hardy, but one could never arrive at Leopold Bloom or *The Waste Land*" (127); on the role of the Modernist literary poet or maker: "Assuming more of the ordinary dress of the twentieth century, the poet [divests] himself of his priestly robes . . . he becomes less the creator and more the compositor who arranges into what he hopes is a functioning unity the various 'givens' of experience. The new role of the poet is that of a medium, an amalgamator . . ." (121–22).

5. Hulme, "Romanticism and Classicism," 118.

6. Kierkegaard, *Sickness Unto Death*, 13–14.

7. Lonergan, *Insight*, 658.

8. Patočka, *Heretical Essays in the Philosophy of History*, 61, 77.

9. Voegelin, *New Science of Politics*, 188.

10. For an account of human knowing that explains why this epistemological supposition is unsound, see Lonergan, *Insight*, chaps. 1 and 9–13.

Chapter One | Emily Dickinson

1. Anderson, "Despair," 35.

2. Vendler, *Dickinson: Selected Poems and Commentaries*, 17.

3. Dickinson, *Poems*, ed. Franklin, 171. All further quotations and numbering of Dickinson's poems are from this edition. For the remainder of this chapter,

poem numbers but not page numbers will be cited. When quotations do not include the first line of the poem, the poem's first line will be referenced. Partial quotations from poems will indicate preceding and/or succeeding lines by the symbol [. . .].

4. On the emergence of American Unitarianism, see Robinson, *Unitarians and the Universalists*, 3–24; and Dorrien, *Making of American Liberal Theology*, 2–34.

5. Robinson, *Unitarians and the Universalists*, 5.

6. Emerson, "Self-Reliance," 148.

7. Diel, "Emerson, Dickinson, and the Abyss," 151–52, 158.

8. See McIntosh, *Nimble Believing*, 14–20; and Gelpi, "Seeing New Englandly," 42.

9. See Sewall, *Life of Emily Dickinson*, 342–45.

10. For an account of the impact of nineteenth-century science on Dickinson (with whose conclusions regarding Dickinson's relation to the Christian idea of God I am in some disagreement), see Wolff, *Emily Dickinson*, 342–48, 451–73.

11. 598: "The brain is wider than the sky."

12. Translation by Eric Voegelin, in his *World of the Polis*, 299. For a slightly different translation of and commentary on this fragment, see Kahn, *Art and Thought of Heraclitus*, 126–30.

13. Dickinson, *Letters,* vol. 3, 926. (In what is obviously a typographical error, this text prints "in" for "is" as the second word in the fragment.)

14. 1433: "What mystery pervades a well!"

15. McIntosh, *Nimble Believing*, 123 (emphasis added).

16. 1260: "Is heaven a physician?"

17. On prayer, see also the crucial poems "My period had come for prayer" (525), "Prayer is the little implement" (623), and "I meant to have but modest needs" (711).

18. Line 3 follows Dickinson's spelling of "it's," as do lines in Poems 1421 and 824 below.

19. This and other Dickinson poems are suggestive of the trend toward "secularization" in the thought and culture of her century is two ways: they detail her abandonment of institutional religious life, and they express her recognition that the natural and everyday—the "secular"—may properly be seen as invested with the high meaningfulness of the sacred. Insofar however as "secular" means the rejection of religious or spiritual reality, Dickinson is obviously a strongly non-secular, or anti-secular, thinker and writer. A recent and impressively ambitious account of what the increasing secularization of modern Western culture has entailed is Charles Taylor's *A Secular Age*; on influential major "narratives of secularization" as "world structures that are closed to transcendence," such as those introduced by Comte and Marx, see 556–89. On diverse and overlapping meanings of the term *secularization*, see Kolakowski, *Modernity on Endless*

Trial, 63–74; and Taylor, *Secular Age*, 1–4. On secularization as the inevitable outgrowth of Christianity's incarnational vision and its radical differentiation of transcendence, see Boyle, *Who Are We Now?*.

20. Dickinson, *Selected Letters*, 173.

21. The biblical phrase goes back to Isaiah 45:15: "Indeed you are a hidden God, you God of Israel, the Savior." For an account of the Gospel epiphany as a revelation of the "Unknown God" through the person of Jesus in continuity with a millennial process of revelation reaching as far back as the Amon Hymns of Egypt, and including Plato's mythical evocations of a divine beyond, see Voegelin, "The Gospel and Culture," 196–212. The concept of the hiddenness of God's essence, of *deus absconditus* or *deus incognitus*, played an important role in the thinking of both Luther and Calvin. See Gerrish, "'To the Unknown God.'"

22. Franke, *On What Cannot Be Said*, vol. 2, *Modern and Contemporary Transformations*, 85. This book and its companion volume (cited below) offer the best available wide-ranging compilation of excerpts from authors of apophatic mysticism in the Western philosophical, religious, and literary traditions, along with excellent introductory remarks.

23. For brief introductions to Pseudo-Dionysius and his impact, see Pelikan, "Introduction I: The Odyssey of Dionysian Spirituality," and Leclercq, "Introduction II: Influence and Noninfluence of Dionysius in the Western Middle Ages," in *Pseudo-Dionysius: The Complete Works*, trans. Luibheid; and Franke, *On What Cannot Be Said*, vol. 1, *Classic Formulations*, 158–61.

24. Dickinson's poems also of course frequently employ "kataphatic" (affirming) symbols to express her experiences of and insights into divine reality, such as "Love" and "Lover," "Beauty," "Friend," Presence" and so on, not to mention the basic kataphatic symbol of Western religious language, "God."

25. Eliot, *Four Quartets*, 44 (*The Dry Salvages*, ll. 201–2).

26. Quoted in McIntosh, *Nimble Believing*, 73.

27. Vendler, *Dickinson*, 9.

28. Dickinson, *Selected Letters*, 242.

29. 670: "One crucifixion is recorded only."

30. Dickinson, *Letters*, vol. 3, 750. The ellipsis after "silence" is Dickinson's.

31. Dickinson, *Selected Letters*, 315.

32. Eberwein, "Dickinson's Local, Global, and Cosmic Perspectives," 42; McIntosh, *Nimble Believing*, 48.

Chapter Two | Marcel Proust

1. Voegelin, "Eternal Being in Time," 329.

2. "[I]ndisputably, there is the author himself who occasionally intervenes with his 'I' and makes generalizations and deductions. . . . [Often] the manner and matter of the comment make it clear that Proust is not merely speaking for Marcel [or the Narrator] but for himself. . . . [I]n his correspondence [Proust

often] claims as his own the opinions expressed in the novel—opinions on art, on love, on friendship, on involuntary memory and the living past, on the lessons of experience in general; so that it is quite safe to assume that the *generalizations* of the novel are those of the author." March, *Two Worlds of Marcel Proust*, 171 (emphasis added).

3. Shattuck, *Proust's Way*, 2.

4. Proust's control over the unity of the book's narrative during its continual expansions and revisions both before and after the 1913 publication of the first volume, *Swann's Way*, was due above all to his having written the first and last parts of the novel early on, between 1908 and 1911—Proust always claiming that he wrote the beginning and end of the story at the same time. The vast bulk of his additions, the initial opportunity for which was provided by the calamity of the First World War which postponed publication of the second volume, *Within A Budding Grove*, for four years, were expansions "from within," enlarging upon previous scenes and themes while adding new ones along with wholly new characters, story lines, and digressive excursions. See Schmid, "Birth and Development of *A la recherche du temps perdu*," 64. On the gradual emergence of the novel from an intended novel-essay entitled *Contre Sainte-Beuve*, see White, *Marcel Proust*, 95–112, and, more extensively, Tadié, *Marcel Proust*, 510–67.

5. As R. C. Zaehner writes of *In Search of Lost Time* in a famous study of mysticism: "[The] mystical element is the key to the whole book as anyone who reads the work carefully must realize." Zaehner, *Mysticism Sacred and Profane*, 52.

6. Proust, *Time Regained*, 262, 264–65, 268, 290, 301, 513.

7. March, *Two Worlds of Marcel Proust*, 216; see 216–28.

8. Proust, *Time Regained*, 298.

9. Cf. Proust, *Time Regained*, 262, where "*diverses impressions bienheureuses*" is translated "diverse happy impressions." The meaning of the French term *impressions* as Proust uses it here is perhaps not best translated by the English word "impressions," though a phrase such as "happy impressions" or "blessed impressions" has the virtue of remaining close to Proust's language. I will rely on the French phrase *impressions bienheureuses* for the most part, but occasionally employ an English substitute such as "epiphanies."

10. White, *Marcel Proust*, 143. The episode appears in Proust, *Swann's Way*, 60–64.

11. Roger Shattuck, in his expert *Proust's Way*, identifies fifteen key *impressions bienheureuses* (or, as he calls them, *moments bienheureux*—although the latter phrase, as far as I can find, does not appear in Proust's novel), the last five of which, occurring in the grand series of "epiphanies" or "reminiscences" midway through *Time Regained*, he presents as a single "event" of linked experiences, yielding him eleven such "events." In appendix 2 of *Proust's Way* he offers a "Table of the *Moments Bienheureux*," with detailed analyses and elucidated patterns pertaining to each *moment*, along with an account of what is common to

all of them; see Shattuck, *Proust's Way*, 257–64. Samuel Beckett, in his 1931 study *Proust*, after mentioning that these moments of "miracle" occur "twelve or thirteen times" in the novel, proceeds to list and describe eleven of these "sacred actions." All of the events identified by Beckett are present in Shattuck's more complete "Table"; but Beckett, with one exception—that arising from Marcel's listening to Vinteuil's Septet in *La Prisonnière* (*The Captive*)—identifies all of the major ones. See Beckett, *Proust;* and *Three Dialogues with Georges Duthuit*, 34, 36–37.

12. Proust, *Sodom and Gomorrah*, 212.
13. Proust, *Swann's Way*, 62.
14. Proust, *Time Regained*, 255–57, 259.
15. Proust, *Time Regained*, 262–63, 290.
16. Beckett, *Proust*, 75.
17. Proust, *Sodom and Gomorrah*, 215, 216.
18. Eliot, *Four Quartets*, 44 (*The Dry Salvages*, ll. 201–2).
19. Proust, *Swann's Way*, 220.
20. Proust, *Time Regained*, 263, 264.
21. Proust, *Swann's Way*, 253–57; *Within a Budding Grove*, 87–91.
22. Proust, *Within a Budding Grove*, 406.
23. Proust, *Swann's Way*, 253.
24. Proust, *Within a Budding Grove*, 406; *Swann's Way*, 438; *Time Regained*, 508. Throughout the novel Proust uses the term "mystery" in an ontological sense, along with phrases that evoke the mysteriousness of eternal reality.
25. Proust, *Within a Budding Grove*, 17.
26. Proust, *Time Regained*, 287.
27. Proust, *Swann's Way*, 61.
28. Proust, *Swann's Way*, 60.
29. Proust, *Swann's Way*, 60, 61, 251–52; *Within a Budding Grove*, 91.
30. Proust, *Time Regained*, 272; *The Captive; The Fugitive*, 347 (*The Captive*).
31. Proust, *Time Regained*, 255, 257, 265.
32. Proust, *Time Regained*, 257.
33. Proust, *Swann's Way*, 60.
34. Proust, *Time Regained*, 264–65.
35. Voegelin, "Eternal Being in Time," 329.
36. Beckett, *Proust*, 35, 69, 93.
37. White, *Marcel Proust*, 8; Bloom, *Western Canon*, 397.
38. Proust, *Time Regained*, 262, 264–65; *Sodom and Gomorrah*, 210, 228; *The Guermantes Way*, 540.
39. Proust, *Time Regained*, 351.
40. Proust, *Sodom and Gomorrah*, 212–13, 215, 228.
41. Proust, *Sodom and Gomorrah*, 216.
42. Quinones, *Mapping Literary Modernism*, 235.

43. Proust, *Time Regained*, 274.
44. Shattuck, *Proust's Way*, 169 (emphasis added).
45. Shattuck, *Proust's Way*, 169.
46. Proust, *Time Regained*, 273, 274.
47. Proust, *Swann's Way*, 251–52.
48. Proust, *The Captive*; *The Fugitive*, 350 (*The Captive*; emphasis added).
49. Proust, *The Guermantes Way*, 155; *Time Regained*, 301.
50. On Proust's parents, see Tadié, *Marcel Proust*, 13–15, 27–31, 37; and White, *Marcel Proust*, 8–14. White states that Adriene Proust was "originally intended for the priesthood" (14); Tadié, whose biography is regarded as the definitive study to date, that he attended "a small seminary" (27).
51. Bucknall, *Religion of Art in Proust*, 18.
52. Gamble, "From *Belle Epoque* to First World War, 20. When the Dreyfus Affair erupted in 1896 and Proust quickly became one of the first Dreyfusards, he took pains to point out his mother's race and faith (March, *Two Worlds of Marcel Proust*, 24); while in 1904 Proust took a "strong public stance" against the anti-clerical act of legislation proposing the formal separation of Church and State, publishing an eloquent article titled "Las Mort des Cathédrales" (Gamble, "From *Belle Epoque* to First World War," 22).
53. Bucknall, *Religion of Art in Proust*, 147.
54. See Zaehner, *Mysticism Sacred and Profane*, 50–61; Bloom, *Western Canon*, 412, where Bloom expresses his agreement with Shattuck; and Bucknall, *Religion of Art in Proust*, 174–98. Shattuck remarks that Proust "had studied Plato and was familiar with this nexus of ideas"; Shattuck, *Proust's Way*, 114.
55. For the influence of Schopenhauer on Proust, see Bucknall, *Religion of Art in Proust*, 13–19, 125–26; on Proust's agreement with Schopenhauer's views but also resistance to German Romanticism, see Jordan, "The Unconscious," 101–2; March, *Two Worlds of Marcel Proust*, 246–47; and Tadié, *Marcel Proust*, 204.
56. Olds, "Literary Symbolism," 156.
57. Olds, "Literary Symbolism," 156.
58. Main, "Baudelaire and Proust," 453.
59. Tadié, *Marcel Proust*, 249–51, 271.
60. Wilson, *Axel's Castle*, 132.
61. Bucknall, *Religion of Art in Proust*, 187.
62. Quoted in Tadié, *Marcel Proust*, 249.
63. Bucknall, *Religion of Art in Proust*, 67.
64. By contrast, Mallarmé's intent, in the words of Paul Valéry, eventually "had reached a point nothing short of deifying the written word." Valéry, "Letter about Mallarmé" (1927), 249.
65. Bucknall, *Religion of Art in Proust*, 18, 122. Leon Chai argues much the same point in *Aestheticism: The Religion of Art in Post-Romantic Literature*.
66. Shattuck, *Proust's Way*, 138, 159–60.

67. Shattuck, *Proust's Way*, 159–60.
68. Wilson, *Axel's Castle*, 145.
69. See Buber, *I and Thou*, 53–68.
70. Buber, *I and Thou*, 123. Love is the unequivocal basis of all revelation of divine transcendence as personal. Even Dickinson's experiences of transcendence as an Abandoner are premised on experiences of loving and being loved by eternal reality; only a Lover can Abandon.
71. Proust, *The Captive*; *The Fugitive*, 388 (*The Captive*; emphasis added).
72. This does not mean that there is no moral effect of the novel on the reader, much less that it subverts a conscientious concern with goodness and promotes "immorality." On the contrary, the unchanging viewpoint of the Narrator is that it is always wrong to be indifferent to suffering, to inflict cruelty, and to be indifferent to truth in the full range of its external and internal complexities and nuances. What might be called the Narrator's "non-morality" consists partly in his avoidance of unreflective, prevalent social habits of ethical bias; but preeminently it is the manifestation of Proust's artistic commitment to accurately *showing*, without intrusive authorial moral sermonizing, how people really are. In this uncensored showing, petty cruelties, self-delusions, close-mindedness, snobbery, willed blindness to suffering, degrading behaviors, and other human foibles and frailties are portrayed with a specificity and unflinching clarity unparalleled in literature. It is in this respect, to be carefully distinguished from the Narrator's "absence of moral sense" regarding justice and responsibility, that Proust shows himself to be a "merciless moralist" and his novel rightly viewed as a masterpiece of moral literature. Wilson, *Axel's Castle*, 162.
73. See Buber, *I and Thou*, 66–67, 123–33; and Levinas, "God and Philosophy," 139–41.
74. Levinas, *Humanism of the Other*, 29–44; "Peace and Proximity," 167–69; and "The Rights of Man and the Rights of the Other," 116–25.
75. How, it may be asked, is this description of *Four Quartets* as a "journey of self-discovery" to be squared with Eliot's famous statement in "Tradition and the Individual Talent" (1917) that the "progress of an artist is a continual self-sacrifice, a continual extinction of personality," and that "the more perfect the artist, the more completely separate in him will be the man who suffers and the mind which creates"? The answer lies in understanding what Eliot means by "impersonality" in artistic creation. The artwork is not understood by Eliot to be divorced from personal experience. On the contrary, as he states in his essay "Shakespeare and the Stoicism of Seneca" (1927), "What every poet starts from is his own emotions [and his struggle is] to transform his personal and private agonies into. . . something universal and impersonal." This impersonality, as he stated in 1940 in a lecture on Yeats, "is that of the poet who, out of intense and personal experience, is able to express a general truth; *retaining all the particularity of his experience*, to make of it a general symbol." Eliot, "Tradition and the

Individual Talent," 7–8; "Shakespeare and the Stoicism of Seneca," 117; and "Yeats," 299 (emphasis added). For an excellent discussion of Eliot's ideas about "impersonality" in art (from which I have received guidance), see Brooker, *T. S. Eliot's Dialectical Imagination*, 82–89.

Chapter Three | Unsought Revelations of the Eternal

1. Such commonalities as exist are not due to any mutual influence. Eliot had an early, but not sustained, interest in Proust's novel. He expressed admiration in 1922 for C. K. Scott Moncrieff's English translation of that year of *Swann's Way*, and soon contacted Proust and his publisher Gallimard requesting an excerpt from the next volume for the first issue of Eliot's new journal *The Criterion*, scheduled for October. Proust was made aware of Eliot's request but nothing came of it. The correspondence between Eliot and Proust has not survived. Carter, *Marcel Proust*, 789, 917. (In 1924, a year and a half after Proust's death, *The Criterion* published a translated excerpt from Proust's novel titled "The Death of Albertine.") In 1949, Eliot remarked in a letter to William Matchett that he was "almost completely ignorant" of Proust's work aside from a few essays and "of course" having "dipped into his first volume." Eliot, *The Poems,* vol. 1, 428. There is no evidence that Proust ever read Eliot's poetry.

2. The work has been described as Eliot's "spiritual autobiography" in the analysis of numerous authors; see, for example, Oser, "Coming to Terms with *Four Quartets*," 216. The philosopher Eric Voegelin also uses the phrase in his "Notes on T. S. Eliot's *Four Quartets*" (1944), 34.

3. Oser, "Coming to Terms with *Four Quartets*," 217.

4. Gardner, *Composition of* Four Quartets, 16.

5. Eliot quoted in Hall, "Interview: T. S. Eliot," 268.

6. Eliot, "Genesis of *Four Quartets*," 23; Gardner, *Composition of* Four Quartets, 18.

7. On the early, decisive impact of the French Symbolists on Eliot's poetic style, especially of the "minor" Symbolist Jules Laforgue, see Crawford, *Young Eliot*, 107–10, 122–27.

8. For example, David Perkins declares that at its best *Four Quartets* "is more honest, more intelligent, more concerned with the essential in human experience, or more of all these in combination, than any other modern English or American poem." Perkins, *History of Modern Poetry*, vol. 2, *Modernism and After*, 25.

9. Eliot, *Four Quartets*, 19. The parenthetical reference here indicates that the phrase is from section 5 of *Burnt Norton*, lines 155–56. Hereafter references to each of the four poems, its sections, and pertinent line numbers will be indicated in the same manner using the following abbreviations: *BN* for *Burnt Norton*; *EC* for *East Coker*; *DS* for *The Dry Salvages*; and *LG* for *Little Gidding*. All further quotes will be from this edition (see Bibliography); page numbers will not be referenced.

10. Kramer, *Redeeming Time*, 235. On Eliot's incorporation of yogic teachings into his Christian perspective as expressed in the third section of *The Dry Salvages*, see ibid., 116–23, and Gardner, *Composition of* Four Quartets, 56–57.

11. On "interspiritual" elements in *Four Quartets*, see Kramer, *Redeeming Time*, esp. 40–42, 90–91, 116–23, 181–82, and the longer notes on 245–56. As a doctoral student at Harvard, Eliot spent two years studying, in the original Sanskrit, Indic traditions and religious writings including the *Bhagavad-Gita* and the *Upanishads*, and an overlapping year in the study of Buddhist scriptures in their original Pali. In 1913/14 he attended another Harvard course on "Schools of Religious and Philosophical Thought in Japan." "No other Western poet of his era," writes Eliot biographer Robert Crawford, "was more profoundly schooled in traditional Indic and Japanese thought." Crawford, *Young Eliot*, 176; see 168–76.

12. Eliot, "Preface" in *Thoughts for Meditation*, 13.

13. Eliot, "Christianity and Communism" (1932), 427–28. Eliot's more discerning biographers and critics have argued the case that Eliot was deeply religious from the beginning—*The Waste Land*, for example, being not the credo of a committed atheist, but the *cri de coeur* of a religious seeker. See Brooker, *T. S. Eliot's Dialectical Imagination*, 118–19.

14. On Eliot's study of literature, religion, philosophy, anthropology, sociology, and psychology, see Crawford, *Young Eliot*, 106–85, *passim*. Crawford notes, "Reading Bergson in French, then in English, he also read Patanjali in the original Pali, the *Upanishads* in Sanskrit, Heraclitus in Greek, Kant in German, Dante in Italian—and, as for Spinoza, he read that great Jewish philosopher in elegant seventeenth-century Latin." (172). On Eliot's early interest and reading in mysticism, see 178–79, 221.

15. Eliot prefaced *Burnt Norton* with two epigraphs drawn from the aphorisms of the pre-Socratic philosopher Heraclitus (quoted in the original Greek), the second of which translates, "The way up and down is one and the same," foreshadowing the poem's presentation of the identical goals and outcomes of the two mystical paths.

16. Kramer, *Redeeming Time*, 20.

17. Gardner, *Art of T. S. Eliot*, 105.

18. This summary is indebted to the descriptions in both Brooker, "From *The Waste Land* to *Four Quartets*," 95–96, and Kramer, *Redeeming Time*, 20.

19. Perkins, *History of Modern Poetry*, vol. 1, *From the 1890s to the High Modernist Mode*, 504.

20. Kenner, *Invisible Poet*, 261.

21. Eliot famously wrote in "Tradition and the Individual Talent," "Poetry is not a turning loose of emotion . . . not the expression of personality, but an escape from personality. . . . The emotion of art is impersonal" (10–11). Placing Eliot's poetry in its context of Modernism, Jason Harding writes: "Analogous to

the techniques of modern art, Eliot's poetic theory proposes an objectification of emotion through a dynamic transformation of personal feelings onto the plane of impersonal structural relations." Harding, "Unraveling Eliot," 4.

22. Donoghue, "On 'Burnt Norton,'" 7.

23. Blamires, *Word Unheard*, 13–14.

24. Blamires, *Word Unheard*, 13. The question of whether the lotos experience is a "hallucination," sometimes raised by critics, is unanswerable; what matters is that the poet presents the experience as a vision of timelessness and enlightenment. See Kramer, *Redeeming Time*, 105.

25. Kenner, *Invisible Poet*, 255.

26. Brooker, *T. S. Eliot's Dialectical Imagination*, 155.

27. Donoghue, "On 'Burnt Norton,'" 7.

28. Brooker, *T. S. Eliot's Dialectical Imagination*, 158.

29. Ellis, "*Four Quartets*," 106.

30. Every reader of *Four Quartets*, as Jewel Spears Brooker remarks, being "compounded of flesh and spirit, mind and matter, provides [an] example of the incarnational principle." The principle thus functions as the key symbol or pattern in the *Quartets*, even as the word points to "the supreme example [of] the meeting of time and eternity, becoming and being, in the Incarnation of Christ." Brooker, "From *The Waste Land* to *Four Quartets*," 105. It is important also to recognize the figure of Krishna, in *The Dry Salvages*, as a "contrapuntal" religious paradigm of Incarnation. Kramer, *Redeeming Time*, 130. Finally, the incarnational principle as presented in *Four Quartets* is, as Elizabeth Drew points out, "active throughout the universe," since everything in the "turning world" instantiates the paradox of the union of time and timelessness: "The shaft of sunlight, the winter lightning, the waterfall, the scent of the wild thyme, the music, are all incarnations; that is, they are all an invisible energy manifesting itself in the phenomena of sense." Drew, *T. S. Eliot*, 187. The incarnational principle, however, is *realized* in human consciousness, where a presence of timeless reality aware of itself as such (to whatever degree this awareness is attended to and understood) co-constitutes a form of created being: "To be conscious is not to be in time" (*BN*, II.85).

31. See Julian of Norwich, *Showings*, 224–25 (Long Text, Chapter 27).

32. Eliot's concluding lines consciously echo Dante's vision, in *Paradiso*, Cantos 31 and 33, of the celestial rose. See Dante, *Paradiso*, 272, 278, 295 (Canto 31, lines 4–21, 118–32; Canto 33, lines 82–93).

33. Donoghue, "On 'Burnt Norton,'" 7; Brooker, *T. S. Eliot's Dialectical Imagination*, 159.

34. Proust, *Time Regained*, 256, 273, 274 (emphasis added).

35. Proust, *Sodom and Gomorrah*, 210–15; *Time Regained*, 253–56, 266–67.

36. Proust, *Swann's Way*, 253–54.

37. *Swann's Way*, 253.

38. *Swann's Way*, 251–52; *Within a Budding Grove*, 91; *Time Regained*, 272; *The Captive; The Fugitive*, 347 (*The Captive*). The exception is the *impression* involving the "sudden revelation" to Marcel, in the seaside hotel at Balbec a year after his grandmother's death, that she is truly dead, and that he has "lost her forever," which elicits in him not a joy but a feeling involving a "painful synthesis of survival and annihilation." Proust, *Sodom and Gomorrah*, 212–13, 215, 228.

39. Proust, *Swann's Way*, 60.

40. Kramer, *Redeeming Time*, 51, 88.

41. Proust, *Time Regained*, 301.

42. Proust, *The Captive; The Fugitive*, 347 (*The Captive*) (emphasis added).

43. Proust, *Time Regained*, 262.

44. Eliot in an interview with Françoise de Castro; quoted and translated from the French by Donald Childs in "Risking Enchantment," 107.

45. Proust, *Time Regained*, 298, 507.

46. Dionysius contrasts the two ways in his short treatise, *The Mystical Theology*; see Pseudo-Dionysius, *Mystical Theology*, 135–41.

47. Johnston, *Inner Eye of Love*, 18. Eastern mystical traditions, in their different conceptual terms, generally agree. Especially in Buddhism, the ground of reality (and thus the essential being of everything existing, including persons) is often symbolized by such terms as "nothingness," "non-being," and "emptiness." See ibid., 106–14.

48. Blamires, *Word Unheard*, 31.

49. Proust, *The Guermantes Way*, 155; *Time Regained*, 301.

50. Proust, *The Captive*; *The Fugitive*, 347 (*The Captive*); *Time Regained*, 264–65.

51. Perkins, *History of Modern Poetry*, vol. 2, *Modernism and After*, 14.

52. Eliot, "Preface to the 1928 edition of *The Sacred Wood*," 414.

53. Eliot, "Poetry and Drama," 94.

Chapter Four | History and Transcendence in Ezra Pound's *Cantos* and T. S. Eliot's *Four Quartets*

1. "Roughly from 1912 to 1925, Pound and Eliot were a front, and Eliot's impact was augmented by this alliance. Their critical statements spread the demand that poetry should 'modernize' its style, and their own poetry exemplified what was meant." Perkins, *History of Modern Poetry*, vol. 2, *Modernism and After*, 5. On Pound, Eliot, and Williams as the three most influential English-language poets of the twentieth century and their lifelong relationships with and attitudes towards each other, see Simpson, *Three on the Tower*.

2. In Western culture, beginning in the eighteenth century, both liberal and utopian secular progressivism became central to philosophical, political, and educational discourse, propelled by thinkers of the Enlightenment (and furthered by some Romantic authors). Eighteenth- and nineteenth-century thinkers

especially important to the articulation of secular progressivist outlooks include Kant, Condorcet, Comte, Marx, and John Stuart Mill. Major critics of secular progressivism's ideas of the inevitability of progress and the perfectibility of society include, in the nineteenth century, Tocqueville, Kierkegaard, Schopenhauer, and Nietzsche, and in the twentieth century, Weber, Solzhenitsyn, and Voegelin. For an overview of the development of the idea of progress from classical times to the twentieth century, see Nisbet, *History of the Idea of Progress*. A classic work on theologies and philosophies of history from which secular progressivist ideas emerged is Löwith, *Meaning in History*. For a brief summary of progressivism in relation to educational reform, see Tröhler, "Progressivism."

3. See Pound's eighteen-poem sequence "Hugh Selwyn Mauberley" (1920), section V, in which his disdain for the crassness and materialism of the modern age reaches a crescendo of disgust at the human waste of the First World War: "There died a myriad, / And of the best, among them, / For an old bitch gone in the teeth, / For a botched civilization." Pound, *Personae*, 191.

4. Pound, "Patria Mia" (1913), in *Selected Prose,* 125.

5. Pound quoted in Kearns, *Guide to Ezra Pound's "Selected Cantos"*, 23.

6. Kenner, *Pound Era*, 408.

7. Read, "Pound, Joyce, and Flaubert," 127.

8. Hyde, *The Gift*, 219. "[T]he images of the gods," Pound writes, ". . . move the soul to contemplation and preserve the tradition of the undivided light." Pound, "A Visiting Card" (1942), in Pound, *Selected Prose*, 307.

9. Pound, *The Cantos*, canto 3, page 11. All further references accompanying quotations will be to canto and page number(s) (e.g., 3/11) in this edition.

10. The "Oirishman" is the Irish theologian and Neoplatonist philosopher John Scotus Eriugena (810–877)—translator into Latin of the writings of Pseudo-Dionysius—whom Pound is quoting: "Omnia quae sunt, lumina sunt" (all things that are, are lights).

11. Kenner, *Pound Era*, 30: "To see gods was a way to see nature, not to use an antique way of talking."

12. Pound, *Guide to Kulchur*, 47, 126.

13. Davenport, "Persephone's Ezra," 151.

14. Kenner, *Pound Era*, 434.

15. Hall, "Interview: Ezra Pound," 333.

16. Clark Emery, *Ideas into Action: A Study of Pound's Cantos*, quoted in Davie, *Ezra Pound*, 216.

17. Kearns, *Guide to Ezra Pound's "Selected Cantos,"* 9.

18. Pound quoted in Hyde, *The Gift*, 216, 264 (emphasis added).

19. Pound quoted in Hyde, *The Gift*, 264.

20. Pearlman, *Barb of Time*, 22.

21. William Carlos Williams quoted in Parkinson, "Pound and Williams," 164.

22. A. David Moody writes that, "on the evidence of the work itself," the themes of the four poems of the *Quartets* can justifiably be associated with what Eliot once described as the four starting points of all poetry: "the emotions experienced by human beings in their relations to themselves, to each other, to divine beings, and to the world about them." Eliot, "From Poe to Valéry," 38. See Moody, *Thomas Stearns Eliot: Poet*, 259.

23. These associations, sometimes questioned by critics, were confirmed by Eliot himself. See Gardner, *Composition of* Four Quartets, 18: ". . . Eliot stated more than once [that] the notion of four poems based on the symbolism of the four elements and the four seasons . . . was a notion that came to him during the writing of *East Coker*. Professor Kristian Smidt reports that in 1948 Eliot told him that it was 'during the writing of *East Coker* that the whole sequence began to emerge, with the symbolism of the four seasons and the four elements. *Burnt Norton* then had to stand for spring in the sequence, though its imagery was perhaps more summery.'"

24. Tracy, "T. S. Eliot as Religious Thinker," 280.

25. Voegelin, *Ecumenic Age*, 47.

26. For an exposition of the presentation of history in *Four Quartets* using Eric Voegelin's explanatory philosophy of history, see Hughes, *More Beautiful Question*, chap. 5 "A Pattern of Timeless Moments: T. S. Eliot's *Four Quartets*" (88–106).

27. Gardner, *Art of T. S. Eliot*, 62.

28. Tracy, "T. S. Eliot as Religious Thinker," 272.

29. Blamires, *Word Unheard*, 35; Kenner, *Invisible Poet*, 262.

30. Dante, *Paradiso*, canto 31, lines 4–21, 118–32; canto 33, lines 82–93. See Dante, *Paradiso*, 272, 278, 295.

31. See Moody, *Thomas Stearns Eliot*, 191, 365n14.

32. Gardner, *Art of T. S. Eliot*, 105.

33. Quoted in Moody, *Thomas Stearns Eliot*, 204. Eliot was raised in a St. Louis Unitarian family of significant social standing, whose religiosity Eliot came to find pallid and insufficiently realistic. The New England Unitarianism that Eliot's notable grandfather (the Reverend William Greenleaf Eliot, graduate of Harvard and founder of Washington University) had brought to St. Louis had been shaped in reaction against Calvinist principles and teachings, including its emphasis on the doctrine of original sin. Eliot early came to feel that Unitarianism's "liberal optimism was shallow by comparison with the pessimistic insight of Christianity into the vanity of human life and the corruption of the heart" (Perkins, *History of Modern Poetry*, Vol. 2, *Modernism and After*, 15), and the poetry of both his adult "atheist" years and his later life of Christian belief is permeated with a sense of human sinfulness. The doctrine of original sin, Kevin Dettmar writes, "seems to have comprised a bedrock component" of Eliot's existence. Dettmar, "'Occupation for the Saint'," 371. On Eliot's Unitarian

upbringing and his response to it, see Crawford, *Young Eliot*, 38–41, 67–68, 73, 96.

34. Kearns, *Guide to Ezra Pound's "Selected Cantos,"* 64.

35. As Jewel Spears Brooker notes, *Four Quartets* shows that any attempt at theodicy "collapses in the face of history itself, which compels the recognition that good and evil . . . are woven into the 'shirt of flame / Which human power cannot remove' (*LG* IV.10–11)." Brooker, *T. S. Eliot's Dialectical Imagination*, 181.

36. The narrator of Beckett's novel *The Unnamable* exclaims, "[T]he question may be asked . . . why time doesn't pass, doesn't pass, from you, why it piles up all about you, instant on instant, on all sides, deeper and deeper, thicker and thicker, your time, other's time, the time of the ancient dead and the dead yet unborn, why it buries you grain by grain . . . no hope of anything, no knowledge of anything, no history and no prospects, buried under the seconds . . ." Beckett, *The Unnamable*, in *Molloy, Malone Dies, The Unnamable*, 446–47.

Chapter Five | Mystic Without Faith

1. Pilling, *Samuel Beckett*, 1.

2. Robinson, *Long Sonata of the Dead*, 28. The quote is from Thomas à Kempis, *The Imitation of Christ*, bk. 4, chap. 31. See also Jacobsen and Mueller, *Testament of Samuel Beckett*, 48–49: "The controlling drive of Beckett's [work], below all its devices, is the frantic motion of the mystic deprived of his vision. . . . The immemorial voice of the most austere of the mystics, asserting that the possession of anything less than God is the possession of dung, speaks through his [works]."

3. Beckett, *Waiting for Godot*, 84: "ESTRAGON: I can't go on like this. VLADIMIR: That's what you think. . . . ESTRAGON: And if [Godot] comes? VLADIMIR: We'll be saved."

4. Rabaté, *Think, Pig!*, 32.

5. Quoted in Fletcher, *About Beckett*, 71 (emphasis added).

6. Van Hulle and Nixon, *Samuel Beckett's Library*, 128–69. On Beckett's important interest in Geulincx, see Knowlson, *Damned to Fame*, 206–07; and Kenner, *Samuel Beckett*, 83–91. Beckett's fluency in five languages, including French, German, and Latin, allowed him to read almost all of these authors in the original.

7. "Whoroscope," written and published in 1930 when Beckett was twenty-four, "has almost as many footnotes as it has lines, [and] is impenetrable without the aid of Adrien Baillet's 1691 *Life of Descartes*," which Beckett was reading at the time. Robinson, *Long Sonata of the Dead*, 55. See Knowlson, *Damned to Fame*, 116–17.

8. Pilling, *Samuel Beckett*, 112–16.

9. Pilling, *Samuel Beckett*, 114.

10. Beckett's formulation at the conclusion of his novel *The Unnamable* has become famous: ". . . you must go on, I can't go on, I'll go on." Beckett, *The Unnamable*, in *Molloy, Malone Dies, The Unnamable*, 476.

11. Beckett, *The Unnamable*, in *Molloy, Malone Dies, The Unnamable*, 423.

12. Beckett, *Worstward Ho*, 7.

13. Toscan and MacGowran, "MacGowran on Beckett: Interview by Richard Toscan," 215.

14. Reid, *All I Can Manage, More Than I Could*, 11.

15. "'Flawless', 'economical', 'haunting' and 'harrowing' were some of the laudatory epithets heaped on the production by critics . . ." when *Krapp's Last Tape* was first produced at the Royal Court Theatre in London in 1958. Fletcher, *Samuel Beckett*, 47–48.

16. Beckett's short story "First Love," written in 1945 (French) and 1946 (English), first published in French in 1970 and in English in 1973, at times, but very mutedly, associates love with a sense of regret: "What goes by the name of love is banishment, with now and then a postcard from the homeland. . . ." Beckett, "First Love," 31. This brief story of the temporary cohabitation of the unnamed protagonist with a prostitute who finds him on a park bench, on which he has taken to sleeping after the death of his father, until he flees her and their newborn child, has sentences suggesting sorrow over beauty and love that tonally prefigure aspects of *Krapp's Last Tape;* but as a whole it exemplifies Beckett's more typical portrayal of life in its mixture of frustration, alarm, anger, and mordant slapstick.

17. "Wearish" is likely an intentional echo of the description of Democritus in Robert Burton's *The Anatomy of Melancholy* (1621), a book Beckett knew well (see van Hulle and Nixon, *Samuel Beckett's Library*, 119–20): "Democritus . . . was a little wearish old man, very melancholy by nature, averse from company in his latter days, and very much given to solitariness . . ." Burton, *Anatomy of Melancholy*, 16.

18. Beckett, *Krapp's Last Tape, and Other Dramatic Pieces*, 10–13.

19. Beckett, *Krapp's Last Tape*, 13.

20. Beckett, *Krapp's Last Tape*, 15–17.

21. Beckett, *Krapp's Last Tape*, 17–20.

22. Beckett, *Krapp's Last Tape*, 21.

23. There is a poem by John Donne (1572–1631) titled "Farewell to Love," whose mood echoes that of Krapp's renunciation—a poem that Beckett would likely have known. On Beckett's erudition and how it is reflected in his works, see van Hulle and Nixon, *Samuel Beckett's Library*.

24. Beckett, *Krapp's Last Tape*, 21–23.

25. Beckett, *Krapp's Last Tape*, 23–27.

26. Beckett, *Krapp's Last Tape*, 27–28.

27. Fletcher, *About Beckett*, 179, 190.

28. Sack, *Samuel Beckett's* Krapp's Last Tape, 3.

29. Cohn, "Beckett Directs," 303; Dougald McMillan and Martha Fehsenfeld, *Beckett in the Theatre*, 261.

30. In Beckett's original direction of this passage of the play, in 1969, he instructed the actor Martin Held to let his head, arm, and body slowly sink to a tender embrace of the machine until he was holding it "erotically." Cohn, "Beckett Directs," 303.

31. Intimately familiar with Proust's novel, Beckett was aware of displaying in his play "the Proustian past of an individual in time" and its "ever-changing identity of the Self" (Robinson, *Long Sonata of the Dead*, 283, 284). His first major prose publication was an extended essay on Proust, written in 1930 (at age twenty-four) and published in 1931; see Beckett, *Proust;* and *Three Dialogues with Georges Duthuit*. On the genesis and writing of the essay, see Knowlson, *Damned to Fame*, 118–22.

32. McMillan and Fehsenfeld, *Beckett in the Theatre*, 298.

33. Knowlson, *Damned to Fame*, 397.

34. Beckett, *Krapp's Last Tape*, 24 (emphasis added).

35. Beckett, *Krapp's Last Tape*, 26.

36. Daniel Sack notes how Krapp's final "cascade of reminiscence" about childhood is linked by the words it dies into to the punt scene ("Lie down across her"), thus merging love of and loss of childhood happiness with love and loss in the realm of romantic communion. Sack, *Samuel Beckett's* Krapp's Last Tape, 19.

37. Dougald McMillan and Martha Fehsenfeld, studying the holographs of the two initial handwritten drafts and four subsequent typed revisions of the play, find "germs" of "Manichean organisation and images" in the first draft, and state that "[i]n the second draft and the four typescripts Beckett devoted much of his attention to expanding and refining the Manichean elements inherent in the first draft" (*Beckett in the Theatre*, 242, 244). James Knowlson asserts, however, that it was only "later"—specifically, in preparing to direct the 1969 German production of the play—that Beckett described the play's "carefully structured pattern of images of black and white, sense and spirit" in terms of a "Manichean dualism" (*Damned to Fame*, 399); and Daniel Sack avers that "Beckett would emphasize that this [Manichean] reading came to him only with the distance of years, that this had not been a conscious principle at the time of writing and does not offer some consummate meaning to the play" (*Samuel Beckett's* Krapp's Last Tape, 32). For details on Beckett's use of Manichaean symbols and imagery, see McMillan and Fehsenfeld, *Beckett in the Theatre*, 243–51, 259, 261, 283.

38. Krapp's "transgression" of Manichaean principles were developed to a highly complex degree in Beckett's construction and interpretation of the play's symbols. See McMillan and Fehsenfeld, *Beckett in the Theatre*, 244–46.

39. McMillan and Fehsenfeld, quoting from Beckett's *Director's Notebook* for the 1969 production, *Beckett in the Theatre*, 261.

40. Beckett: "[N]ote that if the giving of the black ball to the white dog represents the sacrifice of sense to spirit the form here too is that of a mingling." From Beckett's 1969 *Director's Notebook*, quoted in McMillan and Fehsenfeld, *Beckett in the Theatre*, 259.

41. Beckett, *Letters,* Vol. 3, *1957–1965*, 279: Letter of January 4, 1960, to Alan Schneider.

42. Beckett, *Krapp's Last Tape*, 15, 17.

43. Beckett in his 1969 *Director's Notebook*, quoted in McMillan and Fehsenfeld, *Beckett in the Theatre*, 259.

44. Beckett, *Krapp's Last Tape*, 22.

45. Beckett, *Krapp's Last Tape*, 19.

46. McMillan and Fehsenfeld, *Beckett in the Theater*, 248.

47. Cohn, "Beckett Directs," 306; McMillan and Fehsenfeld, *Beckett in the Theatre*, 310.

48. Beckett, *Krapp's Last Tape*, 28.

49. Knowlson, *Damned to Fame*, 474.

50. On this see the comments of Martin Held, who played Krapp in the 1969 Berlin production that Beckett directed, quoted in Fletcher, *About Beckett*, 179.

51. Robinson, *Long Sonata of the Dead*, 285.

52. Beckett, *Letters,* Vol. 3, *1957–1965*, 155: Letter of June 28, 1958, to Marc Wilkinson.

53. Fletcher and Spurling, *Beckett: A Study of His Plays*, 88, 89.

54. Beckett, *Letters of Samuel Beckett,* Vol. 3, *1957–1965*, 123, 127: Letters of April 1, 1958, and of April 10, 1958, to Barney Rosset.

55. French actor Jean Martin quoted in McMillan and Fehsenfeld, *Beckett in the Theatre*, 257; and Fletcher, *About Beckett*, 189. Daniel Sack begins his study *Samuel Beckett's* Krapp's Last Tape by noting that it is Beckett's "most personal and most autobiographical creation" (2). For a general account of the autobiographical elements in the play, see Knowlson, *Damned to Fame*, 319, 346–47, 397–99.

56. See Knowlson, *Damned to Fame*, 319, for parallels between the two "visions."

57. Knowlson, *Damned to Fame*, 346–47.

58. Knowlson, *Damned to Fame*, 397–98.

59. Knowlson, *Damned to Fame*, 91.

60. Unpublished letter of May 21, 1955, to Susan Manning, quoted in Knowlson, *Damned to Fame*, 399.

61. Knowlson, *Damned to Fame*, 397.

62. Fletcher, *About Beckett*, 74.

63. From an interview with Martin Held, conducted by Ronald Hayman, translated by Helen Watanabe, revised by James Knowlson, in Knowlson and Knowlson, *Beckett Remembering, Remembering Beckett*, 186; Cronin, *Samuel Beckett*, 549.

64. Atik, *How It Was*, 22, 33. Less consistently admiring portrayals of Beckett's character can of course also be found. For example, see the sometimes-unflattering portrait in Beckett biographer Deirdre Bair's memoir of working with him in the process of writing his biography. Bair, *Parisian Lives*.

65. Robinson, *Long Sonata of the Dead*, 286.

66. See McMillan and Fehsenfeld, *Beckett in the Theatre*, 257; and Fletcher, *About Beckett*, 179, 189.

Chapter Six | Bob Dylan's Evocations of Mystery

1. "I wanted to do something that stood alongside Rembrandt's paintings," Dylan said in a 2004 interview. Cott, *Bob Dylan: Essential Interviews*, 430.

2. Quoted in Boucher, *Dylan & Cohen*, 6. See, for example, Riley, *Hard Rain*, 133.

3. Stephen Webb indicates a further parallel between Picasso and Dylan by noting how in the recordings of many of his most accomplished songs, Dylan's singing "plays with time" in a manner analogous to Picasso's "reconfiguring [of] space." In such recordings Dylan uses his voice to occupy "multiple levels of temporal progression simultaneously," an effect accomplished in part (I would suggest) through Dylan's singing variously all around (and on) the beat while elongating and abbreviating syllables and alternating line entrances and word emphases in surprising ways—always, though, in service of the emotional meanings of the lyrics. Webb, *Dylan Redeemed*, 13–14.

4. Dates for songs refer to composition and/or recording, not necessarily to dates of official album release. Dates for albums refer to years of official release.

5. See Kant, *Critique of Judgement*, 168.

6. Lonergan, "Art," 216.

7. Lonergan, "Art," 221.

8. As to recordings: as early as 1959/60, while still in Minneapolis playing folk music in the bohemian area of the city known as Dinkytown, Dylan was listening to what Greil Marcus has called the "founding document of the American folk revival," Harry Smith's six-album *Anthology of American Folk Music* (1952). Marcus, *Invisible Republic*, 87; Webb, *Redeeming Dylan*, 116. The *Anthology*, a diverse compendium of eighty-four songs recorded mostly in rural areas in the 1920s and 1930s, became the "bible" of the Greenwich Village folk scene, as singer and guitarist Dave Van Ronk recalled, "We all knew every word of every song on it, including the ones we hated" (quoted in Marcus, *Invisible Republic*, 88). With his preternatural ability to adopt "folk" music as his own, the

more oddly authentic the better, Dylan had found here a treasure of forgotten, haunting styles; eerie voices; and weirdly mythical stories, which had an obvious impact on his early compositional imagination.

9. For the respective influences of Guthrie and Johnson on Dylan, see Dylan, *Chronicles*, vol. 1, 243–48, 280–88.

10. See Hajdu, *Positively 4th Street*, 10; Wilentz, *Bob Dylan in America*, 334; and Marqusee, *Chimes of Freedom*, 151. For the impact of the song "Pirate Jenny" on Dylan's songwriting, see Dylan, *Chronicles*, vol. 1, 272–76; Wilentz, *Bob Dylan in America*, 42–43; and Heylin, *Revolution in the Air*, 151–54.

11. Marqusee, *Chimes of Freedom*, 151.

12. Ricks, *Dylan's Visions of Sin*, 19.

13. Dylan wrote of his early immersion in the worlds of folk songs and ballads: "I loved all these ballads right away. . . . I was beginning to feel like a character from within these songs, even beginning to think like one. . . . I could rattle off all these songs . . . as if all the wise and poetic words were mine and mine alone." Dylan, *Chronicles*, vol. 1, 240.

14. This gift is especially apparent in the young Dylan's recordings of the traditionals "No More Auction Block" (recorded live in 1962) and "Moonshiner" (recorded 1963), both released on *The Bootleg Series, Volumes 1–3 (Rare & Unreleased), 1961–1991.*

15. Riley, *Hard Rain*, 31.

16. Marcus, *Bob Dylan by Greil Marcus*, 124, 144, 366.

17. Wilentz, *Bob Dylan in America*, 12.

18. Lonergan, "Art," 220.

19. The literary and cultural critic George Steiner states: "In ways so obvious as to make any statement a tired cliché, yet of an undefinable and tremendous nature, music puts our being as men and women in touch with that which transcends the sayable, which outstrips the analysable. Music is plainly uncircumscribed by the world as the latter is an object of scientific determination and practical harnessing. The meanings of the meaning of music transcend." Steiner, *Real Presences*, 218.

20. Lonergan, "Art," 217–19, 229.

21. All quoted lyrics are as sung on cited recordings, not as printed in the sometimes-misleading versions in Dylan, *Lyrics, 1961–2012.* More dependable transcriptions, including alternate recorded and sung versions, are in the deluxe Dylan, *The Lyrics. Since 1962.*

22. "I don't know about other people's sympathy," Dylan said in 1966, "but my sympathy runs to the lame and crippled and beautiful things." Cott, *Bob Dylan: Essential Interviews*, 106.

23. Tarkovsky, *Sculpting in Time*, 239.

24. Hughes, *Invisible Now*, 139. See Marcus, *Bob Dylan by Greil Marcus*, 49; and Heylin, *Revolution in the Air*, 294.

25. Typical of many of his comments on human sinfulness, in a 1986 interview Dylan told Bill Flanagan, "Most people walking around have this strange conception that they're born good, that they're really good people—but the *world* has just made a mess out of their lives. I have another point of view." Quoted in Webb, *Redeeming Dylan*, 92. For appearances of the term *sin* in Dylan lyrics, and detailed accounts of some treatments of the seven deadly sins in his songs, see Ricks, *Dylan's Visions of Sin*, 2–5, 51–218. "Dylan's is an art in which sins are laid bare. . . ." (2).

26. Cott, *Bob Dylan: Essential Interviews*, 119. For a concise summary of the influence of the Bible on Dylan's lyrics and work, see Gray, *Song & Dance Man III*, 392–93. Gray's long, scholarly study is probably the single best source for investigating specific biblical references and allusions in Dylan's lyrics; see his index under the heading of "religion" and its sub-headings "Bible," "Christ," "Christianity," and "God." Christopher Ricks identifies many specific references in Dylan's lyrics from twenty-seven biblical books and epistles in his *Dylan's Visions of Sin*; see the heading "Bible" in the general index. Clinton Heylin is also helpful for identifying biblical references in Dylan's lyrics in his two-volume chronological song-by-song snapshots of Dylan's compositions; see Heylin, *Revolution in the Air*, and *Still On the Road.*

27. Quoted in Marcus, *Invisible Republic*, 30.

28. Cott, *Bob Dylan: Essential Interviews*, 98.

29. In comments introducing his interview with Dylan published in *Rolling Stone* in December 2001, Mikal Gilmore wrote, "[O]ne senses that [Dylan] carries a dignified knowledge of enduring mysteries that probably unsettle him every bit as much as his awareness of them distinguishes him." Cott, *Bob Dylan: Essential Interviews*, 413.

30. Dylan quoted in Heylin, *Still On the Road*, 23: "[T]hose are the kind of songs I [now] wanted to write. The ones that do have the break up of time, where there is no time, [while] trying to make the focus as strong as a magnifying glass under the sun."

31. Dylan quoted in Boucher, *Dylan & Cohen*, 71. Dylan has credited the artist Norman Raeben, a New York painter from whom he took lessons for two months in 1974, for helping him to break up the sense of linear time in his songs and create a sense of simultaneous past, present, and future. See Wilentz, *Bob Dylan in America*, 137–40; Cott, *Bob Dylan: Essential Interviews*, 260–61.

32. Voegelin, *Science, Politics, and Gnosticism*, 311.

33. See King, "Where Do We Go From Here?" (1967), 179.

34. Major compositions with pronounced eschatological imagery include "Gates of Eden" (1965), "I Shall Be Released" (1967), "The Wicked Messenger" (1967), "All Along the Watchtower" (1967), "Changing of the Guards"

(1978), "Jokerman" (1983), "Ring Them Bells" (1989), "Not Dark Yet" (1997), "Ain't Talkin'" (2006), "Key West (Philosopher Pirate)" (2020).

35. "I believe in the Book of Revelation," Dylan said in an interview in 1984; Ricks, *Dylan's Visions of Sin*, 384–85. For useful discussion of the topic, see pertinent passages (by index) in Gray, *Song & Dance Man III*; and Ricks, *Dylan's Visions of Sin*.

36. "[The sense that] every day is a judgment," Dylan said in his sixties, "is instilled in me by the way I grew up; where I come from: early feelings." Quoted in Heylin, *Still On the Road*, 468.

37. Performing "Blind Willie McTell" in concerts beginning in the 1990s, Dylan took to singing these last two lines as "All the way from New Orleans / To *New* Jerusalem." The lyric change names the "heavenly city" whose establishment at the end of time is promised by the Bible, emphasizing the song's eschatological focus.

38. Critics have complained that the apocalyptic prophesizing in Dylan's Christian songs are marred by a Jeremiah-like wrath. (As if furious anger were new to his songs.) Equally prevalent, though, are expressions of spiritual gratitude and love; see for example "Precious Angel" and "I Believe in You" from *Slow Train Coming*; "Saved," "Covenant Woman," "What Can I Do for You?" and "Saving Grace" from *Saved*; and "In the Summertime" and "Every Grain of Sand" from *Shot of Love*.

39. Wilentz, *Bob Dylan in America*, 12. On the "flux of divine presence" in human experience and history, see Voegelin, *Ecumenic Age*, 404–10.

40. For excellent discussions of the symbolic intricacies—historical, biblical, and existential—of "Blind Willie McTell," see Marcus, *Bob Dylan by Greil Marcus*, 155–61; and, especially, Gray, *Song & Dance Man III*, 517–47.

41. Clinton Heylin notes that Bert Cartwright, in his *The Bible in the Lyrics of Bob Dylan*, identifies over sixty biblical allusions in the songs of *John Wesley Harding*. Heylin, *Bob Dylan*, 285–86.

42. The lyrics of "Joe Hill" originated as the poem "I Dreamed I Saw Joe Hill Last Night" by Alfred Hayes, written in 1930, which Earl Robinson set to music in 1936.

43. See Heylin, *Revolution in the Air*, 362–64; and Wolff, *Grown-Up Anger*, 89–91.

44. Buber, *I and Thou*, 67.

Conclusion

1. Karpeles, "Translator's Introduction" to Józef Czapski, *Lost Time: Lectures on Proust in a Soviet Prison Camp*, ix. Czapski describes the "treasure" of Proust's novel as "a new apparatus with an unforeseen precision for psychological assessment" (12).

2. Steiner, *Real Presences*, 64.

3. Pound, *The Cantos*, notes for cantos CXVII et seq., p. 802: "That I lost my center / fighting the world. / The dreams clash / and are shattered— / and that I tried to make a paradiso / terrestre."

4. See Steiner, *Real Presences*, 216: "The meaning of meaning is a transcendent postulate."

5. On imaginative oblivion, see Voegelin, "Foreword," 37; and Voegelin, *In Search of Order*, 76–77.

6. Proust, *Time Regained*, 299.

BIBLIOGRAPHY

Abrams, M. H. *Natural Supernaturalism: Tradition and Revolution in Romantic Literature*. New York: W. W. Norton, 1971.

Albaret, Celeste. *Monsieur Proust: A Memoir*. Translated by Barbara Bray, edited by Georges Belmont. New York: McGraw-Hill, 1976.

Andersen, Anders Thyrring. "Hard Rain: The End of Times and Christian Modernism in the Work of Bob Dylan." In *A God of Time and Space: New Perspectives on Bob Dylan and Religion*, edited by Robert W. Kvalvaag and Geir Winje, 183–212. Oslo: Cappelen Damm Akademisk, 2019.

Anderson, Charles R. "Despair." In *Emily Dickinson*, edited by Harold Bloom, 9–35. Bloom's Modern Critical Views. New York: Chelsea House Publishers, 1985.

Atik, Anne. *How It Was: A Memoir of Samuel Beckett*. N.p.: Shoemaker & Hoard, 2005.

Bair, Deirdre. *Parisian Lives: Samuel Beckett, Simone de Beauvoir, and Me: A Memoir*. New York: Doubleday, 2019.

Beckett, Samuel. "First Love." In *The Complete Short Prose: 1929–1989*, edited by S. E. Gontarski, 25–45. New York: Grove Press, 1995.

———. *Krapp's Last Tape, and Other Dramatic Pieces*. Evergreen Edition. New York: Grove Press, 1960.

———. *The Letters of Samuel Beckett.* Vol. 2, *1941–1956*. Edited by George Craig, Martha Dow Fehsenfeld, Dan Gunn, and Lois More Overbeck. Cambridge: Cambridge University Press, 2011.

———. *The Letters of Samuel Beckett.* Vol. 3, *1957–1965*. Edited by George Craig, Martha Dow Fehsenfeld, Dan Gunn, and Lois More Overbeck. Cambridge: Cambridge University Press, 2014.

———. *The Letters of Samuel Beckett.* Vol. 4, *1966–1989*. Edited by George Craig, Martha Dow Fehsenfeld, Dan Gunn, and Lois More Overbeck. Cambridge: Cambridge University Press, 2016.

———. *Molloy, Malone Dies, The Unnamable*. Everyman's Library. New York: Alfred A. Knopf, 1997.

———. *Proust*; and *Three Dialogues with Georges Duthuit*. London: John Calder, 1965.

———. *Waiting for Godot*. New York: Grove Press, 1954.

———. *Worstward Ho*. London: John Calder, 1999.

Blamires, Harry. *Word Unheard: A Guide Through Eliot's* Four Quartets. London: Methuen, 1969.

Bloom, Harold. *The Western Canon: The Books and School of the Ages*. New York: Harcourt Brace, 1994.

Boucher, David. *Dylan & Cohen: Poets of Rock and Roll*. New York: Continuum, 2004.

Boyle, Nicholas. *Who Are We Now?: Christian Humanism and the Global Market From Hegel to Heaney*. Notre Dame, IN: University of Notre Dame Press, 1998.

Brée, Germaine. *Marcel Proust and Deliverance from Time*. Translated by C. J. Richards and A. D. Truitt. New York: Grove Press, 1955.

Brooker, Jewel Spears. "From *The Waste Land* to *Four Quartets*: Evolution of a Method." In *Words in Time: New Essays on Eliot's* Four Quartets, edited by Edward Lobb, 84–106. Ann Arbor: University of Michigan Press, 1993.

———. *T. S. Eliot's Dialectical Imagination*. Baltimore: Johns Hopkins University Press, 2018.

Buber, Martin. *I and Thou*. Translated by Walter Kaufmann. New York: Charles Scribner's Sons, 1970.

Bucknall, Barbara J. *The Religion of Art in Proust*. Urbana: University of Illinois Press, 1969.

Burton, Robert. *The Anatomy of Melancholy*. New York: New York Review Books, 2001.

Carter, William C. *Marcel Proust: A Life*. New Haven, CT: Yale University Press, 2013.

Chai, Leon. *Aestheticism: The Religion of Art in Post-Romantic Literature*. New York: Columbia University Press, 1990.

Childs, Donald J. "Risking Enchantment: The Middle Way between Mysticism and Pragmatism in *Four Quartets*." In *Words in Time: New Essays on Eliot's* Four Quartets, edited by Edward Lobb, 107–30. Ann Arbor: University of Michigan Press, 1993.

Cohn, Ruby. "Beckett Directs: 'Endgame' and 'Krapp's Last Tape.'" In *On Beckett: Essays and Criticism*, edited by S. E. Gontarski, 291–307. New York: Grove Press, 1986.

Cookson, William. *A Guide to the Cantos of Ezra Pound*. New York: Persea Books, 1985.

Cott, Jonathan, ed. *Bob Dylan: The Essential Interviews*. New York: Wenner Books, 2006.

Crawford, Robert. *Young Eliot: From St. Louis to* The Waste Land. New York: Farrar, Straus and Giroux, 2015.

Cronin, Anthony. *Samuel Beckett: The Last Modernist*. New York: HarperCollins, 1997.

Czapski, Józef. *Lost Time: Lectures on Proust in a Soviet Prison Camp*. Translated by Eric Karpeles. New York: New York Review Books, 2018.

Dante Alighieri. *Paradiso*. Translated by Allen Mandelbaum. Berkeley: University of California Press, 1982.

Davenport, Guy. "Persephone's Ezra." In *The Geography of the Imagination: Forty Essays*, 145–73. San Francisco: North Point Press, 1981.

Davie, Donald. *Ezra Pound: Poet as Sculptor*. New York: Oxford University Press, 1964.

De Masirevich, Constance. *On the Four Quartets of T. S. Eliot*. London: Vincent Stuart, 1965.

Dettmar, Kevin J. H. "'An Occupation for the Saint': Eliot as a Religious Thinker." In *A Companion to T. S. Eliot*, edited by David E. Chinitz, 363–75. West Sussex, UK: Wiley Blackwell, 2014.

Dickinson, Emily. *The Letters of Emily Dickinson, Vol. 3*. Edited by Thomas H. Johnson, associate editor Theodora Ward. Cambridge, MA: Belknap Press of Harvard University Press, 1958.

———. *The Poems of Emily Dickinson: Reading Edition*, edited by R. W. Franklin. Cambridge, MA: Belknap Press of Harvard University Press, 1999.

———. *Selected Letters*, edited by Thomas H. Johnson. Cambridge, MA: Belknap Press of Harvard University Press, 1994.

Diel, Joanne Feit. "Emerson, Dickinson, and the Abyss." In *Modern Critical Views: Emily Dickinson*, edited by Harold Bloom, 145–59. New York: Chelsea House, 1985.

Donoghue, Denis. "On 'Burnt Norton.'" In *Words in Time: New Essays on Eliot's* Four Quartets, edited by Edward Lobb, 1–19. Ann Arbor: University of Michigan Press, 1993.

Dorrien, Gary. *The Making of American Liberal Theology: Imagining Progressive Religion, 1805–1900*. Louisville, KY: Westminster John Knox Press, 2001.

Drew, Elizabeth. *T. S. Eliot: The Design of His Poetry*. New York: Charles Scribner's Sons, 1949.

Dylan, Bob. *Chronicles: Volume One*. New York: Simon and Schuster, 2004.

———. *Lyrics, 1961–2012*. New York: Simon & Schuster, 2016.

———. *The Lyrics. Since 1962*. Introduction by Christopher Ricks. New York: Simon & Schuster, 2014.

Eberwein, Jane Donahue. "Dickinson's Local, Global, and Cosmic Perspectives." In *The Emily Dickinson Handbook*, edited by Gudrun Grabher, Roland Hagenbüchle, and Cristanne Miller, 27–43. Amherst: University of Massachusetts Press, 1998.

Eliot, T. S. "Christianity and Communism." In *The Complete Prose of T. S. Eliot: The Critical Edition*. Vol. 4, *English Lion, 1930–1933*, edited by Jason Harding and Ronald Schuchard, 422–31. Baltimore: Johns Hopkins University Press, 2015.

———. *Four Quartets*. London: Faber and Faber, 1970.

———. "From Poe to Valéry." In *To Criticize the Critic, and Other Writings*, 27–42. Lincoln: University of Nebraska Press, Bison Book printing, 1991.

———. "The Genesis of *Four Quartets*." Excerpt from *The New York Times Book Review*, November 29, 1953. In *T. S. Eliot: Four Quartets: A Casebook*, edited by Bernard Bergonzi, 23. Basingstoke, UK: Palgrave, 1969.

———. *The Poems.* Vol. 1, *Collected and Uncollected Poems: The Annotated Text.* Edited by Christopher Ricks and Jim McCue. Baltimore: Johns Hopkins University Press, 2015.

———. "Poetry and Drama." In *On Poetry and Poets*, 75–95. New York: Farrar, Straus and Cudahy, 1957.

———. "Preface." In *Thoughts for Meditation: A Way to Recovery from Within*, edited by Nagendranath Gangulee, 11–14. London: Faber & Faber, 1951.

———. Preface to the 1928 edition of *The Sacred Wood: Essays on Poetry and Criticism*. In *The Complete Prose of T. S. Eliot: The Critical Edition,* vol. 3: *Literature, Politics, Belief*, edited by Frances Dickey, Jennifer Formicelli, and Ronald Schuchard, 413–15. Baltimore: Johns Hopkins University Press, 2015.

———. "Shakespeare and the Stoicism of Seneca." In *Selected Essays, 1917–1932*, 107–20. New York: Harcourt, Brace, 1932.

———. "Tradition and the Individual Talent." In *Selected Essays, 1917–1932*, 3–11. New York: Harcourt, Brace, 1932.

———. "Yeats." In *On Poetry and Poets*, 295–308. New York: Farrar, Straus and Cudahy, 1957.

Ellis, Steve. "*Four Quartets*." In *The New Cambridge Companion to T. S. Eliot*, edited by Jason Harding, 103–15. Cambridge: Cambridge University Press, 2017.

Emerson, Ralph Waldo. "Self-Reliance." In *The Essential Writings of Ralph Waldo Emerson*, edited by Brooks Atkinson, 132–53. New York: Modern Library, 2000.

Everdell, William R. *The First Moderns: Profiles in the Origins of Twentieth-Century Thought*. Chicago: University of Chicago Press, 1997.

Fletcher, John. *About Beckett: The Playwright and the Work*. London: Faber & Faber, 2003.

———. *Samuel Beckett: Waiting for Godot; Endgame; Krapp's Last Tape*. London: Faber & Faber, 2000.

Fletcher, John, and John Spurling. *Beckett: A Study of His Plays*. New York: Hill and Wang, 1972.

Franke, William, ed. *On What Cannot Be Said: Apophatic Discourses in Philosophy, Religion, Literature, and the Arts*. Vol. 1, *Classic Formulations*. Notre Dame, IN: University of Notre Dame Press, 2007.

———. *On What Cannot Be Said: Apophatic Discourses in Philosophy, Religion, Literature, and the Arts.* Vol. 2, *Modern and Contemporary Transformations*. Notre Dame, IN: University of Notre Dame Press, 2007.

Gamble, Cynthia. "From *Belle Epoque* to First World War: The Social Panorama." In *The Cambridge Companion to Proust*, edited by Richard Bates, 7–24. Cambridge: Cambridge University Press, 2001.

Gardner, Helen. *The Art of T. S. Eliot*. New York: E. P. Dutton, 1959.

———. *The Composition of* Four Quartets. New York: Oxford University Press, 1978.

Gelpi, Albert. "Seeing New Englandly: From Edwards to Emerson to Dickinson." In *Emily Dickinson*, edited by Harold Bloom, 37–64. Bloom's Modern Critical Views. New York: Chelsea House Publishers, 1985.

Gerrish, B. A. "'To the Unknown God': Luther and Calvin on the Hiddenness of God." *Journal of Religion* 53, no. 3 (July 1973): 263–92.

Gray, Michael. *Song & Dance Man III: The Art of Bob Dylan*. London: Continuum, 2000.

Hajdu, David. *Positively 4th Street: The Lives and Times of Joan Baez, Bob Dylan, Mimi Baez Fariña and Richard Fariña*. New York: Farrar, Straus and Giroux, 2001.

Hall, Donald. "Interview: Ezra Pound." In *Their Ancient Glittering Eyes: Remembering Poets and More Poets*, 316–35. New York: Ticknor and Fields, 1992.

———. "Interview: T. S. Eliot." In *Their Ancient Glittering Eyes: Remembering Poets and More Poets*, 261–76. New York: Ticknor and Fields, 1992.

Hampton, Timothy. *Bob Dylan's Poetics: How the Songs Work*. New York: Zone Books, 2019.

Harding, Jason. "Unraveling Eliot." In *The New Cambridge Companion to T. S. Eliot*, edited by Jason Harding, 1–25. Cambridge: Cambridge University Press, 2017.

Harvey, Giles. "Bob Dylan After the Fall." *New York Review of Books*, November 25, 2010.

Heylin, Clinton. *Bob Dylan: Behind the Shades Revisited*. New York: William Morrow, 2001.

———. *Revolution in the Air: The Songs of Bob Dylan, 1957–1973*. Chicago: Chicago Review Press, 2009.

———. *Still On the Road: The Songs of Bob Dylan, 1974–2006*. Chicago: Chicago Review Press, 2010.

Hughes, Glenn. *A More Beautiful Question: The Spiritual in Poetry and Art*. Columbia: University of Missouri Press, 2011.

———. *Transcendence and History: The Search for Ultimacy from Ancient Societies to Postmodernity*. Columbia: University of Missouri Press, 2003.

Hughes, John. *Invisible Now: Bob Dylan in the 1960s*. New York: Routledge, 2016.

Hulme, T. E. "Romanticism and Classicism." In *Speculations: Essays on Humanism and the Philosophy of Art*, edited by Herbert Read, 111–40. London: K. Paul, Trench, Trubner, 1936.

Hyde, Lewis. *The Gift: Imagination and the Erotic Life of Property*. New York: Vintage Books, 1983.

Jacobsen, Josephine, and William R. Mueller. *The Testament of Samuel Beckett*. New York: Hill and Wang, 1964.

Johnston, William. *The Inner Eye of Love: Mysticism and Religion*. San Francisco: Harper & Row, 1978.

Jones, Tudor. *Bob Dylan and the British Sixties: A Cultural History*. London: Routledge, 2019.

Jordan, Jack. "The Unconscious." In *The Cambridge Companion to Proust*, edited by Richard Bales, 100–16. Cambridge: Cambridge University Press, 2001.

Julian of Norwich. *Showings*. Translated by Edmund College, OSA, and James Walsh, SJ. New York: Paulist Press, 1978.

Kahn, Charles H. *The Art and Thought of Heraclitus: An Edition of the Fragments with Translation and Commentary*. Cambridge: Cambridge University Press, 1979.

Kant, Immanuel. *The Critique of Judgment*. Translated by James Creed Meredith. Oxford: Clarendon Press, 1980.

Karpeles, Eric. *Paintings in Proust*. London: Thames & Hudson, 2008.

———. "Translator's Introduction." In Józef Czapski, *Lost Time: Lectures on Proust in a Soviet Prison Camp*, translated by Eric Karpeles, ix–xxxiv. New York: New York Review Books, 2018.

Kearns, George. *Guide to Ezra Pound's "Selected Cantos."* New Brunswick: Rutgers University Press, 1980.

Kenner, Hugh. *The Invisible Poet: T. S. Eliot*. University Paperbacks Edition. London: Methuen, 1965.

———. *The Poetry of Ezra Pound*. Lincoln: University of Nebraska Press, 1985.

———. *The Pound Era*. Berkeley: University of California Press, 1974.

———. *Samuel Beckett: A Critical Study*. 2nd ed. Berkeley: University of California Press, 1968.

Kiberd, Declan. Ulysses *and Us: The Art of Everyday Life in Joyce's Masterpiece*. New York: W. W. Norton, 2009.

Kierkegaard, Søren. *The Sickness Unto Death: A Christian Psychological Exposition for Upbuilding and Awakening*. Translated and edited by Howard V. Hong and Edna H. Hong. Princeton, NJ: Princeton University Press, 1980.

King, Martin Luther, Jr. "Where Do We Go From Here?" In *I Have A Dream: Writings & Speeches That Changed the World*, edited by James M. Washington, 169–79. New York: HarperOne, 1992.

Knowlson, James. *Damned to Fame: The Life of Samuel Beckett*. New York: Simon & Schuster, 1996.

Knowlson, James, and Elizabeth Knowlson, eds. *Beckett Remembering, Remembering Beckett: A Centenary Celebration*. New York: Arcade Publishing, 2006.

Kolakowski, Leszek. *Modernity on Endless Trial*. Chicago: University of Chicago Press, 1990.

Kramer, Kenneth Paul. *Redeeming Time: T. S. Eliot's* Four Quartets. Lanham, MD: Cowley Publications, 2007.

Leclercq, Jean. "Introduction II: Influence and Noninfluence of Dionysius in the Western Middle Ages." In *Pseudo-Dionysius: The Complete Works*, translated by Colm Luibheid, 25–32. Mahwah, NJ: Paulist Press, 1987.

Levinas, Emmanuel. "God and Philosophy." In *Basic Philosophical Writings*, edited by Adriaan T. Peperzak, Simon Critchley, and Robert Bernasconi, 129–48. Bloomington: Indiana University Press, 1996.

———. *Humanism of the Other*. Translated by Nidra Poller. Urbana: University of Illinois Press, 2006.

———. "Peace and Proximity." In *Basic Philosophical Writings*, edited by Adriaan T. Peperzak, Simon Critchley, and Robert Bernasconi, 161–69. Bloomington: Indiana University Press, 1996.

———. "The Rights of Man and the Rights of the Other." In *Outside the Subject*, translated by Michael B. Smith, 116–25. Stanford, CA: Stanford University Press, 1994.

Lonergan, Bernard. "Art." In *Topics in Education: The Cincinnati Lectures of 1959 on the Philosophy of Education*, edited by Robert M. Doran and Frederick E. Crowe, revised and augmenting the unpublished text prepared by James Quinn and John Quinn, 208–32. Vol. 10 of *The Collected Works of Bernard Lonergan*. Toronto: University of Toronto Press, 1993.

———. *Insight: A Study of Human Understanding*, edited by Frederick E. Crowe and Robert M. Doran. Vol. 3 of *The Collected Works of Bernard Lonergan*. Toronto: University of Toronto Press, 1992.

Löwith, Karl. *Meaning in History*. Chicago: University of Chicago Press, 1949.

Main, M. "Baudelaire and Proust: The Symbolistic Technique as Applied to the Novel." PhD diss., University of London, 1953.

March, Harold. *The Two Worlds of Marcel Proust*. Perpetua Edition. New York: A. S. Barnes, 1961.

Marcus, Greil. *Bob Dylan by Greil Marcus: Writings 1968–2010*. New York: Public Affairs, 2010.

———. *Invisible Republic: Bob Dylan's Basement Tapes*. New York: Henry Holt, 1997.

Marqusee, Mike. *Chimes of Freedom: The Politics of Bob Dylan's Art*. New York: New Press, 2003.

McIntosh, James. *Nimble Believing: Dickinson and the Unknown*. Ann Arbor: University of Michigan Press, 2000.

McMillan, Dougald, and Martha Fehsenfeld. *Beckett in the Theatre: The Author as Practical Playwright and Director.* Vol. 1, *From* Waiting for Godot *to* Krapp's Last Tape. London: John Calder, 1988.

Moody, A. David. *Ezra Pound: Poet: A Portrait of the Man and His Work.* Vol. 1, *The Young Genius, 1885–1920*. Oxford: Oxford University Press, 2007.

———. *Ezra Pound: Poet: A Portrait of the Man and His Work.* Vol. 2, *The Epic Years, 1921–1939*. Oxford: Oxford University Press, 2014.

———. *Ezra Pound: Poet: A Portrait of the Man and His Work.* Vol. 3, *The Tragic Years, 1939–1972*. Oxford: Oxford University Press, 2015.

———. *Thomas Stearns Eliot: Poet*. 2nd ed. Cambridge: Cambridge University Press, 1994.

Moss, Howard. *The Magic Lantern of Marcel Proust: A Critical Study of* Remembrance of Things Past. Philadelphia: Paul Dry Books, 2012.

Nisbet, Robert. *History of the Idea of Progress*. New York: Basic Books, 1980.

Olds, Marshall C. "Literary Symbolism." In *A Companion to Modernist Literature and Culture*, edited by David Bradshaw and Kevin J. H. Dettmar, 155–62. Malden, MA: Blackwell Publishing, 2006.

Oser, Lee. "Coming to Terms with *Four Quartets*." In *A Companion to T. S. Eliot*, edited by David E. Chinitz, 216–27. West Sussex, UK: Wiley Blackwell, 2014.

Parkinson, Thomas. "Pound and Williams." In *Ezra Pound Among the Poets*, edited by George Bornstein, 149–67. Chicago: University of Chicago Press, 1985.

Patočka, Jan. *Heretical Essays in the Philosophy of History*. Translated by Erazim Kohák, edited by James Dodd. Chicago: Open Court, 1996.

Pearlman, Daniel D. *The Barb of Time: On the Unity of Ezra Pound's* Cantos. New York: Oxford University Press, 1969.

Pelikan, Jaroslav. "Introduction I: The Odyssey of Dionysian Spirituality." In *Pseudo-Dionysius: The Complete Works*, translated by Colm Luibheid, 11–24. Mahwah, NJ: Paulist Press, 1987.

Perkins, David. *A History of Modern Poetry*. Vol. 1, *From the 1890s to the High Modernist Mode*. Cambridge, MA: Belknap Press of Harvard University Press, 1976.

———. *A History of Modern Poetry*. Vol. 2, *Modernism and After*. Cambridge: Belknap Press of Harvard University Press, 1987.

Pilling, John. *Samuel Beckett*. London: Routledge & Kegan Paul, 1976.

Pound, Ezra. *ABC of Reading*. New York: New Directions, 1960.

———. *The Cantos of Ezra Pound*. New York: New Directions, 1972.

———. *Guide to Kulchur*. New York: New Directions, 1970.

———. "Patria Mia." In *Selected Prose, 1909–1965*, edited by William Cookson, 99–141. New York: New Directions, 1973.

———. *Personae: The Collected Shorter Poems*. New York: New Directions, 1971.

———. "A Visiting Card." In *Selected Prose, 1909–1965*, edited by William Cookson, 306–35. New York: New Directions, 1973.

Proust, Marcel. *Swann's Way*. Vol. 1 of *In Search of Lost Time*. Translated by C. K. Moncrieff and Terence Kilmartin, revised by D. J. Enright. New York: Modern Library, 1992.

———. *Within a Budding Grove*. Vol. 2 of *In Search of Lost Time*. Translated by C. K. Scott Moncrieff and Terence Kilmartin, revised by D. J. Enright. New York: Modern Library, 1992.

———. *The Guermantes Way*. Vol. 3 of *In Search of Lost Time*. Translated by C. K. Scott Moncrieff and Terence Kilmartin, revised by D. J. Enright. New York: Modern Library, 1993.

———. *Sodom and Gomorrah*. Vol. 4 of *In Search of Lost Time*. Translated by C. K. Scott Moncrieff and Terence Kilmartin, revised by D. J. Enright. New York: Modern Library, 1993.

———. *The Captive; The Fugitive*. Vol. 5 of *In Search of Lost Time*. Translated by C. K. Scott Moncrieff and Terence Kilmartin, revised by D. J. Enright. New York: Modern Library, 1993.

———. *Time Regained*. Vol. 6 of *In Search of Lost Time*. Translated by Andreas Mayor and Terence Kilmartin, revised by D. J. Enright; and *A Guide to Proust*, compiled by Terence Kilmartin, revised by Joanna Kilmartin. New York: Modern Library, 1993.

Pseudo-Dionysius. *The Mystical Theology*. In *Pseudo-Dionysius: The Complete Works*, translated by Colm Luibheid, 135–41. Mahwah, NJ: Paulist Press, 1987.

Quinones, Ricardo J. *Mapping Literary Modernism: Time and Development*. Princeton, NJ: Princeton University Press, 1985.

Rabaté, Jean-Michel. *Think, Pig!: Beckett at the Limit of the Human*. New York: Fordham University Press, 2016.

Read, Forrest. "Pound, Joyce, and Flaubert: The Odysseans." In *New Approaches to Ezra Pound*, edited by Eva Hesse, 125–44. Berkeley: University of California Press, 1969.

Reid, Alec. *All I Can Manage, More Than I Could: An Approach to the Plays of Samuel Beckett*. New York: Grove Press, 1968.

Riasanovsky, Nicholas V. *The Emergence of Romanticism*. New York: Oxford University Press, 1992.

Ricks, Christopher. *Beckett's Dying Words*. Oxford: Clarendon Press, 1993.

———. *Dylan's Visions of Sin*. New York: Ecco Press, 2003.

Riley, Tim. *Hard Rain: A Dylan Commentary*. New York: Alfred A. Knopf, 1992.

Robinson, David. *The Unitarians and the Universalists*. Westport, CT: Greenwood Press, 1985.

Robinson, Michael. *The Long Sonata of the Dead: A Study of Samuel Beckett*. New York: Grove Press, 1969.

Rosenblum, Robert. *Modern Painting and the Northern Romantic Tradition: Friedrich to Rothko*. New York: Harper & Row, 1975.

Sack, Daniel. *Samuel Beckett's* Krapp's Last Tape. London: Routledge, 2016.

Schmid, Marion. "The Birth and Development of *A la recherche du temps perdu*." In *The Cambridge Companion to Proust*, edited by Richard Bales, 58–73. Cambridge: Cambridge University Press, 2001.

Schwartz, Sanford. *The Matrix of Modernism: Pound, Eliot, & Early 20th-Century Thought*. Princeton, NJ: Princeton University Press, 1985.

Selnes, Gisla. "Bob Dylan's Conversions: The 'Gospel Years' as Symptom and Transition." In *A God of Time and Space: New Perspectives on Bob Dylan and Religion*, edited by Robert W. Kvalvaag and Geir Winje, 163–82. Oslo: Cappelen Damm Akademisk, 2019.

Sewall, Richard B. *The Life of Emily Dickinson*. New York: Farrar, Straus and Giroux, 1980.

Shattuck, Roger. *Proust's Way: A Field Guide to* In Search of Lost Time. New York: W. W. Norton, 2000.

Shelton, Robert. *No Direction Home: The Life and Music of Bob Dylan*. New York: Beech Tree Books, 1986.

Simpson, Louis. *Three on the Tower: The Lives and Works of Ezra Pound, T. S. Eliot and William Carlos Williams*. New York: William Morrow, 1975.

Sounes, Howard. *Down the Highway: The Life of Bob Dylan*. Updated edition. New York: Grove Press, 2011.

Spurr, Barry. *'Anglo-Catholic in Religion': T. S. Eliot and Christianity*. Cambridge, UK: Lutterworth Press, 2010.

Steiner, George. *Real Presences*. Chicago: University of Chicago Press, 1989.

Sudol, Sister Barbara, CSFN. *Mystical Elements in the Poetry of T. S. Eliot*. Saarbrücken, Germany: VDM Verlag Dr. Müller Aktiengesellschaft, 2008.

Tadié, Jean-Yves. *Marcel Proust: A Life*. Translated by Euan Cameron. New York: Viking, 2000.

Tarkovksy, Andrey. *Sculpting in Time: Reflections on the Cinema*. Translated by Kitty Hunter-Blair. Austin: University of Texas Press, 1987.

Taylor, Charles. *A Secular Age*. Cambridge, MA: Belknap Press of Harvard University Press, 2007.

———. *Sources of the Self: The Making of the Modern Identity*. Cambridge, MA: Harvard University Press, 1989.

Toscan, Richard, and Jack MacGowran. "MacGowran on Beckett: Interview by Richard Toscan." In *On Beckett: Essays and Criticism*, edited by S. E. Gontarski, 213–25. New York: Grove Press, 1986.

Tracy, David. "T. S. Eliot as Religious Thinker: *Four Quartets*." In *Literary Imagination, Ancient and Modern: Essays in Honor of David Grene*, edited by Todd Breyfogle, 269–84. Chicago: University of Chicago Press, 1999.

Tröhler, Daniel. "Progressivism." In *Oxford Research Encyclopedia, Education*, edited by George W. Noblit, 1–36. Oxford: Oxford University Press, 2016.

Valéry, Paul. "Letter about Mallarmé." In *Leonardo, Poe, Mallarmé*, translated by Malcom Cowley and James R. Lawler, 240–53. Vol. 8 of *Collected Works of Paul Valéry*. Bollingen series 45. Princeton, NJ: Princeton University Press, 1972.

Van Hulle, Dirk, and Mark Nixon. *Samuel Beckett's Library*. Cambridge: Cambridge University Press, 2013.

Vendler, Helen. *Dickinson: Selected Poems and Commentaries*. Cambridge, MA: Belknap Press of Harvard University Press, 2010.

Voegelin, Eric. *The Ecumenic Age*. Edited by Michael Franz. Vol. 4 of *Order and History*, vol. 17 of *The Collected Works of Eric Voegelin*. Columbia: University of Missouri Press, 2000.

———. "Eternal Being in Time." In *Anamnesis: On the Theory of History and Politics*, edited by David Walsh, translated by M. J. Hanak, based upon the abbreviated version originally translated by Gerhart Niemeyer, 312–37. Vol. 6 of *The Collected Works of Eric Voegelin*. Columbia: University of Missouri Press, 2002.

———. "Foreword." In *Anamnesis: On the Theory of History and Politics*, edited by David Walsh, translated by M. J. Hanak, based upon the abbreviated version originally translated by Gerhart Niemeyer, 33–38. Vol. 6 of *The Collected Works of Eric Voegelin*. Columbia: University of Missouri Press, 2002.

———. "The Gospel and Culture." In *Published Essays, 1966–1985*, edited by Ellis Sandoz, 172–212. Vol. 12 of *The Collected Works of Eric Voegelin*. Baton Rouge: Louisiana State University Press, 1990.

———. *In Search of Order*, edited by Ellis Sandoz. Vol. 5 of *Order and History*, vol. 18 of *The Collected Works of Eric Voegelin*. Columbia: University of Missouri Press, 2000.

———. *The New Science of Politics: An Introduction*. In *Modernity Without Restraint: The Political Religions; The New Science of Politics; and Science, Politics, and Gnosticism*, edited by Manfred Henningsen, 75–141. Vol. 5 of *The Collected Works of Eric Voegelin*. Columbia: University of Missouri Press, 2000.

———. "Notes on T. S. Eliot's *Four Quartets*." In *The Drama of Humanity and Other Miscellaneous Papers, 1939–1985*, edited by William Petropulos and Gilbert Weiss, 33–40. Vol. 33 of *The Collected Works of Eric Voegelin*. Columbia: University of Missouri Press, 2004.

———. *Science, Politics, and Gnosticism*. In *Modernity Without Restraint: The Political Religions; The New Science of Politics; and Science, Politics, and Gnosticism*, edited by Manfred Henningsen, 243–313. Vol. 5 of *The Collected Works of Eric Voegelin*. Columbia: University of Missouri Press, 2000.

———. *The World of the Polis*. Edited by Athanasios Moulakis. Vol. 2 of *Order and History*, vol. 15 of *The Collected Works of Eric Voegelin*. Columbia: University of Missouri Press, 2000.

Webb, Eugene. *The Dark Dove: The Sacred and Secular in Modern Literature*. Seattle: University of Washington Press, 1975.

Webb, Stephen H. *Dylan Redeemed: From* Highway 61 *to* Saved. New York: Continuum, 2006.

White, Edmund. *Marcel Proust*. New York: Viking, 1999.

Wilentz, Sean. *Bob Dylan in America*. New York: Doubleday, 2010.

Wilhelm, James J. *The Later Cantos of Ezra Pound*. New York: Walker and Co., 1977.

Wilson, Edmund. *Axel's Castle: A Study in the Imaginative Literature of 1870 to 1930*. New York: Charles Scribner's Sons, 1931.

Wolff, Cynthia Griffin. *Emily Dickinson*. New York: Alfred A. Knopf, 1987.

Wolff, Daniel. *Grown-Up Anger: The Connected Mysteries of Bob Dylan, Woody Guthrie, and the Calumet Massacre of 1913*. New York: HarperCollins, 2017.

Zaehner, R. C. *Mysticism Sacred and Profane*. London: Oxford University Press, 1961.

INDEX

PERMISSIONS

Chapters or chapter sections in this book originated as presentations at conferences that, in revised and expanded form, appeared as essays in various publications. Chapter 1 has been adapted from "Love, Terror, and Transcendence in Emily Dickinson's Poetry," published in the journal *Renascence: Essays on Value in Literature* (2014). Chapters 2 and 3 are expanded and altered versions of "Proust, Transcendence, and Metaxic Existence" and "Unsought Revelations of Eternal Reality in Eliot's *Four Quartets* and Proust's *In Search of Lost Time*," which appeared in *The Timelessness of Proust: Reflections on* In Search of Lost Time, edited by Charles R. Embry and Glenn Hughes (South Bend, IN: St. Augustine's Press, 2019). An early version of chapter 4 was published as "History in Ezra Pound's *Cantos* and T. S. Eliot's *Four Quartets*" in the journal *Anamnesis* (2012). All appear here by gracious permission of the editors and publishers.